3rd Edition - August 2009

Death, Heaven & Back

(The True Story of
One Man's Death and Resurrection)

Lonnie Honeycutt

For Sarah — Thank you so very much for being there for your Mom & Dad during this most difficult time. I pray that the Lord, our God, will bless you and your family as you seek His will for your lives!

Cover Art: Sam Noerr
Picture of Lonnie Honeycutt: Bill Starling
Proofreaders: Linda Caldwell & Margaret Forstchen

In Christ,

Rev. Lonnie Honeycutt can be contacted by writing, calling, or emailing him at the following:

Jer. 29:11

Lonnie

Rev. Lonnie Honeycutt (RevLon)
3350 Dawes Rd.
Mobile, AL. 36695
251-421-4166
www.DeeperLifeEast.com
LonnieHoneycutt@yahoo.com or RevLonnie@gmail.com

Contents

Death, Heaven, & Back
(The True Story of One Man's Death and Resurrection)
By Rev. Lonnie Honeycutt

"Who are you man of clay? Whose life is a vapor that fades away. With vanity as your only shield, you scoff and you curse at God's will. You challenge Him as your strength it ebbs and you act as though your God is dead. But just for a moment for the briefest time, won't you consider Him just one more time?" Lonnie Honeycutt, from his song Canvas and Tapestry©

Special Thanks

I'd like to first thank my Savior, Jesus Christ, Who is and Who was, and Who is to come, Jehovah God, the Lord Almighty. It is to Him my life is dedicated and it is for Him I have penned the following book. Without His, His Father's and the Holy Spirit's graciousness I wouldn't be alive today to tell of what He has allowed me to experience. It is for His glory that our lives should be lived and for that same glory that I declare that without God my life and every other life would be in vain. It is my most sincere desire that everyone would choose Jesus to be their Lord and Savior and would then have their own tale of redemption, of being brought from death into life and that they could then join me in Heaven for all eternity. Remember as you read this book that it's all about Jesus. Everything in our lives should be about Jesus because Jesus is the way, the truth, and the life. Amen.

Secondly, my thanks go to my amazingly sweet, altogether wonderful wife, Dawn. Without her, my life, before my death and most certainly after it, would be so much less special. Dawn, you really are the love of my life and I thank you for "hanging in there with me" through the worst part of my life. I promise I'll spend the rest of the days the Lord gives me trying to be the best husband and friend you could ever have.

To my pastor, Mark Wyatt, I'd like to say thanks for being my friend. You really are a stand-up guy and I pray daily for you and your family. You've modeled for me what it is to be someone who expects the unexpected and who craves for the Kingdom of God to be made manifest in the here and now.

If there were two people in this world that I think would be great for everyone to mimic it would be Libby and Melvin. Guys, the two of you are the most wonderful people I've ever met. Melvin, you are the father I never had and I so appreciate your kindness, your correction, and your love. I only hope that I can become half the father you are to my own children. Libby, you've been my confidante, my counselor, my friend, and the closest thing to a Mom I have besides my real mother.

To my Mom (Eddie Honeycutt), thanks seems such a small word for all the times you've been there for me and with me. Through the trials and tribulations of growing up with health problems and the teenage years (which I know were very 'special' times for you because of me) and even as an adult, you've always been there for me. You were the one who first introduced me to the love of Jesus and for that and so much more I thank you and I love you dearly!

Jay, my brother, you've been more than a friend to me. As I was growing up you were a surrogate father, one of my best friends, and a giant to me in the Christian faith. Thanks so very much for being around when I needed to talk and especially when I didn't want to talk.

To Helena, Lillian (Gay), and David, I love you all! A man could not ask for any better siblings than you have been to me. And to Steve I'd like to say "I Love You" and I hope you'll decide to join me in Heaven.

To Rev. Mike and Rev. Patti Woods, what more can I say but Praise God that the two of you were put into our lives. Mike, you've been such an inspiration to me because of your faithfulness in prayer and the love you've shown me as your friend. Patti, your kindness and empathy and prayers, tempered by a level head and strength, has been such a source of comfort for my family. I dearly love you both.

Mark Strick, my brother-in-law and, more importantly, my Brother-in-Christ, you are one of the sweetest guys I've ever met. Your love, compassion, and gentleness have made you a hero in my eyes and that of your sisters. Thanks so very much for allowing God to mold you into the man you are today.

Honestly, I could go on and on and on for pages thanking people who have taken part in my life and made me a better man. But, if I tried to do that I'm certain I'd forget someone and I wouldn't want to offend anyone. So, with that being said, I'd like to simply say THANKS to YOU (my friends, my associates, my neighbors, and my family) for being there for my family and me. When we all get to Heaven (and I do hope you'll join me there), I'll give you proper thanks. Until then, please know that I cherish you more than you'll ever know on this side of eternity.

Note: Something you'll find missing in this book is the recognition of the hospitals and medical professionals involved in my case. This wasn't an oversight. I sincerely believe that each and every person involved in my treatment tried their level best to give me the best care possible and that they succeeded in doing so. However, I am fully convinced that God used and continues to use the cancer, the treatments, my death, and my subsequent resurrection for His glory and that no one, regardless of their expertise, could have kept me from dying or could have brought me back to life. As such, I would never want to denigrate the service provided by these incredible people by implicating them in my death. To all those who gave of themselves to me medically I have this to say: Please know that I am incredibly grateful for the time you spent with me, the prayers you prayed for me and my family, and for the attention you gave my case. May the Lord, our God, bless you as you continue to do His will.

Foreword

Reverend Mark Wyatt
Pastor of Deeper Life Fellowship in Mobile, Alabama

When I first began to hear and read stories of miracles, of people encountering the power of God today, it became a matter of settling one issue first: these people are either telling the truth or they aren't. If they are not telling the truth, then I can write this off and go on with my life. However, if they are telling the truth, it is going to require something of me. I'm going to have to decide what impact it has on my life if God speaks and heals today. Do I want to be a part of it or not? Will I be limited by my understanding, or will I learn how to embrace mystery? What if it's true and I ignore it? What will I be missing?

A few weeks ago, the father of one of the men in my church passed away after a brief battle. When my friend David called to tell me about his dad, I raced to the hospital to be with him and his family. On my way there, David called and said, "*I just wanted to let you know that I called Lonnie to come be with us tonight as well. I wanted my family to hear his story.*" You see, David had just heard Lonnie share at our church about his trip to Heaven, and David thought that it just might be what they all needed right now.

As I approached the front doors of the hospital, David met me with a smile. I followed him down to where his children, his wife, his mother, his brother, and his whole family sat wide-eyed and smiling, Lonnie sitting in front of them, telling them what Heaven is like, painting a picture for them of what their beloved "Poppy" was seeing at that very moment. It was a moment of incredible peace and joy. It was a moment of the substance of things hoped for. It was as if Heaven had settled into that room.

The story you are about to read is true. I, for one, have been changed by it forever. If you are willing to believe it too, then a whole new world will open up for you – a world of miracles, a world of infinite possibilities, a world that Jesus called "*the Kingdom of Heaven.*" And, as you will see, that world is separated from this world by the thinnest of veils. So the only question for you is, if this is real, what does it mean for you? If you seek the Kingdom, what might you see? If you ignore it, what wonders, what moments, what kinds of resurrections will you miss?

Read this story. Embrace it in all its mystery. Let it lead you to seek the unveiling of the rule and reign of God in your life. But whatever you do, both in this life and the next... don't miss Heaven.

Mark Wyatt

Pastor, Deeper Life Fellowship – Mobile, Alabama – August 2008

Prologue

After a brutal battle with cancer, on February 16, 2008, I died.

But then, as my friend Brumbaugh says, I got better. What happened after I died changed my life forever!

I sincerely hope that all who read this story will pardon the unconventional way in which it was written – utilizing both first person commentary from me as well as copies of previously written email communications from me to others and their subsequent responses. The reason I've chosen to write my story like this is because it's the most honest form I can't think of since I suffer from short-term memory loss. As such, I've had to rely on my wonderful wife and friends (and the aforementioned emails) to fill in the gaps. While the email section is the longest section of the book, I highly suggest you read through them as they'll give you a better picture of my mental state than will the main copy of the book itself. You'll also be entertained by stories that include '*Greg, the 81 Year Old Atheist,*' my '*Tribble episode*' (of Star Trek fame) that occurred after I came back from Heaven, and many other funny stories.

What About Scoffers?

I know that there will be many people who will not believe that I, or anyone else for that matter have ever gone to Heaven and returned. I'm okay with that. I know what the Lord has told me to do and that is to obey Him by telling my story to everyone I can. Since it's up to Him to deal with issues of the heart, I know everything will be okay. If people believe me, fine. If they don't believe me, fine. Either way, it's Him and His ways they have to agree or disagree with – not me. So, all the pressure's off.

It's interesting to have died and, yet, lived to tell about it. But, that's exactly what happened to me. I really did die on that day in February in at least two different ways: cardiac arrest (no pulse or blood pressure) and cerebral hypoxia (brain death). What occurred between the time of my death and resurrection forever changed my outlook on life and on death. I was transported to Heaven, experienced peace beyond measure, met a person whom I immediately knew but whom I'd never met on Earth (she had died nearly 30 years before I did), and was asked if I wanted to return.

Even if a person doesn't believe I truly went to Heaven or, at the very least, that I had a vision of the same, the one thing that no one can deny – ever – is the physical healing that took place in my body immediately after my 'Heaven Experience.' It's medically impossible for a body to undergo the trauma that mine did via chemo, radiation burns, and death and then to return to a baseline of normalcy as quickly as I did. Yet, that's precisely what occurred. The following is my story…

1
The Ordeal Begins

"In this you greatly rejoice, though now for a little while, if need be, you have been grieved by various trials, that the genuineness of your faith, being much more precious than gold that perishes, though it is tested by fire, may be found to praise, honor, and glory at the revelation of Jesus Christ ... receiving the end of your faith, the salvation of your souls."
1 Peter 1:6,9

My ordeal with cancer began about four years prior to my actually being diagnosed as having the disease. In 2003 I went to my doctor complaining of a swollen lymph node on the left side of my neck. I was given a round of steroids and antibiotics and told to 'watch it.' Sure enough, the lymph node reacted to the medicine and reduced in size. The reduction lasted a few months and then I was back in my doctor's office. At that time I was again given another round of steroids and antibiotics and told to 'watch it.' Again, the lymph node seemed to react favorably to the medicine for a few more months. To make a very long story much shorter, this 'up and down' reaction kept occurring until, finally, in early 2007, I began to be seriously concerned that there was something 'up' with my lymph system. The reason for my concern was because nothing had appreciably gotten better the last couple of times I'd taken both antibiotics and steroids and because I'd noticed that there were two swollen lymph nodes whereas before there had only been one.

I convinced my doctors to do a needle biopsy but the results came back as 'inconclusive.' I was then told that *we* (meaning myself and my medical team) would watch it. This same procedure was performed twice more until, finally, one of the oncology specialists suggested that we go ahead and take the lymph node out. That was more than fine with my wife and me – especially since we were both told that the chance of it actually being cancer was minimal.

In mid-September, I underwent surgery.[1] Several hours later my wife was told by the physician, "*It is cancer, just as I suspected.*"

This was one of the first times that the word 'cancer' had been uttered by a physician as being a possibility and, yet, it was what I had. The diagnosis came as quite a shock to both my wife and me and the prognosis was grim. During the course of the next several weeks we came to know the name for the disease in my body as oropharyngeal cancer. It was staged and graded as IVa – which is one of the worst stages and grades possible. To make matters seem more grim, my own personal research found that the recurrence rate for oropharyngeal cancer has remained at about 65% for the past 40 years – even after surgery, chemotherapy, and radiation treatments. Further, I found that only half of those diagnosed with the disease will survive more than five years. As for my overall life expectancy, the clinical data provided by the American Cancer Society presents the following answer:

"Survival advantages provided by new treatment modalities have been <u>undermined</u> by the <u>significant percentage</u> of patients cured of head and neck squamous cell carcinoma (HNSCC) <u>who subsequently develop second primary tumors</u> (emphasis mine)."

In short, the treatment I'd be getting (called field cancerization) often actually <u>creates other cancers</u> that are, in their words, a *"major threat to long-term survival after successful therapy of early-stage head and neck squamous cell cancer."*

Out of about 40,000 cancers like the one in my body that were diagnosed a couple of years ago (2006), over 11,000 people died from the same. Regardless of who you are, this was sobering information. All-in-all, it was a very dark time in our lives.

As already noted, I underwent surgery to remove the masses that were in my neck. What I didn't know, until I awoke, is how invasive the surgery was. Once inside my head and neck the surgeon found that nine out of fourteen of my lymph nodes were infected with cancer. These nodes, as well as a nerve, my jugular vein, part of my tongue and about six inches of muscle tissue were all removed. I was left with a thin but prominent scar that extends from just behind my ear in an upward loop that encompasses most of my esophagus.

The surgeon who performed the operation told my wife and me that two of the tumors were slightly larger than a golf ball though they were more elongated. He explained that one of the tumors had been up in my head (behind my left ear) about two inches and a second tumor (about 12 cm long) had been deep in my chest – so deep that he was within minutes of cracking my chest open and removing my left clavicle in order to get it all. Fortunately, he was able to tug and pull and scrape until the entire mass was excised. Due to the fact that the cancer that had invaded my body was so uncommon, the tumors that were removed were sent to one of the pathology centers of the AFI (Air Force Institute) for classification.

As a result of the surgery, every time I extend my arm it feels as though my 'funny bone' is being compressed. Thankfully, this sensation has decreased (or I've gotten used to it) over time. The removal of the nerve and muscle tissue has caused a partial paralyzation on the left side of my face. I can still feel pressure and my smile hasn't diminished but my left ear now feels as though it's made out of wood. There is also a definite depression in my neck and trapezoid muscle.

2

The Cancer Treatments Begin

"And not only that, but we also glory in tribulations, knowing that tribulation produces perseverance; and perseverance, character; and character, hope."
Romans 5:3

On October 24, 2007 I underwent a PET Scan (a Positron Emission Tomography scan is used as a way for a doctor to examine the chemical activity in certain parts of the body to detect abnormalities in those areas. Since cancers use more energy (glucose) than surrounding tissues, they normally appear brighter on the PET scan). On October 31, 2007, the results of the PET Scan came back and it was determined that I still had cancer in my body. We were told that because of the nature of the cancer I had (the AFI had determined it to be oropharyngeal cancer), aggressive treatment was called for. So, over the next few months (beginning on November 14, 2007) I underwent 40 radiation treatments plus concurrent chemotherapies.

I use the plural 'chemotherapies' because my body reacted so violently to the first type of chemo drug (Cisplatin) that my physician changed me to another drug (Erbitux). In most cases, from what I understand, chemo patients don't usually experience major side effects (such as raging nausea and vomiting) to Cisplatin until around six to eight weeks after beginning their treatment. Unfortunately, my body proved to be an exception to the rule. My reaction to the drug started about four hours after my first treatment and continued for hours and then days. I vomited so much that I had to go into the clinic and have I.V. fluids administered.

Within a few days of starting the Cisplatin, my physician changed me to Erbitux – a non-platinum-based drug. The primary drawbacks to Erbitux were the common side effects of sudden cardiac arrest, anaphylactic shock, and sudden death. I was told that I had a heightened chance of each of these due to the fact that I live with a congenital heart defect (2 holes in my heart) and because I don't have a spleen. Consequently, each time Erbitux was administered, I was forced to wait at the hospital for an hour so that medical help would be available should one of the aforementioned side effects occur. While I escaped these side effects I did develop others. For instance, I developed a rash that went from the top of my head to the bottom of my feet. The rash caused pustules to form everywhere on my body and, at one point, the skin on my head became so brittle that when I would vomit my scalp would break open and blood would pour forth from it.

Although I was already taking double doses of an anti-nausea medicine (okayed by my doctor) as well as another that should have prevented headaches, I suffered from a fairly consistent migraine whose quality was unlike most I've ever experienced – easily an 8.5 out of 10.

As the treatments continued, my throat became more and more blistered from the radiation. They irradiated both sides of my neck as well as parts of my head and my chest. By December 4, 2007, my goatee, which I had sported for several years, started coming out in clumps and I had to shave it off. My son, Brance, who had never seen me without a goatee or a beard asked my wife: *"Why does Dad look so weird?"* and *"Is he always going to look that way?"* Leave it to an 8-year-old to say something that simultaneously makes you laugh and feel worse at the same time!

Concurrent with my beard falling out, I noticed that I was beginning to experience advanced signs of what is technically termed photo-aging. Less technically, some of the skin around my neck and face was beginning to lose integrity and had started to wrinkle (this was especially the case around the scar that now graced my neck and throat). Speaking of my neck and throat, my jaw line was causing me almost constant pain and it was extending into my gums. What all of this meant is that the radiation I was being bombarded with was not only cooking the inside of my body, the effects were showing up on the outside by way of capillary fragility, loss of collagen, et cetera.

By the seventh of December my saliva had begun drying up. I can tell you now that no one should ever underestimate the value of spit. It's one of those things that we all take for granted until it's gone (I know I did). Having very little saliva meant that I had to make allowances for things I'd never had to consider before. Allowances such as sleeping through the night or, rather, not sleeping through the night. I began to wake during the night some 15 times because I'd be choking due to a dry throat. It's impressive how dry your throat can become even if you're not a 'mouth breather' like I used to be.

Having dry mouth (technically called xerostomia) is the pits.

Thankfully, there's always water available. Unfortunately, when I'd wake up to take a drink of water (which I began to keep at my bedside), it tasted like liquid salt to me. That's right, salt. In fact, until after I died, water tasted like pure sodium to me. Thankfully, I was able to handle the taste (what choice did I have?) and I began drinking multiple bottles or glasses of water every single day (up to a gallon and a half). Nothing else helped and nothing else tasted even close to the goodness of water (if you can call salty tasting water 'good'). As a side note, my taste buds got so used to water tasting like salt that even after water started tasting like water to me again, my body actually craved the taste of salt for several days.

You probably already know that saliva is used to moisten and cleanse our mouths by helping to control bacteria and fungi as well as to digest food. Well, it's also needed for taste buds to activate correctly and for your vocal chords to work properly. As you might imagine, not having enough saliva to properly moisten the inside of your mouth could potentially cause many problems. In my case, I began to lose my voice and my taste buds quit working to such an extent that not only did foods not taste the same, but most of the foods I'd liked before my treatments began either simply did not have any taste or they began to taste rotten.

During the midst of all of this, our family pet, who was nearly 19 years old, Margaret Ann (a precious little kitty-cat), died. Whew, talk about a depressing time in our lives.

In the middle of December, the rash I'd spoken of before had become so painful that my doctors upped my dose of pain medications to three times what they had been and I was still having a bit of trouble coping. By this time, the majority of what I was 'eating' was in the form of liquid nutrition (i.e., Boost® or Ensure®). In case you've ever wondered if drinking your food would get redundant and boring after awhile, imagine only tasting salt when you drink *anything* (milk, soft drinks, tea, fruit juice) – it redefines the term boring.

As the salivary glands in my mouth continued to decrease in function, the other mucous membranes in my mouth, nose and eyes followed their lead. I began using a tremendous amount of eye drops and had pretty much stopped wearing contacts. Due to the fact that my wife had lost her job by this time (the company she'd worked for had closed its doors), I was unable to purchase any glasses. My lips were so tender and raw that they began to split open for no apparent reason and it seemed as though I had blisters popping up on my tongue and on the inside of my mouth almost every single day (the most impressive one was about the size of a dime – ouch!).

What little voice I had remaining was slowly but surely waning although I couldn't tell if it was just from the inflammation caused by vomiting or if it was a side-effect from the radiation treatments (it was probably a combination of the two).

The rash that was over my entire body became worse than ever and my oncologist ordered a reduction in the amount of Erbitux I was getting because he said, *"It's working too good."* He also ordered stronger meds to help alleviate some of the pain from the sores in my mouth and on my tongue.

3
Feeding Tube

"My brethren, count it all joy when you fall into various trials, knowing that the testing of your faith produces patience. But let patience have its perfect work, that you may be perfect and complete, lacking nothing."
(James 1:2)

To be quite honest, by this time I was getting tired of it all. Not knowing how well the treatment was actually going and having to live through the problems of the treatment was getting to me. Due to the fact that my white blood cell count had dropped significantly, I couldn't afford to be around people, so I was, for the most part, homebound. This was very difficult for me as I am a people person. I wasn't even able to attend the church at which I was the pastor and I had a hard time not saying to heck with all of it, stopping treatment, and just seeing what would happen. But, my personality is such that I needed to know that I had done all I could to lick this disease so that I could look into the eyes of my wife and children and tell them that I had done everything possible.

Fortunately, I could associate with people at the clinics where I was receiving treatments and I took full advantage of those times. As you'll read in the emails I sent out (starting on page 100), I was actively trying to talk with those who would listen about the love of our Lord Jesus Christ and of His wonderful Kingdom. I truly believe that if I had not had these times for ministry that I may not have made it through the months of treatments I endured. In trying to comfort others, I found comfort.

While I was supposed to have from the 17th of December until the 26th of December 'off' from treatments, six days before Christmas the day came that I'd been expecting but dreading. Ever since my treatments for cancer had begun I'd been losing weight due to my inability to eat or drink much. So, it was decided that the time had come to have a feeding tube inserted into my stomach. As it was explained to my wife and me, the procedure was relatively simple; all they would have to do is to feed a tube down my throat into my stomach, shine a light towards the outside, and puncture my flesh so that the feeding tube could be inserted.

Of course, with me, it wasn't that simple at all.

As I've mentioned before, I was born with some physical defects. Two of those defects were a diaphragmatic hernia and a twisted spleen. The diaphragmatic hernia (more specifically, a Bochdalek hernia in which my stomach and intestines had migrated into my chest cavity) had to be repaired while my spleen, which was necrotic (dead tissue), had to be removed. The operation to repair and remove said organs resulted in my having a large amount of very thick scar tissue that runs the length of my belly vertically. This being said, you can probably already guess what happened. The surgeon, upon trying to insert the feeding tube, found that it was impossible for him to simply puncture the tissue of my abdomen and, so, he was forced to perform a full, vertical, midline incision from my sternum to my belly button.

About the only good thing to come out of that day was that I got a PICC line[2] put in so they wouldn't have give me so many shots. Regrettably, the veins in my arms had already begun to collapse and to develop scar tissue, which made blood draws very painful.

While undergoing the procedure to have the feeding tube inserted, I began having horrible nightmares and imagining things. My wife, after speaking with my doctor, was told that they were '*fairly certain that it wasn't from the medications*' I was on but that it was more likely from a progression of the cancer or a stroke. You can just imagine the joy that this thought brought to my wife.

Once the feeding tube had been placed in my body (which required me to be hospitalized and to have a spinal block and took two days for what should have been an outpatient procedure), I went to sleep and Dawn, my wife, found that she was unable to revive me. Medical staff was called in and it was decided that I should be given a shot of Narcan® (naloxone).

Narcan, once administered, wiped-out all the pain medications in my body and I woke up in excruciating pain. I experienced practically every symptom possible from the use of Narcan including body aches, increased heart rate, fever, sweating, nausea, vomiting, irritability, trembling, weakness, and increased blood pressure. To say that it was horrible would be a dramatic understatement. This was the first of two times that I had to be given Narcan during the course of my treatments.

4

Going From Bad to Worse

"Therefore we do not lose heart. Even though our outward man is perishing, yet the inward man is being renewed day by day. For our light affliction, which is but for a moment, is working for us a far more exceeding and eternal weight of glory, while we do not look at the things which are seen, but at the things which are not seen. For the things which are seen are temporary, but the things which are not seen are eternal."

2 Corinthians 4:16

Through all of this, the blessings that we received were mighty.

Strangers, people we had never met, began sending us money. Several churches including one pastored by Rev. Charles Lewis (New Life Baptist, Converse, Tx.) and another pastored by Rev. Clyde Pressley (United Methodist Church, Mt. Vernon, Al.) sent us gifts. I mention this because I was so very impressed (and still am) that these churches were able to look outside of themselves, to step out of any preconceived denominational 'boxes,' as it were, and see the need of a Brother- and Sister-in-Christ and then truly follow Jesus' instruction to "...*love one another*" (John 13:34). Friends and the friends of our friends brought my family food and donated their time to help us. People I barely knew from a local food bank (the Prodisee Pantry – operated by DeAnn S.) enabled my family to eat well during this time. Friends and neighbors (Bob and Jenny P., Garland B., Gary M., and others) had been regularly donating their time to take me back and forth to my oncology appointments. Our children's Christmas presents were taken care of and people rallied around my family as if they were my blood relatives. I do not have the words to express my thanks to everyone for the loving kindness we received.

I came home from the hospital on Christmas Eve and don't remember Christmas day, arguably my favorite day of the entire year, at all. What I do remember is that being fed through the feeding tube wasn't going well. I could stomach (if you'll pardon the pun) just a few ounces of food or water at a time and so I was only absorbing about 500 calories every 24 hours.

By the first week of January I'd lost a serious amount of weight and both my doctors and I were getting worried. Frankly, as it was getting close to the end of my treatments, I thought I'd be able to 'tough it out.' Regrettably, over the course of the next three weeks, they increased the dose of radiation (called a 'boost') and that caused me considerable agony. In an attempt to prepare me for what was to come, my oncologist told me that the next three weeks would be as painful as all the previous six weeks combined. He wasn't joking. After the first treatment, my neck was burnt and continued to redden over the weekend. I had another treatment and my neck began to look like a combination of raw and cooked hamburger (that was the description my wife gave). To make matters worse, my neck and face also began to crack open and bleed. I went back to the hospital to receive another dose of radiation but was vomiting so severely that they were unable to treat me. Instead, they sent me home with a sack full of medications (lotions, ointments, gauze) to topically treat the open sores on my neck. I was also told that by the end of the week my jawbone would probably be painful too. As you might imagine, neither my appetite nor my eating improved.

On January 10, 2008, Dawn drove me to the Municipal Civic Center in Mobile, Alabama, and a couple of the prayer warriors from Bill Johnson's team (Brent and Kyle) came over to pray for and with me. For those of you who aren't familiar with Bill Johnson, he is an evangelist who pastors Bethel Church in Redding, California. Bethel is also home to the Bethel School of Supernatural Ministry (BSSM) – a school that is committed to the truth that God loves people, gave Himself for them and has given His Church supernatural power to bring individuals and nations into wholeness. In any case, about 12 hours after being prayed for by Brent and Kyle, I was at a luncheon with Bill Johnson himself. Actually, I hadn't planned on going to the luncheon until I was invited to be the *man on the mat* by some dear friends of mine who wanted Bill to pray for me in person. That was accomplished as Bill walked through the door and was escorted by my pastor, Mark Wyatt, to where I had taken a seat.

I came away from this meeting thoroughly convinced that God had healed me of cancer even though I was still suffering from the residual effects of the cancer treatments I'd been through. About ten days after my initial prayer session with Bill in Mobile, Alabama, my wife and I had the opportunity to fly to Redding, California and to actually attend Bethel Church. It was a wonderful treat. Several people, including Bill, prayed for me and, again, I returned home honestly believing that the cancer in my body had been banished. I was so convinced of this that on my very next trip to see my oncologist I asked if there was a possibility of getting a PET Scan earlier than I was scheduled to in order to determine if I was indeed cancer free. Sadly, it was explained to me that this wouldn't be possible because the injury to my neck, face and throat would register a false positive owing to the fact that the body uses glucose to heal itself and cancers use it to grow. So, while I truly believe that I was healed of cancer that night, there's no way to prove it.

Even if I had been healed of cancer I still had to endure the problems associated with the treatments for the same. Due to the radiation damage to my neck I sent out an email to any and everyone requesting them to send me pull-over shirts that they wouldn't mind being destroyed. I had to cut the shirts at the collar so that they didn't rub against my wounds and make them bleed – actually the bleeding wasn't as bad as the pain but it was profuse when it occurred. The response to my request was overwhelming. I received shirts from as far away as Texas and California.

At this point my face and neck were in very bad shape and I was told that it would be at least a week (most likely two to three weeks) before I could resume treatments. The new date for the end of my treatments was now set at February 1, 2008.

The fact that my treatments were being extended, along with the pain I was experiencing and the pain meds I was taking, made me extremely depressed. Of course, not having the energy to play with my children (4 and 8 years old) or to even help my wife with basic, essential housework didn't help my overall attitude either.

By the time February rolled around, I'd lost 40+ pounds, my energy levels had dropped to almost non-existent levels, and I was sinking lower and lower into depression. I had already begun to take Zoloft (an antidepressant) but it didn't seem to be doing much for me.

Like most everything else concerning my treatment protocol, the time line of the first of February didn't hold true. It wasn't until the sixth and eighth of the month when my chemo and radiation therapies were over with. But, they were finally over and my wife and I began to prepare to rejoice in the fact that I'd made it through the entire ordeal.

1. I believe on my DVD I state that I had the surgery in Mid-July. That is incorrect. The correct timeframe is mid-September 2007.

2. A PICC line is a Peripherally Inserted Central venous Catheter that is advanced into the body in the veins until the internal tip of the catheter is in the superior vena cava, one of the central venous system veins that carries blood to the heart.

5

My Perspective by Dawn Honeycutt

"But this is what I commanded them, saying, 'Obey My voice, and I will be your God, and you will be My people ; and you will walk in all the way which I command you, that it may be well with you.'"
Jeremiah 7:23

Over the last year, my favorite song has been "*The Voice of Truth*" by Casting Crowns. I'd like to say that I was constantly tuned to the 'voice of truth' but I must admit that there were an awful lot of times when the 'voice of lies' got the best of me.

I remember the day of Lonnie's surgery as clearly as if it were yesterday. It was the day my life became a time of complete oxymorons: trusting God but crying out to him for abandoning us.

I recall being concerned because Lonnie has had so many health problems throughout his life that even this simple surgery was a big deal. When we arrived at the waiting room for the outpatient clinic some of our friends were already there. By the time Lonnie was escorted back to prep him for surgery, the waiting room at the hospital was filled with so many friends who were offering support that my thought was 'wow, it is cool that Lonnie is so loved'. At this point in my journey I really did believe that they were all there for Lonnie. However, during this ordeal I learned that they were there to support me as well. You know that is one of the big lessons my heart learned during this time. The deceiver of mankind (satan) had convinced me that people *loved* Lonnie and they *liked* me because I was Lonnie's wife. The truth that grew in my heart was that people loved me as well and it has completely changed my perspective on relationships. I used to serve out of my love for others, but more often than not felt invisible. For the most part that was okay because I still served with Christ's heart but it was still terribly lonely. The way I felt that people perceived me and because of my lack of understanding or acceptance that I was really and truly loved by others for the value that I brought to the relationship caused me to be filled me with fear and dread whenever I was around most people. Now, after experiencing God's love for me through so many people, I actually enjoy being around people and long for the fellowship.

Back to my perspective…

I was in the waiting room during the surgery with all of our friends. The surgeon had told me that he would call during the surgery to let me know how it was going. At this point the word 'cancer' had not been used in connection with the lumps that were in Lonnie's neck so I wasn't concerned.

As time dragged along and no call was received from the doctor, fear began to weasel its way into my soul. When the surgeon finally called, his comment of "*It is cancer, just as I suspected*" hit me like a freight train.

Please understand that up until this time we had both really been walking in God's power and authority over all things. We had seen someone healed from Parkinson's Disease. So, even though the word 'cancer' was frightening I honestly believed that it was just another thing that God had authority over and I struggled to not give the word too much power. Instead I chose to believe that God was still in control, the surgery would be successful and that was the last we would deal with cancer.

When I told the others in the waiting room, my tears began to flow and there were so many to offer comfort. At that time I was mostly stunned and working hard to not let the word cancer scare me, but, rather, to trust that God had it under control. I remember folks telling me it was okay to cry and be upset. I could tell that they were concerned about me because I did not become overly upset at that time (only the momentary tears that I cried). Try as I might, I couldn't convince them that my trust in God was sufficient enough not to warrant a breakdown at that time.

My first major bout of concern came when the surgery was over and I got to speak with the surgeon. He told me that they hadn't identified the origin of the cancer yet and more tests would have to be done. He had brought a radiologist into the operating room so he could show him what areas would need to undergo treatment, as far as they could tell. We would know what we were really dealing with after a PET scan. This scared me. Truly frightened me. I'd been thinking all along that the surgery would be the last of the cancer that had invaded Lonnie's body and, yet, now I was being told that there was so much of it that further treatment would be needed.

To make matters worse, Lonnie was still unconscious from the surgery and I was going to have to be the one to break the news to him. I didn't know how that was going to go but I had a feeling it would be a very emotionally trying thing for him to accept. Surprisingly, when I told Lonnie the prognosis, he took it extremely well. His attitude was one that seemed to belie the seriousness of the situation. Instead of becoming depressed or angry or scared, he and I agreed that the best thing we could do at the time was to trust that God was still in control and that the surgeons had actually gotten all the cancer out of his body.

The next period of time was worry and fear mixed with trusting God to handle things. Lonnie has always been big on researching things. The Internet is a wonderful tool, but also contains so much information it can be overwhelming. This was part of the 'other' voice we allowed into our lives – too much information. While knowing it was important to know what was ahead and just as important (especially for Lonnie) for us to be informed about treatment options and side effects, his research also brought into light some frightening statistics that tried to raise fear and doubt about our trusting in God to handle things.

Then our first opportunity arose. A wonderful man of God (Brian H.) offered to fly us wherever we needed to go for treatment or another consultation. We asked him to fly us to California to Bill Johnson's church in Redding, CA. We had heard Bill speak of the wonderful healings he had been blessed to be a part in and that they were working toward a cancer-free zone in Redding. So, my Aunt Margaret and Uncle Fred came to stay with the children and we took off for California, full of hope and eagerness for what the Lord was going to do. It was a wonderful time of prayer and seeking the Lord and we came back trusting that God had worked a miracle and the PET scan would show that Lonnie was cancer free.

It didn't happen that way.

While the tests showed that the cancer hadn't spread beyond his neck, it had metastasized from the base of his tongue into several of his lymph nodes. God hadn't come through. While that was devastating and the future was scary, there was still hope and trust that God was in control and all would ultimately be okay. Of course, my idea of okay at that time was that Lonnie would be cured with the treatment and, while this time might be difficult, God would see us through it because He wasn't done with Lonnie yet.

The coming months were very difficult with very little sun in our lives. We thought Lonnie would get through the first portion of the treatment with little difficulty. The reality was that he got sick the very first week. Between the chemo and the radiation he grew weaker and sicker almost with each passing day. As the doctors increased his pain meds, his ability to cope diminished. When the chemo began causing constant nausea and producing painful rashes that would crack open and bleed and the radiation produced sores in his mouth and throat, it all seemed like some cruel, sick joke.

I tried to minimize the trauma on my children by shielding them from the seriousness of what their dad was going through, but my 4-year-old daughter grew increasingly frightened of her father. His vomiting, as it was so violent and frequent, would see her running to her room and crying inconsolably. I prayed constantly that God would protect them from the horror Lonnie was experiencing.

About 10 days before Christmas, Lonnie had lost a lot of weight because he was unable to keep any food down and because his throat was extremely raw from the radiation and chemo. His doctor decided the best method of treatment was to put Lonnie in the hospital to receive IV fluids, get the vomiting under control, and have a feeding tube inserted. At this point we welcomed the feeding tube (something that was amazing in and of itself as Lonnie had been adamant about not having to have a feeding tube when this ordeal began) and looked forward to some improvement in his condition. As it turned out, nothing with Lonnie through this ordeal was simple.

The first attempt to put the feeding tube in was unsuccessful because Lonnie has so much scar tissue built up from an operation he underwent as an infant to repair a hernia and to remove his spleen. The first procedure was abandoned and Lonnie was taken back to his room. The doctors had trouble waking him up. This is something that everyone said should not have happened. In order to wake him, it was decided that they should give Lonnie a shot of Narcan. For anyone unfamiliar with Narcan, it is a medication that wipes all other pain drugs from your system. This had the effect of waking Lonnie immediately but also sent him into a pain crisis. After the failed feeding tube attempt Lonnie had a terrible dream that left him in torment (so much so that he would often forgo sleep so as to not dream the dream again) and he regularly hallucinated until the day he died.

It was decided that they were going to have to do a midline incision to insert the feeding tube. This is where they make an incision from below the sternum down to the belly button. This is a much more complicated procedure that was made even more difficult by the fact that the anesthesiologist was afraid that inserting a breathing tube into his esophagus would cause the airway to collapse because of the damage done by the radiation. Lonnie was also terrified of going under anesthesia because of the pain episode and terrifying dream he'd had. The anesthesiologist decided to do a spinal block instead.

The surgery went well but we had more problems on the horizon.

My brother, Mark Strick, and his family arrived to celebrate Christmas with us. He was able to take the children home from our friend's house where they had been staying and I stayed at the hospital with Lonnie.

Before telling you what happened next, I feel it's only right that I tell you that the hospital we were at was staffed by wonderful and highly qualified nurses. However, the modern healthcare system has left these folks stretched between many patients and with very little external monitoring. With that being said…

Lonnie was given a great deal of medication to help him with the pain of his surgery as well as the pain from the cancer treatment. At 11:00 p.m. that night a nurse gave him a shot of morphine and left the room. About 10 minutes later I noticed he was having trouble breathing. I alerted the nurses and they were not able to wake him. I hate to think what would have happened that night if I hadn't stayed. Because of his throat trouble, again it was decided that intubating him was not a good option so he was given another shot of Narcan. This episode was even worse than the one before because on top of the pain he was going through due to the chemo and radiation, his stomach had been sliced open. I've never seen anyone in so much pain and to have the person going through such trauma to be your spouse is almost unbearable. Lonnie told me after the pain crisis was over, that if I hadn't been there holding his hands and talking him through it, he believes he would have hurt himself or someone else.

You know, it is wonderful when someone has that much trust in you but it brings with it great responsibility. I know that some thought I was overboard in my care of Lonnie, but I was dedicated to him through this struggle and I wouldn't change a minute of what I did for him. Lonnie and I have enjoyed a relationship that I would wish everyone could have. I really feel that God brought us together and through Him we complete each other. The way Lonnie treats me is such a beautiful picture of the love Christ has for each one of us. My love for Lonnie can't be measured or diminished by circumstances. God is dedicated to us in this way and I believe He was honored by my service during this year.

Up to this point Lonnie had been an incredible witness and servant of the Lord. He was always witnessing to the others while receiving treatments, to the doctors and to those he touched by email. He spent many hours in prayer for others.

After Christmas we entered a time of true crisis. The radiation burned his neck and he suffered from 2nd and 3rd degree radiation burns and had to lay off treatment for two weeks so his neck could heal. The pain was excruciating and I spent many hours holding his hands while he cried. I also lost my job during this time and we threw the loss of insurance and income on top of the pile of stress that was already threatening to bury us. Looking back I can say that during those times when I was the weakest, God was at his greatest in my life. During this time I got to see just how alive and well the body of Christ is and just how many people there are out there who hear God's voice and obey His leading. My great friends, Garland and Alicia B., employed me at their gymnastics business and provided us with insurance. People we didn't even know began sending us money to help us financially through this time. Friends sacrificed of themselves to help us through this. The love of Christ was tangible in those around us.

Even after the feeding tube was in place Lonnie was never able to take in enough nourishment to halt his weight loss. He also continued to get nauseous and would vomit several times a day. The difference was that now we had a bag that hooked up to the feeding tube so that instead of throwing up, the bag just sucked the stomach contents out. At least now he could find relief without having to do more damage to his throat. The best way to control all this was to be diligent in feeding and administering medication. Every 2 – 4 hours, 24 hours a day, I would put medication and food into his feeding tube. For a couple of months I didn't get more than 2 hours of sleep at a time. But each day God gave me the grace to go on.

Finally, the end of January came and the last of Lonnie's treatments passed. We knew that it would take awhile for him to recover, but at least, we thought, things should have started to improve.

A couple weeks into recovery, Lonnie wasn't feeling very well. His throat and mouth were so damaged that he wasn't even able to swallow water. His stomach still wouldn't hold much nutrition. The doctor said that he was dehydrated and that I should bring him in for I.V. fluids. Once again, what should have been a simple thing turned into another crisis. Lonnie had an allergic reaction to the anti-nausea medication given with the fluids and he began getting physically jumpy. Nothing the doctor did seemed to have any effect in reversing this reaction and the oncologist decided to admit him to the hospital.

Over the next 13 hours, Lonnie was given enough medication to drop an elephant – literally. By this time he was down to about 130 pounds. He was given five different medications that, according to the nurse, each dose should have been enough to stop a man more than twice his size. Still, nothing improved. For 13 hours, he was so jittery he was unable to stay still for more than 10 seconds. He would leap from bed and walk around the room although this became more difficult as the hours passed and the medication made him unstable. It was exhausting. A dear friend, Gary M. came to the hospital and took turns sitting with Lonnie. Gary even rubbed Lonnie's feet – something that my husband finds soothing. To see a man's-man like Gary rubbing the feet of another man made me realize what a special friend he really is. Finally, about 3:00 a.m. Lonnie fell asleep and so did I. Two hours later he was awake, feeling better and wanting to go home. It was amazing. He kept badgering the nurses about seeing his doctor and when his doctor came, he insisted that he was well enough to go home. I was convinced that there was no way under the sun his doctor would release him, but, like I said, Lonnie was insistent and he was released just before noon.

Honestly, Lonnie was doing better than he had in months. He was actually doing so well I left him home alone for a while that day. He went next door and visited the neighbors by the campfire. He cooked dinner for us that night and he sounded more like his old self. I was so relieved. It seemed like we had turned the corner on this whole mess and I was praising God for getting us through. Lonnie played with the children and when nightfall came he laid down with our son Brance that night to watch a show (either Smash Lab or Mythbusters) with him. He fell asleep there in our son's bed after taking the sleeping pill that had been prescribed to him by his physician. Figuring he would get uncomfortable after a while and come to bed, I left him sleeping and crawled into bed myself, thoroughly exhausted but feeling better than I had in months. Little did I know that Lonnie would almost never wake up from his nap that night.

6

The Day Lonnie Died
by Dawn Honeycutt

"Jesus said to her, 'I am the resurrection and the life.
He who believes in Me will live, even though he dies.'"
John 11:25

The morning of February 16th was a beautiful day. I woke to find that I had actually slept all the way through the night! It was the first time in I couldn't recall how long. Lonnie wasn't in bed with me but I assumed he had just been so tired that he never left Brance's bed. That was unusual, but after all that we had been through, what was normal? I got dressed and showered, which seemed like a luxury, while the house slept. The children had a gymnastics exhibition that morning so around 8:00 a.m. I decided it was time to get everyone up and moving so we would be on time. We never made it…

I went in to wake Brance and Lonnie first. Lonnie didn't stir and his color was horrible. He was snoring a raspy snore but only once every 40-45 seconds. I started shaking him and pinching but couldn't wake him. Trying to control the fear that arose within me, I sent Brance to get the phone and call 911. I got Lonnie off the bed and onto the floor. I could detect a faint pulse but he was blue. The 911 operator had me begin giving Lonnie artificial respiration. I was terrified that I was too late. I wanted to comfort my children, who I knew must be so scared, but I couldn't leave Lonnie and I needed Brance's help. I had to have him lock our dogs up and open the gate for the ambulance. I've always known that I was good while I was needed during a crisis, but once the professionals arrived I would fall apart. That is exactly what happened this time.

The paramedics arrived and took over. I told them of Lonnie's medical history and got his oncologist on the phone. They decided that they wouldn't intubate him because of the throat damage. While they worked on Lonnie, our neighbors (Bob and Jenny P. and Larry and Cindy J.) arrived. As they took Lonnie out of the house, one of the paramedics was asked by Cindy, point blank: *"Is he going to make it?"* She was told, *"No, I don't expect him to make it. It doesn't look good for him at all.”*

I called a friend to come get the children and the neighbors watched them while I went to the hospital with Lonnie. I was terrified for the children and for Lonnie and prayed all the way to the hospital. I prayed over Lonnie for him to start breathing. I began to imagine, for the first time, a life without my sweet husband. It was more than I could handle.

My pain and fear made it impossible to hear God or feel His presence. I felt completely abandoned and betrayed. How could He walk us through this and then let me down like this? This was crazy!!! What was going on!

Friends began showing up in the ER. Family was contacted out of state and arrangements were made for them to get there quickly. The doctors were telling us that it didn't look good. Lonnie started having seizures in the ER and they had to put him on a ventilator to breathe. I was told that his flailings didn't mean that he was responsive but that his body was basically in death throes due to cerebral hypoxia. Everyone wanted to know if he had a living will. Since he did not, I was asked what I wanted to do? Would I sign a DNR (Do Not Resuscitate) order?

The pain and loss I felt was overwhelming. This was really happening. All the fears I had held at bay since September threatened to crush me. Where was the God who was so good? Why had He abandoned us? How could He let this happen? We were so faithful!?!?

Lonnie was eventually moved to the ICU. I was told that his pupils were fixed and dilated which indicated significant brain damage due to terminal anoxia. I found out that if both eyes have fixed or dilated pupils (such as Lonnie had), the prognosis is generally very poor since this can indicate significant damage to the brain-stem – the area of the brain responsible for regulating such basic functions as breathing. The medical staff told me that the outcome was not promising.

The attending physician told me that he believed that all the medication Lonnie had been given two nights before had caught up with him on Friday night and he had, in effect, overdosed.

At one point the medical staff rushed out into the waiting room and asked me about signing a DNR because they couldn't find a blood pressure or pulse. They were putting in a central line, but needed to know what to do. Lonnie and I had discussed this and I knew that he didn't want to live if there was no hope. I told them I would sign it.

Fortunately, they never had to hand me the paper.

There were many friends gathered by this time. A group of men and women gathered together in the courtyard of the hospital after hearing this latest bit of news (that my husband had neither blood pressure nor a pulse and his eyes were fixed and dilated). They began praying and calling Lonnie forth from death. A short time later, the doctor came out and said that they now had a pulse. There was much celebrating. Lonnie was back!

The nurse who came on the night shift that night poured a huge bucket on ice water on the hope we had. She wasn't afraid to tell us what the doctors wouldn't. She let me know that Lonnie's chances of waking up were very slim and that he would be in the ICU on the ventilator for at least 3 weeks. She also said that if he ever did wake up, he wouldn't be the same because he had suffered major brain damage. I was told that due to the damage to his brain that I'd probably spend the rest of my life changing his diapers and spoon-feeding him.

About midnight all their efforts to regulate his blood pressure failed. His blood pressure bottomed out again. The nurse rushed to call the doctor to ask what to do. The doctor replied, *"What do you want me to do, the man has a hypoxic-anoxic brain. He's brain dead. You need to tell his wife."* The nurse said, *"I expect you to give him something so he has a chance to live."* The doctor then prescribed one last-ditch medication, but said if it didn't work it was over.

The nurse told me of her conversation with the doctor and I was told, in no uncertain terms, that Lonnie was brain dead. I immediately started praying over Lonnie and, to my surprise, the nurse joined me. Thankfully, she never had to give Lonnie the last medication as his pressure came back up while we prayed and he continued to improve. She checked his pupils and there was some reaction this time. There seemed to be hope!!

After the doctor made rounds in the morning he indicated that we now had 'a little' hope. Still not very encouraging. I sat in the waiting room and cried again. Ten minutes later the nurses came out and said that Lonnie was awake and asking for me! I ran back there to find him awake indeed. They asked if he knew me and he nodded his head

"*Yes*" and signed "*I Love You,*" something we always do in our family! He was awake and really knew me!! They sedated him at this point to help him rest. The next day they started weaning him from the vent and the day after he was off the ventilator and moved to a private room! God had really come through!

While we were in the private room, one of the nurses came in and said that he had spoken with the doctors, nurses and medical instructors and they all said the same thing "...*they had never seen someone who was so bad off, recover so quickly and so well.*" It was truly something that "...*defied medical reason.*" Praise God, Lonnie was truly back from the dead!

He continued to progress from 'dying' at an incredible rate. The other astonishing healing was that after only 3 days in ICU, he was able to eat with no problem. Three days earlier he couldn't even swallow water and now he could eat anything and everything. His throat and mouth were healed.

Remember back in my perspective when I said that my trust in God was that all would be okay? Well, I have to say that one of the biggest things I've learned about God is that HE IS GOOD – ALWAYS!!!! And always means always. Even when He doesn't come through the way I think He should, that doesn't change His goodness. He is there in everything and just because I don't understand or like it, doesn't mean that God is anything but good. That gave me hope each day.

There is a song by David M. Bailey that helped me during this time. It is called "*When*" and the final section says that when you stumble and fall, you might look around and see no one around, but maybe they have fallen too and might need you. "*So rise up my friend and welcome the new day with a shout and cherish every second. Drive away the doubt and walk right through the shadows. I promise there's a way to find out why the Good Lord has given you one more day.*"

Remember that there is always a way you can serve and love God, even in the midst of your own crisis. During one of the times in the ICU waiting room, one of my friends came to me and said there was someone in the ICU that they needed me to pray for. I was able to enter into someone else's pain and help them have some hope. I found out later that this encounter made a lasting impact on their lives. I can proudly say that there were many lives touched during this time, by us, by friends and family members and by those that we were able to touch. The world doesn't stop because you do, so please don't miss the opportunities for God to use you in whatever your current situation might be. Help Him reach others with His hope and love. It might actually help you find His hope and love for you.

I've been asked often how I got through all this. I can honestly say that it was only through God and my listening to the *'Voice of Truth.'* This isn't to say that I was always the strongest of Christians. There were definitely times when my pain kept me from feeling God's love, even though it was always there. My friends who listened to me cry during these times always helped me lift that veil of pain and find God's love again. The prayers of others kept both Lonnie and I going. It was and is truly humbling when I consider the number of those who became involved in our pain and trials. I thank each and every one of you for your love and dedication. Thanks also to each of you who have done this for someone else. You may never know how your prayers have helped, but never doubt that they did.

7

My Ascension Into Heaven

"He will wipe every tear from their eyes. Death will be no more;
mourning and crying and pain will be no more,
for the first things have passed away."
Revelation 21:4

Before I begin to recount the time I spent in Heaven, I'd like to say a few words concerning my theological bent. I am very conservative when it comes to the Bible. I take the Word of God seriously and am not prone to come to many conclusions that can't be found by the most conservative of evangelical scholars. As such, I told no one about my visit to Heaven for almost a month after I'd died and was resurrected. It was only after I had prayed and diligently sought the Lord concerning the validity of my 'experience' that I told the first person (my wife).

I would also like to thank Brother Don Piper, whom I've never met but with whom I share a great deal as far as it concerns our individual trips into Heaven. While I'd certainly heard of his wonderful book *'90 Minutes In Heaven'* I'll be eternally grateful that I had not read the book prior to my death. The reason is simple: Nearly three months after I had died and gone to Heaven myself, I was given the book to read, and, once I had, I was more convinced than ever that what I had experienced was really and truly a true experience because what Mr. Piper experienced in Heaven mirrored my own experience so closely. Obviously, there are divergences, but, if you get the chance to read his book you'll see what I mean. With that being said, here is what I experienced while in Heaven…

Unlike many, many people who have had a near death or death experience, I did not see a 'light at the end of the tunnel.' Instead, my memories of Heaven begin with my being on a road, flanked by three angels (one on either side and one in behind me). People I speak with often ask me if the angels were tall? As I tell them, 'tall' is a relative term and because I'm so short (I used to be 5' 3" before I lost all my hair), almost everyone is tall to me. But, in all seriousness, the angels were rather tall, maybe 6' 5" to 7' tall. So, while they were tall, they weren't 'Goliath' tall. I noted that all four of us were wearing traditional flowing white robes (traditional in the sense of what you might have seen people wearing around the first century, not the flimsy, silky type of robe we often see Jesus depicted in), although mine was slightly whiter or brighter than those of the angels around me.

Some very inquisitive individuals have pressed me to give them a more thorough description of the angels that were escorting me and have been disappointed that I'm not able to. I fully realize that there have been dozens upon dozens of books, tracts, and booklets (and more internet blogs than a person can shake a stick at) written about angels, what they look like, descriptions of their appearances, et cetera, but I'd like to point out that the angels who were accompanying me, to me at least, were simply beings who were there with me solely as escorts. As for a physical description of the angels, besides their height, I hesitate to tell you much about them for fear of a misunderstanding as it concerns 'races' (which is purely an evolutionary concept). With that being said, I'd tell you the following: One of the angels was black (like onyx or ebony – not merely black but the blackest of black) and the other two had kind of an olive complexion. However, their complexions had nothing to do with their inner natures. In other words, when the term 'black' is used in America we often think of 'African or African American' and when the term olive is used in connection with skin color we many times think of a 'Jewish or Mexican or a Middle Eastern' person). But, the angels who accompanied me were not African American or Jewish or any other particular ethnicity. It wasn't as if their color held any ethnic distinction, it was just what they looked like to me.

Honestly, the angels weren't overly exciting to me because I knew that I was going to New Jerusalem and whom I was going to see – Jesus Christ, in person. Knowing this I think that you can understand why the presence of angels weren't all that exciting to me. I often ask the question: Who or what among all of creation, can possibly awe us when compared to the King of Kings and Lord of Lords – the most AWESOME being in the universe? The answer is no one and nothing!

Also, in my mind, I expected and have always expected to see many angels in Heaven. So, to me, while it was great to have the angels around, they weren't a 'big deal.' I honestly don't believe that anyone who goes to Heaven (any and all of those who have accepted Jesus as their Savior) will be all that awed by angels. Will we be impressed? I think so. I know that I was. But the reason I was impressed was because these beings had already spent millennia in the presence of the Almighty God whereas I had yet to personally meet Him – at least face-to-face. So, while angels who appear here on Earth are sure to impress and to strike a godly fear into people, in Heaven, they are simply beings who attest to His greatness – but not nearly as much as a single saint who resides there.

As I said, I was immediately transported into Heaven. The road upon which we stood was the most beautiful pathway I've ever imagined. It was translucent gold. Now, when I say 'translucent, I really mean *translucent*. It was a road of transparent, see-through gold and there was light shining up through it in a myriad of colors. There was a brilliant, brilliant light all around us – all around me and everything else. In fact, the word I choose to describe my entire time in Heaven is brilliant! Everything that I saw and experienced there felt more real than anything I've ever known here on Earth.

Again, the light I was bathed in seemed to permeate everything to such an extent that all I saw almost glowed from it. Yet, the light, being ever so bright, didn't hurt my eyes. As I walked with my escort of angels I remember looking behind them and me and towards our feet. I'm fairly certain I did this to see if there were any shadows. There weren't. None at all. No shadows of any type, anywhere that I could see. None under us, none behind us or in front of us, none around the trees or the flowers that lined the sides of the road. Shadows simply didn't exist in Heaven. Also, the light didn't seem to have any particular source. What I mean is that there was no sun or other basis of light from which it was emanating. So, I have to conclude that God was the source of the light!

While on this road, I also experienced something that I've rarely experienced here on Earth and that was… peace. Peace that is literally beyond human comprehension. If there is anything that I truly long for on this side of Heaven it's the feeling of peace that seemed to permeate every cell in my body. I now know what it's like to experience a deep, abiding sense of peace and I want to enter into that presence of mind again. Prior to my trip to Heaven I never knew that such peace actually existed. Since that time, I've only experienced the same type of peace twice and it comes from knowing that God really does have everything under His control.

My wife asked me if I had been aware of people here on Earth (those that were praying for me, herself and my children) and, I have to say, I was. I knew that I had left behind my wife and children and mother and brothers and sisters but it was okay. I knew, in my heart of hearts, that everything was going to be all right, that everything *was* all right *because* I was in Heaven. I was at peace with everything.

Others have asked me if I was aware of people who were not in Heaven (i.e., those that were in Hell). Again, the answer is Yes. But, again, it was okay. This is perhaps the most difficult thing that I have to try and explain – how one cannot feel remorse or sadness for people (even some of my own family members) who are in Hell. Still, it's true.

Not to sound callous or cavalier (which I'd never be concerning the eternal destination of anyone), but I knew, in my heart of hearts, that the reason the people I saw were in Hell was because they'd made a conscious decision not to accept Jesus as their personal Lord and Savior. As such, it wasn't that Jesus (God) had sent them there because of anything they'd done (i.e., sin) but because they chose not to accept the one Person (Jesus) who could and would have pardoned them.

I now know what it means to have all tears of sadness wiped away because, for the briefest of moments, I truly believe that my understanding was like that of the mind of Christ. I understood the ramifications of our decisions here on Earth and their eternal consequences. Today, those I grieve for are those who, like my step-brother, have not accepted Jesus as their personal Savior and, as such, are going to miss out on the glories of Heaven. It is for these people I weep. But, after a person has died, it is too late.

Yet, even though I was aware of all of this, while I was in Heaven, my soul was absolutely tranquil but I was very excited at the same time. How could I have been anything but excited? I was in the 'other country,' the abiding place of my Lord and Savior.

As far as being aware of people on Earth goes, I was able to see people *here* on Earth while I was *there*. I've been asked how I was able to see people on Earth from Heaven and I must admit that words fail to allow me to describe exactly how it was that I could see the events taking place. If I had to try to describe the manner in which I was viewing the happenings on Earth it would be like I was looking through a very thin, extremely pale membrane or veil. I could see people praying for me, I knew what people were doing and I could hear those who were praying for me.

At one point I remember looking *down* and *through* the road on which I was walking and seeing people in the hospital and the courtyard of the hospital. Another time I remember looking to the side of where I was standing and seeing others who were in prayer for me. So, while the manner of how I was able to 'see through to Earth' escapes me, I know I did it. As I explained to one young man who asked me what it looked like, I told him that it was like seeing through a pane of glass – one that was clear and thin but also one that acted as a barrier between the two worlds.

I later became impressed by the knowledge that those I met were aware of the prayers of saints and the events that were occurring on Earth but I was only aware of those who were directing prayers to God for me. Perhaps this was because I wasn't yet a *permanent* member of Heaven, perhaps not. Perhaps I wasn't aware of the prayers and lives of others because I was so attuned to what was going on around me at the time that I was simply distracted. Whatever the reason is it's the way it was. What I do know as a fact is that God is moved by the prayers of the saints (anyone who has taken Jesus as their personal Savior) and that I heard David B. asking me to come back. Specifically, I heard him say, "*Lonnie, come back. I love you.*" David, as I was told after I returned, had chosen to 'stand in' for me while everyone else prayed for me to be allowed to return and, as my friend, David and I do share a love for one another. I'm so appreciative for every prayer sent to God on my behalf because, as Mary Ann Wyatt aptly stated, the prayers were the 'hinge point' on which hung the decision of God to allow me a choice to return to my family and friends.

I remember that the air was clean and fresh and the sky was an amazing array of blue and white. The white I initially assumed was due to clouds but, as I looked closer, I saw that the white was due to angels. There were countless legions of angels flying to and fro above us as we walked and their ranks stretched as far as my eyes could see in every direction. As I walked along the road, I noted that my vision was much better than it had ever been on Earth. Or, perhaps, my vision seemed better due to the fact that the environment I was in was completely pure. As such, every tree and every flower, even the blades of grass I saw along the side of the road nearly burst with the most vibrant of colors. I remember taking in deep, deep breaths of air and feeling the coolness filling my lungs. It was exhilarating and my pulse seemed to race as I thought of where I was.

One of the most enduring memories I have is of the breeze and the smell of Heaven. While walking along the road, I felt the most wonderful breeze – not too warm or too chilly or too hard – but it was steady and constant. And, on that breeze, there was a smell unlike anything I can describe. It was so very, very sweet though not overpowering.

I've been asked to attempt a description of what I smelled that day and the closest I can come to doing so is this: If you've ever been to a fruit orchard when the trees are full of blossoms and you've smelled the sweetness of the fruit trees wafting in the air, you'll have some pale idea of the deliciously delicate, sweet smell I smelled. Come to think of it, since there were trees that lined the road on which I was walking and because we're told that there are fruit trees in Heaven, the smell may have come from them. Whatever the source, I'll never forget the breeze or the smell.

The road on which we were walking was wide and long. Very wide and very long and I was the only person on it. I mention this fact because I wondered why I was the only one on the road at that moment. I remember thinking that I certainly couldn't have been the only person who had died that day or even that hour. Honestly, I didn't give it much thought at the time because I was excited about getting into the city I saw at the end of the road. But, afterwards, when I was telling this story to my wife, I did begin to think about whether or not it made sense that I would have been the only person on the road at that time. I've decided that if what I experienced was real (and I certainly believe it was), that I had crossed over into eternity. The reason this point is important is because, in eternity, time has no meaning. So, since we're told that each person will have to make a personal account of his or her actions to God, why couldn't it be that each person who goes to Heaven will get his or her own time on the same road?

As I said, I didn't take any time to really contemplate these types of questions while I was in Heaven because they simply didn't matter and because I wanted to reach the Heavenly city I saw in the distance.

Unlike Brother Don Piper, I didn't see pearly gates of any type. It could have been that I was already past them at the time my memory begins or it might simply be that I didn't notice them (although I think that giant pearls or even pearlescent gates would be terribly difficult to miss). But, what I did see was a wonderfully large building amongst other relatively small ones. I think that the building captivated my attention so much because of its size. Huge doesn't even come close to describing it. The height and breadth of the building was such that I don't remember being able to see the end to its top or sides. What I do remember though was that in the building I saw arched windows (very similar to the Spanish-style windows we see in some homes) and, as I walked nearer and nearer to the entrance of the city, people were gathering at the windows and looking out towards me. I distinctly remember that there were, at different windows, one, two, three, four, five, and six people who gathered together in the windows to peer out at me (the larger groups pressed into one another in a cluster).

Both to the left and the right of the large building (which seemed to me to be concave, rather than square and seemed to be located somewhere in the center of an extremely large area) I saw what I can only describe as spires and bridges and walkways and what, for the lack of a better word, seemed to be gardens. I saw people strolling along the pathways, milling about among beautiful flowers and trees and purposefully walking to and fro. The other structures that I saw seemed to be made of a material similar to that of the road I had walked into New Jerusalem on – a golden metal but a metal that was as clear as it was shiny. Something that struck me is that I saw no means of transportation other than walking. That doesn't mean that there aren't other modes of going from one place to another, I simply didn't notice any.

There was also a massive number of people gathering at the entrance of the city waiting for me to get there. And, at the ground level of the huge building, there were smaller buildings. One child recently asked me how big those structures were and I had to admit that I had no idea because I don't have any idea as to how large the huge building was. I've also been asked if I knew what the huge building or smaller buildings were and, again, I have to say that I don't. I would assume, based on the fact that I saw some people coming out of the smaller structures, that they were homes of some type but I could be incorrect. Whatever function they served, I can hardly wait to find out.

The most unforgettable and remarkable thing that I remember from my entire trip to Heaven was the feeling that I got from the people who were waiting for me to cross the threshold into the city. The only way I can describe what I *felt* is as a *pressure*, but I know and knew exactly what it was that the people were feeling. They were giddy; absolutely excited about the fact that I was coming to join them and that I would be spending the rest of eternity with them and with Christ. The feeling was palpable. The pressure was tangible. It was as real as anything I've ever experienced before in my life and I will never forget it.

These people, most of whom I'm convinced that I did not know while on Earth, were happy about me being there with them. Now that's what I call a wonderful welcoming committee!

As I came closer to the entrance of the city, which we know as New Jerusalem, I noticed that not everyone was dressed the way I was. While the angels and I were dressed in traditional white robes, some of the people I saw were dressed in what I would consider run-of-the-mill, everyday clothes while others did have on white robes like mine. I've been asked what I believe the significance of the white robes is and I truly have no clue. Obviously I know that they are a symbol of purity (we see, in the book of Revelation that the robes are made white by the blood of the Lamb) but why everyone wasn't wearing them at the time I don't know. Maybe everyone shows up in white robes and then we get a chance to change once we're 'at home.' Who knows? I don't. But, again, I'm not concerned about it and I don't think anyone else should be either.

For whatever reason, I don't remember going very far into New Jerusalem itself (but I guarantee that the next time I get to Heaven I'll run into it). Nor do I remember ever meeting Jesus. I may have and I probably did, if my 'gut feeling' is true, but I simply don't remember doing so at the present time. This is probably a good thing because, I truly believe that if I remembered meeting Jesus face-to-face then I would be miserable here on Earth.

What I do know is that I was asked by someone (I have a strong feeling that it was either the Holy Spirit or Jesus Himself) if I wanted to return to Earth or stay. I said *"Yes,"* I wanted to return to Earth.

At this point I must confess that the reason I chose to return was because of my wife, not my children, as much as I love them. I knew that everyone would be able to get along well enough without me, God would see to that, but I also knew that my wife truly needed me back. Whereas, my children, a little girl who was four at the time, and my son, an eight-year old, would eventually either forget me (which would be okay because I'd see her again if she accepted Jesus as her Savior – my son has already made the decision to have Jesus as his personal Savior) or would adapt fairly quickly to my absence, I sensed, probably from all the prayers being prayed on her behalf, that Dawn would be devastated without me. So, I chose to return to Earth because of my wife. When I first told Dawn this, she confessed to me that while I was in a coma, she had told me that it was *"Okay if I needed to go be with Jesus."* Then she asked me if I was sad about returning to her. I told her, *"No, I'm not sad at all. It's what I wanted to do and it was my decision."* But, as I've told everyone who has heard this story, not a single day goes by that I don't think about Heaven and all of its wonders.

I honestly can't wait until the day comes when either Jesus comes back for all those who have accepted Him as their Lord and Savior or when this world is delivered from the Curse of sin and is resurrected into a New Earth or when I die and get to go be with Christ permanently.

Just before I left Heaven, I remember, as clear as day, that a woman I had never met before (she had died some 30 years before I had) came through the crowd of people and I immediately knew her identity. She was the first one to reach me and when she had she hugged me and smiled and gave me a message for someone very close to me. The lady was also someone who wasn't wearing white robes like I was. Instead, she was dressed in a blue dress that had puffy sleeves. Her hair was curly/wavy, dark brown and she looked to be 35ish. In fact, everyone I saw in Heaven looked to be around 35 years old.

I mention this specific encounter with the lady in blue because I want everyone who reads this to know that it's true what the Bible says *"For now we see in a mirror, dimly, but then face to face. Now I know in part, but then I shall know just as I also am known.*" (1 Cor. 13:12)

By the way, the woman I met in Heaven was my mother-in-law, June. She's another reason, besides Brother Piper's own experience, that I'm convinced that my experience in Heaven was real. The reason June helped me come to believe that what I experienced is real is because of what she had told me to tell my wife, her daughter.

As I've said, June died some 30+ years before I did, in a different state, and a long, long time before my wife and I met. While Dawn and I had talked about her mom before, she never told me any intimate details about their relationship. So, the fact that when June gave me the message she wanted delivered to her daughter she used a cherished nickname for my wife (one that I'd never heard Dawn mention), gives me (and my wife) reason to believe that what I saw and who I met in Heaven was real.

As I just mentioned, everyone I saw while in Heaven looked to be around 35 years of age. But, in the case of my mother-in-law, she had died when she was in her 60's and her body had been ravaged by disease (she died of emphysema). The fact is that I'd never, ever seen a picture of her when she was around 35 years old (the only ones I recall ever seeing were those of when she was already sick and advanced in years). So, the fact that I knew who she was astounds me even today. Still, there was something about her and everyone I met that day that allowed me to know if they were older or younger when they died. It was an almost intangible quality – sort of like when you meet a person who is wise beyond their years or who is younger in character than their actual body says they are. It's one of those tangible intangibles. I can't explain it any better than that at the moment.

I feel very blessed, for three reasons, that the first person I was able to share this story with is my wife. The first reason is because she knows me better than anyone else and would know if my vision of Heaven were simply my imagination running wild. Secondly, due to the fact of what her mom said to her through me, Dawn is now convinced that I actually visited Heaven. In fact, prior to my telling her what June had given me for her, my wife honestly says that "*Well, I had taken what Lonnie was saying about Heaven with a grain of salt because I know how his imagination works. But, after hearing what my mom said to me, I now believe his story wholeheartedly and without reservation.*"

The third and last reason I feel blessed to have been able to tell my wife this story is because it assuaged a long-held fear of hers. As a child, a well-meaning teacher in Sunday school had once told her that when you die, *"it's just like going to sleep."* That is, when you die you don't know anything at all; it's just silence and inactivity when you die. This is called *soul sleep* in some circles and it is the unbiblical doctrine that refers to the belief that when we die, the soul ceases to exist, or sleeps. During this period of soul sleep the believer is not conscious of anything and the soul is completely inert until the time of the final resurrection of the dead. I'm very happy to say that this simply isn't what happens. As the Apostle Paul stated, *"To be absent from the body is to be present with the Lord"* (2 Corinthians 5:8) and *"For to me, to live is Christ and to die is gain. But if I am to live on in the flesh, this will mean fruitful labor for me; and I do not know which to choose. But I am hard-pressed from both directions, having the desire to depart and be with Christ, for that is very much better"* (Philippians 1:22-23). As we see in the story of the unnamed Rich Man and the beggar named Lazarus (Luke 16), a person is either immediately transported to Heaven or Hell upon death. There is no limbo or purgatory. It is one of the two destinations and I hope that you'll choose to one day join me in Heaven.

An interesting and totally unexplainable blessing came about from my knowing the details of the dress that my mother-in-law wore to greet me. Thea S., Dawn's cousin, heard about my testimony from my wife's Aunt Margaret and Uncle Fred F. (June's brother). Upon hearing the details of the dress – it was blue and had puffy shoulders – and before she was told that the person wearing it was her aunt, she declared, *"That was Aunt June. I know that dress. I remember Aunt June was so thin and I told her that blue dress looked too big on her because of the puffy sleeves."* This is simply another confirmation to the reality of my trip to Heaven. It was also a confirmation for June's brother (Fred) who had prayed with his sister just a week prior to her death that she would accept Christ. I know of no other reason that I would have remembered the details of the dress June wore the day I met her other than for confirmation to me that I'd actually been to Heaven and to June's family that she was waiting for them. By the way, since that day, I've searched through every picture of June and in none of them is she wearing anything that remotely resembles a blue dress with puffy sleeves. Praise God!

To be fair, I must note that there are things I saw, experienced and was told while in Heaven that I'm not allowed to reveal at this time. One day, perhaps, I will be allowed to talk about these things. Perhaps not. In either case, I hope you'll take the message of Heaven I've been sent to spread as hope for a better future in a very real place – a place that makes any wonder on Earth pale in comparison.

8

My Friends and Family Weigh In On that Fateful February Day in 2008

"Jesus saw a commotion, with people crying and wailing loudly. He went in and said to them, 'Why all this commotion and wailing? The child is not dead but asleep.'"

Mark 5:38b-39

Eddie Honeycutt (Mother)

When I got the call from Dawn that you had stopped breathing and she had had to perform CPR on you until the paramedics arrived and that you had died and were now in a coma, the first thing that popped into my mind was, *"No more, I can't take this."*

Then when I was calling your brothers and sisters to tell them the news, I thought, *"I can't lose him. We have gone through too much together."* Then I prayed and said, *"He is in Your hands as he has been since the day he was born. As I said to You on that day, Lord, I place him in Your hands because that's where he has been and still is. Your will be done."*

On the way to the hospital, all the way from Texas to Alabama, my thoughts were with you.

Now, when I got to the hospital, I saw you and all the thoughts and feelings that I had when you were 16 came rushing back to me. If you'll remember, when you were 16 you had developed endocarditis and almost died then as well. To me this was twice as bad because at least when you had endocarditis you never went into a coma.

I kissed you and told you, *"You have to quit doing things like this because I couldn't take any more."*

Later, as I was holding your hand and I told you that I loved you, your fingers gave mine a tiny squeeze and I said to myself, *"Yes, Lord, he will be okay."*

I can't tell you the emotions that a mother goes through whenever her child is going through what you were. It's terrible and heart wrenching.

The day at the hospital when they took you off life support and you opened your eyes and acknowledged us was almost more than I could stand. I knew at that moment you were back to stay for a while longer.

Lonnie, you were my miracle when you were born and you're still my miracle by the grace of God and I give Him my thanks for I know if it wasn't for Him, I wouldn't have you. Mom

Cindy J. (Next-Door Neighbor and Friend)

Lonnie, we invited you over to sit around the campfire with us the night before you died on February 16, 2008. Everyone was so excited because you had just finished your treatments and it was a real pleasure to be able to once again sit with you and just chat. You had been concerned about our son Lee because he was in a car wreck that same week.

We were all talking about how blessed we are and how good God is. You shared with us about some of the things you were looking forward to doing as soon as you regained your strength.

As most of our conversations always included our love for food and chocolate you told us a story we'd never heard before. It was about a time when you and Dawn had first begun dating and you'd found out that she liked white chocolate. You told us that you had driven over an hour away from where you lived in California to buy it for her as a gift on Valentine's Day. What you didn't know is that they actually sold white chocolate in the grocery store right next door to where you lived. We all were laughing and excited to see you feeling better.

The next morning I was walking my dog, when I heard sirens and saw a fire truck and an ambulance coming down our street. I immediately thought that they were going to the house of our elderly neighbor, Mrs. Nancy. I went inside to get the spare key to her gate and house and just before I entered my house, I noticed my parents, who live one house up from me, were already in their car and following the ambulance to what I assumed was Mrs. Nancy's home. I was shocked when I came back outside to see they had pulled up into your family's yard. My parents called me on my cell phone as I was walking next door and said, *"Lonnie has taken a turn for the worst and it doesn't look good."*

As I approached the ambulance, I asked the driver how you were doing. He said *"No, I don't expect him to make it. It doesn't look good for him at all."*

I stayed at the house with Brance and Danielle and packed some clothes for the kids to take while waiting for Alicia B. to pick them up.

The children were fully aware of what had happened with their daddy and kept saying how he had stopped breathing. The kids and I agreed to just pray while we gathered things up for them to leave. Cindy J.

Bob and Jenny P. (Next-Door Neighbors and Friends)

Bob and I (Jenny) were leaving to go to Wal-Mart at about 8 AM on February 16, 2008. I had stopped in the street waiting for Bob to shut and lock the gate. That's when a fire truck and an EMS unit turned onto our street. Our first thought was of the elderly neighbor lady who lives at the end of the street. Bob rushed back in to get the keys to her house and gate, thinking that they were going to her house to help her. We turned the car around and drove down the street. That's when we saw that the EMS vehicle had driven into your driveway.

We parked and rushed inside. Bob went straight to Brance's bedroom because that's where the three EMT's went. You had slept in Brance's room that Friday night. When Bob arrived at the door of the bedroom, he saw you lying on the floor, on your back with your arms down by your side in your underwear. You were not breathing, not moving, totally unresponsive. Your color was dark blue and black all over and you appeared to be dead.

One of the EMT's asked Bob if you had signed any papers to revive you. Bob said, "*I don't know, but I'll find out.*" Bob asked Dawn if you had signed any kind of papers regarding being revived and she said "*No,*" you had not signed any papers. During all of this, Dawn was very upset and crying, and was on the phone with either your pastor or the doctor.

Bob told the EMT, "*No, he has not signed any papers,*" and he immediately placed a large squeeze bulb with a mask over your mouth and nose. They tried to get a blood pressure reading and a pulse, but there was none. After they worked on you for approximately 30 seconds without getting a response, one of the guys looked at Bob and shook his head negatively, then said, "*We need to get him on a stretcher and into the ambulance right now.*"

Bob stepped out of the bedroom to make room for the men to get you onto the stretcher. They quickly loaded you on the stretcher. In Bob's personal opinion, you were physically dead.

To back up to when we first went into your house through the back door, Bob went on down the hall to Brance's room, and I saw Brance sitting with his knees drawn up to his chest. He was sitting on the sofa that is in front of the front windows. He was so quiet and so worried-looking, just listening and 'taking it all in.' I went over and sat down beside him. I can't remember just what I said to him, but he said that his daddy slept in his room last night and that you had trouble breathing. He had tried to wake you up but couldn't.

While we were sitting there, he could hear his mother crying and the things that were said and knew that the EMT's were with his dad. He looked like he was trying to make sense of it all.

I asked him if he would like to get his shirt on and go next door to Ms. Cindy's and he said, *"I think that I need to pray for my dad."* So he turned toward the back of the sofa and, with his face behind a cushion, he prayed.

I went into the kitchen to make a phone call to Alicia B. to come pick up Brance and Danielle, and then I called Cindy to come stay with them until Alicia got there. While Bob and I were in the kitchen, the EMT's wheeled you out through the dining room to the back door. I could see your legs and feet and they were dark blue.

After Cindy arrived at your house, Bob and I left and went to the hospital where you were taken to the emergency room.

Cindy said that while she was waiting for Alicia to arrive, Brance was walking through the house praying.

Cindy came to the hospital as soon as she could. Your pastor arrived right away, many other friends arrived, and prayers were being prayed for you and Dawn. God has obviously answered our prayers for you and miracles have happened.

We love you all, Lonnie, Dawn, Brance and Danielle.

Bob and Jenny P.

Brumbaugh (Friend)

This is to my Friend Lonnie – He used to be dead, but he got better!

It was Saturday February 16, 2008, and we had a full day planned. God had been doing a lot and I was going to go to Paul and Jaime T.'s to celebrate.

I had been doing some volunteer work that day and I didn't have time for one more interruption. My day was planned. I would work, rest, relax, process what was happening with my relationships with my friends …

I had a voice message from Paul that Lonnie was in the hospital *again*! He was just done with chemo and things were supposed to be on the mend. He'd stopped breathing during the night and his wife, Dawn, had found him, performed CPR and called 911. He was rushed to the hospital. He was in critical condition.

SIGH, Dawn didn't need this AGAIN. I decided I would stop by and give her a little encouragement and get on with my day. I finished my volunteer work and drove to the hospital. I have to admit, it was mostly out of duty, not love. When Lonnie had first gotten sick, I challenged the cancer in front of God and everybody at church and was sure that somehow there would be a victory, but I was tired of it.

When I got there, it was more serious than I had thought. They were talking major brain damage. Mark Wyatt and Lee McDougald were there as were Mrs. Libby B. and Alicia B., and several other people. The enemy was clearly accusing God to Dawn and making a very strong case against God's goodness. People were trying, with various degrees of success, to both acknowledge the depth of Dawn's pain and the truth of God's goodness. But the enemy was making a strong case against God and the battlefield was Dawn's heart and mind. I was grateful to my sense of duty, because now I was there out of love.

I sent a text message to Jaime to bring in reinforcements and to get them there *fast*. This was major spiritual warfare and the good guys were on the ropes. While I knew that ultimately the victory would be God's, the question was, will we win *this* battle. So many hearts, so many choices, so many people were on the line. So much was at stake. So many of us had been declaring the goodness of God and talking about healing and miracles and Lonnie and Dawn had been on the forefront of all that! The thought that was lurking in all our minds, because the enemy was whispering to us, was… *"God's going to make fools of you, by letting this one die… He set you up."*

Alicia asked me to pray for Dawn, to shield her and strengthen her against this attack on her mind. So, I did. I don't remember exactly what I said or what I felt, but it seemed pretty weak and pathetic at the time. I was sure I'd fought greater battles against the enemy and had sent him running with his tail between his legs, but this seemed almost proforma and I didn't see the enemy flee at all.

The women continued to pray for Dawn and encourage her. Soon, she began to declare her knowledge of the goodness of God.

I started pouring out my heart to God; out loud and with 100% honesty. Again, I don't remember exactly what I said, but evidently, some of it could have been construed as offensive to other people in the room. Fortunately, Pastor Mark had already preached being 'unoffendable' enough that nobody there was truly offended (I hope!).

The word came back from the critical care unit that they could not find a pulse or blood pressure. Sometime during that time Paul and Jaime T. and David B. arrived.

Then they started talking about having Dawn sign a Do Not Resuscitate Form and that, even if Lonnie lived, his brain had been without oxygen for so long that he would never be the same again. Lonnie would not be Lonnie. He would simply be a shadow of his former self.

I called Beez (John B.). I told him we were going to either heal him or raise him from the dead, but he wasn't going to stay dead. Beez started asking me questions like, *"What if he doesn't want to be raised..."* This is an important role Beez has played in my life; he reminds me that just because we *can* do something doesn't mean we *should* do it and that includes 'good things' like calling people back from the dead.

He wasn't convinced that this was something we *should* do. I was just as sure that it *was*. When he heard the determination in my voice, he began to instruct me on love and power. He told me that if we focus on the power and not the love, then we would lose Lonnie.

I called Paul and David into the corner for a quick conference; one of us was going to have to 'take point' in the spirit world. The logical and obvious choice was me because I had the most experience in this type of intervention of the three of us. But, the one thing Beez had successfully taught me when dealing in the supernatural was brutal honesty before God. I knew it couldn't be me. I would be distracted not only by the power but by all of the little social issues between my friends and me. I was not in any spiritual condition to take point. And I had to admit it to two other men. Fortunately, these men love me regardless of where I am.

Paul hugged David and said, *"It's you, brother."* So, we went to the courtyard with Jaime. The phone rang. It was Beez, I put him on speaker. He said, *"NOW is the time, Lonnie's dying."* I told him David was going to take point. He said, *"Good! Everybody focus love on David."*

Kellie B. came out to join us. I anointed everyone's hands with fragrant oil. We were all holding hands and praying silently. John was providing some verbal guidance on the phone. I was distracted. My love for these people who were holding my hands was distracting me. The stuff I was planning that day was distracting me. Beez's voice was distracting me. Then I remembered that Beez had told us to focus all our love on David so he could take it into the spirit realm. So, I began to thank God for each thing that was distracting me and thanked God for my friendship with David and poured it into him.

I became aware that I was not going into the spirit realm, but instead I was looking out into the natural realm and becoming aware of the spirits that were there. It became clear that my job was to watch for the enemy and keep him out. I was aware of, but did not see, my spiritual allies standing on the wall with me, keeping the enemy at bay.

At some point, I heard Beez ask Jaime to pray. I don't remember what she said, but I do remember just how much love I heard in her voice. Love for Dawn. Love for Lonnie. Love for God. Love for Paul. Love for each of us.

I know Kellie prayed. I think Paul prayed. I don't remember if I did or not or what any of us said, except that it was a general declaration of God's goodness and our petition to God for Lonnie's sake.

Then I heard Beez say, *"Lonnie, come forth!"*

Not long after that David finally spoke. He said, *"God said, "Don't pray past the miracle."*

We stopped. We were in agreement that something had happened and, whatever it was, God was happy with it. We didn't know whether Lonnie was alive or dead. But we knew it was good.

Kellie told us that she had awoken that morning with a vision of Joshua and Aaron holding Moses' hands up. In retrospect, it was clearly instructions for what we were supposed to do with David.

Instead of going back to the ICU waiting room to check on Lonnie, we went to the cafeteria. We were all hungry. We needed to be with each other and just enjoy one another's company. We talked and we ate. On the surface, it looked like just a group of friends enjoying each other's company. But we knew we had all been through something extraordinary and the ordinary was a necessary part of it.

When we went back to the waiting room, everyone was excited and giving each other high-fives. It seems that in a heartbeat, they went from being unable to find a pulse to Lonnie fighting the doctors. One of the nurses said that it had gone from a 'worst case' to 'best case' scenario almost instantly.

The medical staff was in agreement that whatever had happened was beyond medical science. Brumbaugh

David B. (Friend)

OK, Beez said I needed to write down what I saw when Lonnie was raised. Let me start earlier in the day. I got the call to pray from Julie T. who told me that Lonnie was back in the hospital. I was playing on the Internet and continued playing instead of stopping and praying. Then I got the call to come to the hospital. The enemy started telling me right away that if I really loved Lonnie, I would have stopped what I had been doing and prayed.

Skip ahead to when we started praying outside in the hospital courtyard. I started to think about God and the Holy Spirit and Jesus. For a short time, I saw Lonnie and was talking to him, telling him that I loved him. One thing I remember clearly was rubbing the top of his head and telling him that I wanted another chance to rub his bald head and laughing with him. Suddenly everything went black and I started to see pulses of a textured green pulsing toward a point just off to the right of center of my 'sight.' It was fairly fast-paced at first. When I would start losing focus, it would pulse away from the center point. So I really tried to stay focused.

At one point the pulsing stopped and I couldn't start it again. Then I heard Paul say, "*Sweet Holy Spirit.*" He said it like 4 times. The first 3 sent pulses again. I think it was then that Beez said, "*Lonnie, come forth! Now!*" Then it was kind of like a Doppler radar. The green was being spread around like a radar.

That happened for a little bit and then I heard God say, "*Don't pray past the miracle.*" I stood up. I wanted to tell everyone what I saw but

I felt like it would defile it. It wasn't until I was alone with Paul and Brumbaugh that I could talk about it.

When we went to eat, I was shaking and weak and started becoming really agitated. I wanted people to talk but not to me. I wanted people to talk, but it was annoying to hear them. I was also dizzy and had to grab the wall a couple of times on the way to the cafeteria..

As I told Lonnie, after his ordeal, my prayers were centered around and for his wife, Dawn. I knew, without question, that she needed Lonnie back. I also knew that, while I truly loved Lonnie, that she loved him much more than I did so I prayed for God to return Lonnie for her sake – she was an emotional wreck.

Anyway, that is my perspective on what God did. David B.

Kellie B. (Friend)

I woke up on the morning of February 16 with a vision of Joshua and Aaron holding Moses' hands up. Whenever I wake up with that kind of vision, I know it is from God and I know it means something important is going to happen. I just didn't know at the time that it was because of the battle Lonnie was facing at the moment.

While everyone was praying in the courtyard of the hospital, I saw God and an angel with Lonnie and I was overcome by the love that Lonnie has for people.

I began praying, *"Lord, you know if you gave Lonnie a choice to stay or go He would stay (on Earth with us), no matter what kind of pain he is in because of the love he has for Your people."*

After this, I began asking God to answer Dawn's prayers and to honor and bless her for all the prayers she had given out to others at the hospital that day – what an AWESOME woman of God. I believe the hand of the Lord, the same hand of the Lord that caused Elijah to be able to excel past the Chariots (1 Kings 18:46), sped up the resurrection of Lonnie that day in February. Kellie B.

John B. (Friend)

I feel that I must begin my testimony by giving a very firm note on my troubles with my gifting from God. There are things that every one of us will have to deal with concerning our natures. Mine happens to be a fear of what I can do inadvertently or by design. I have spent years disciplining my actions and thoughts to always be under control.

It has also led me to look deeply into the nature of things to understand how things are put together to better work within the will of Papa God.

The thing that has brought this to the forefront of my heart is a resurrection that just happened a couple of days ago. A dear man of God, Lonnie Honeycutt, had and, at the writing of this, may still have cancer. It progressed to the point of debilitation. His sweet wife was living with the dying process. It would become a situation just like Jesus faced outside the city when he came upon the funeral procession of the widow burying her son.

On February 16, 2008, she found Lonnie unconscious and called 911 to get him quick medical care. While he was being rushed to the hospital, the calls began to get everyone praying. The team responded in love.

I had been out helping a neighbor split wood and had come in with the mail when the call came in to me. Things weren't right for some reason. I must admit that when talking with Brumbaugh I asked some very hard questions when he told me they were either going to pray for his healing or a resurrection. Just because we CAN do something, doesn't mean we SHOULD. Acting on good intentions is the battle of the immature.

Now please know that I have been helping people die well for several decades. Many times, a death is a good thing. And, many times, it is a needed thing. I can't tell you the number of people I have walked to God. The joy they know is unbounded! Of course, there have been others for whom it became a horror. But such is their (and our) choice.

As I said, the questions I put to Brumbaugh were hard. I so appreciate his love for me. I wanted to be very sure that the resurrection would be done for the *right* reasons. It is never enough to simply use the authority we have because we want something. And in the questioning I knew that something was just not right. Brumbaugh had to get off the phone to keep me from being any more of a distraction. We ended with me giving him some instructions on how to do a resurrection.

I dwelt in God for a time and called back when I saw Lonnie leaving us. The team was in prayer with David B. in the room with Lonnie. I asked to be put on the speakerphone to join with them in prayer. It was such a time of faith and of love.

Now, was I convinced that a resurrection was the right thing? No. Remember that I was still dealing with a feeling of something not quite open and known. But once a team decision was made, it became something for me to see through. I prayed a small tendril of God's creative material through David to Lonnie, telling everyone that they needed to open themselves up to David so that he would have access to the strength of our combined faith. Then it struck me what was missing.

I called out to Jamie to pray out loud. She is a little shy when it comes to taking the lead in prayer. I told her to not worry about the words. It was her heart and intention that was important! And the prayer she gave and the presence of God she invoked in that prayer was truly wonderful. There is a great deal that comes about because of wielding the love God has given us.

After her prayer, there was a spike of power three or four times. And each time joy filled my soul. But nothing was happening. That happens sometimes. We don't always get a "*Yes*" answer from Papa.

Then it hit me. We were seeking to lead Lonnie back from the dead. That is a valid method of resurrection. But sometimes, and especially when dealing with a person who so greatly loves God, our love just doesn't compare to the realization of love the dead experience. Our leading will not be enough.

So I looked Lonnie right in the soul. I called out in command, "*Lonnie come forth. Now.*" I knew it was his decision and that it must be made at that time. And he came back – slowly (in the spiritual realm – his actual return in the natural was almost immediate). At times like this, the dead person must make a decision to come back or not, simply based upon love. There is the realization that the love of God will always be with us, and it is a testimony to how much Lonnie loves his wife that he came back. It is also a testimony of her love for him. John B.

David Easterbrooks (Friend)

I was pushing my cart in Kroger's, picking out a dozen eggs, cottage cheese, and some yogurt. It was Sunday or Monday evening, February 24 or 25, and it was just days after I got the call from Dawn telling me of Lonnie's critical and seemingly hopeless situation. My phone rang, I saw that it was Dawn calling me, and I had a jolt of grief as I anticipated the news. I put back the cottage cheese and answered my cell phone.

A few days prior I had received a call from Dawn. She was so sad as she related some of the emergency events that had led to Lonnie being in the ICU on a ventilator and with no signs of hope in the natural realm.

Without me asking for details, Dawn basically painted a picture of DOA (dead on arrival), certain massive brain death and destruction, and no hopeful signs for survival or life from the hospital staff. She told me that she had spoken to our friend Dr. Bill Frazier, and that many local friends were at the hospital praying for Lonnie.

I immediately called Dr. Bill and he confirmed the sadness and dire or hopeless condition and that it seemed we had already lost Lonnie. Dr. Bill and I prayed for Lonnie and his family and had a wonderful touch as the Holy Spirit joined us. I now was planning a trip to Mobile, for what I expected to be a funeral… and I kept praying.

A day or so later, in the early evening, I got the call from Dawn that, against all medical possibilities, Lonnie had opened his eyes, and had 'signed' to Dawn "*I love you.*" I was astonished and excited! This isn't how dead people behave!!

So, in spite of all the bad medical reports, something was going on with Lonnie. In the natural, however, the situation was grave and Dawn said that the doctors and medical staff gave her little or no expectation for brain function. I still somewhat expected that if removed from the ventilator, Lonnie could not live.

I am no stranger to the helpless and hopeless reality of ICU ventilators and brain death. In 1999, my father entered a brain dead coma, was kept alive for 4 days for family members to arrive, and then I watched his body lose all life after being removed from the ventilator. I had spent hours with him in ICU as the ventilator would expand his lungs with air and the strange sounds of that machine are still with me today.

Back to Kroger's…

As I answered the phone, a hoarse voice said "*David*? David?" to which I replied, "*Lonnie?? Lonnie… It's YOU!!! It's REALLY YOU!!*"

Lonnie replied, "*Sorry my voice is so hoarse, they just removed the tube that was down my throat.*"

I immediately abandoned my cart and ran for the front door of Kroger's, as I was afraid of losing my cell phone connection in the supermarket. I was giddy and felt like I was talking to a friend that was gone for good. Hearing Lonnie's voice was like Houston's Mission Control hearing John Glenn's voice after the re-entry blackout. He's Alive!!!

Jubilation and astonishment is how I felt. I remember saying, *"Lonnie, we've got to get you out of that place, it's dangerous in the hospital."* And Lonnie laughed and said, *"Yeah, they're trying to kill me here!"*

We had a great coherent conversation (about 5 minutes) and Lonnie really sounded like the Lonnie I know. Other than being tired and hoarse, I would have had no idea of the extreme week Lonnie had just experienced.

Apparently, Lonnie was alone in his hospital room and picked up the cell phone on the table, and called me. Again, this is not the behavior of brain dead people!

Lonnie has been sent back to us to complete the Lord's purposes through him. Lonnie has been sent out again. We should pay close attention to the message.

In Luke 10:16 Jesus said, *"He who listens to you listens to Me; he who rejects you rejects Me; but he who rejects Me rejects him who sent Me."*

Lonnie's story clearly shows us how much God Loves us and wants our wholehearted love and relationship with Him. Listen to Lonnie's story, and know that the God who created you gave everything so that you would choose Him as your Lord. Come as the little children came to Jesus.

What if Lonnie's story is true? Again, What if it's true??

What will I do with this story as it relates to my relationship with the Lord?

What will I do with this story as it relates to God's plans and purposes for my life?

What will my life look like when it's finished? It may finish today, tomorrow, or in decades. Remember, everything we do today and tomorrow matters forever.

Lonnie's friend, David Easterbrooks.

Mark Strick (Brother-in-Law)

I arrived the day after Lonnie had died two times and really didn't know what to expect. When I finally got the chance to go in and see him, what I saw said there was no chance. He had the respirator tube down his throat and he just looked terrible. As I would have put it, he looked like death warmed over.

As time went by and we prayed for him, miracles started to happen. It was a day later when things started to turn around, the respirator was removed, and he started to look better. He would talk but very carefully, since the respirator had irritated a throat that had been blistered by radiation treatment.

A day later he was moved from ICU to a room and he continued to improve significantly. He continued to improve dramatically the rest of the week and even the doctors said they had never seen such a dramatic and quick turnaround – from dead to walking around and off the respirator within three days is unheard of. This just goes to show the power of prayer and the Lord's care for those who put their faith and trust in Him. Mark Strick.

John (Jay) Honeycutt, Jr. (Brother)

Mom called me and told me that Dawn had called and was very upset. Mom said that Dawn had found you not breathing and without a pulse. She told us that you had been taken to the hospital and that your condition was critical. Mom was a little unclear as to what exactly had occurred, but it was clear that you were in very serious condition.

Mom had also said that Brance had called 911. As soon as I hung up from talking with Mom, I immediately called Dawn to try and get clarification. Dawn was clearly upset and told me that you had lain down with Brance, the night before, and had fallen asleep. When she went to wake you in the morning, she found you with no pulse and not breathing. She said she woke Brance screaming at you and trying to get you to respond. She told Brance to call 911 and tell them 'your daddy is not breathing.' Brance apparently did as he was told and the ambulance arrived a short time later. I was very proud of Brance and the courage he demonstrated during this time.

Dawn told me that no one knew how long you had gone without

breathing and one of the main concerns, if they were able to revive you, was brain damage. She told me that you had to be revived a second time by the paramedics and that you were in the hospital in a coma. Dawn told me she was very afraid for you and she kept repeating that she could not lose you.

I got off the phone and told Valerie that I was heading to Mobile. You are my brother and I love you.

I explained the situation and that based on what Mom and Dawn had told me, I was convinced that you might not live until I arrived. I was praying steadily during this whole time. Valerie told me she was coming with me and called her boss to tell him the situation and he said 'go.' I called Mom and told her I was leaving as soon as I could contact my boss and get packed. I asked if she wanted to go with me and in the end, she and our sister, Gay, came along. I called Helena and asked if she was going, but she could not go. I then called David and asked if he was able to go, but he was sick. David and Helena asked me to keep in touch and David said he would try to come down as soon as he could.

Valerie and I pulled out, picked up Mom and Gay, and headed to Mobile.

Lonnie, Valerie and I took our funeral clothes, because I truly thought that I was coming to bury you. It was difficult to concentrate and drive.

We arrived in Mobile, checked in and went straight to the hospital. Once at the hospital, we spoke to Dawn and got an update. There were several people from your church there but I cannot remember their names. I went in to see you as soon as they would let me and I did not want to leave your room. Once, Dawn, myself, and another member of your church were in your room when the ICU had a lockdown and we could not get out for about 20 minutes. That was okay with me. Another time, Mom and Dawn and Gay started crying and I told them they would have to leave if they did not stop as people in comas tended to pick up on the feelings and sounds from those around them.

Lonnie, I held your hand, kissed your forehead, and prayed fervently. I have never prayed such as I did during this time. I would step out to let others in, but I came back in as soon as I could. The nurses often let me stay when others came in, several of them thought I was your dad and I did not correct them. I talked to you a lot, especially when I found myself alone with you. From time to time, you would squeeze my hand or I thought you did.

Man, watching you lie there, unresponsive, and with tubes and wires all over you was a difficult thing, but I would not have been anywhere else. Even now, as I write this, it is hard to keep the tears from my eyes. I know that I was prepared to stay until you were out of trouble or the worst occurred. I am happy that the former occurred. During our time in your room and in the waiting room, I met some wonderful people and was so happy that you and Dawn had the support group there. I was very concerned about that.

Somewhere in here, we arranged to go and see Brance and Danielle at the gym. At the gym, we watched Danielle. The women watched her longer than I did. Ballet is okay, but I chose to go and find Brance and spend a little time with him. I sat with him, in the floor, while he and a young girl made forts and attacked each other's fortresses. Brance was very creative. Then he sat on the steps while I spoke to one of the owner's sons about karate. Later, we sat in the gym and watched them do their routines. It was a lot of fun.

We came back to the hospital after that. Over the four days we were there, there was a good deal of waiting. I would do it again without hesitation. You started to show improvement and eventually you were moved to a private room.

While in this room, one of the roving chaplains came in (Mike Woods – a guy from your church) and we prayed together for you. Once you were talking to us and you were out of danger, we decided to go home. You were talking, but not a lot. During the following days and weeks, I kept in touch with you and certainly kept you in my prayers. I still pray for thanks to God for His generous protection over you and your family every day. Love, Jay

David Easterbrooks and Lonnie Honeycutt before he died (2006).

P.J. T. and Lonnie after surgery (May 30, 2007).

Scar from the surgery to remove cancer-infected lymph nodes, a nerve, my jugular vein, part of my tongue and six inches of muscle tissue – Staples still in (Sept 28, 2007).

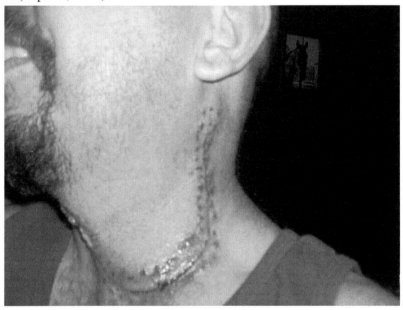

Staples removed from scar (October 1, 2007).

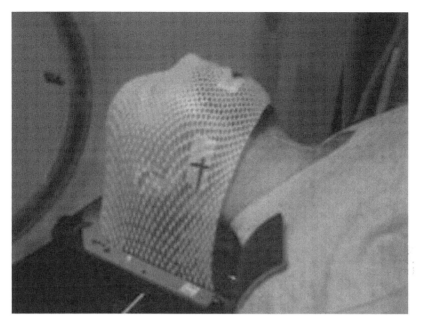

Lonnie strapped to table in radiation mask (October 24, 2007).

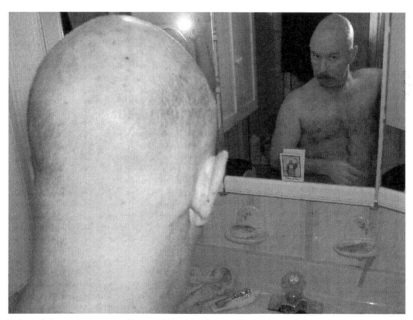

Me taking pictures of myself and the rash that covered my body (December 14, 2007).

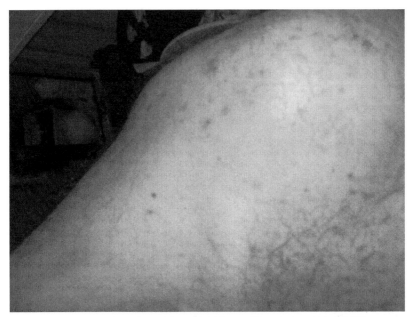

Rash on the top of my head from Erbitux (December 14, 2007).

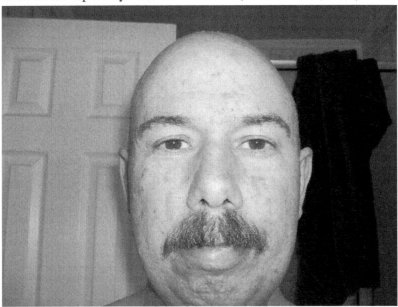

Rash on my face from Erbitux (December 14, 2007).

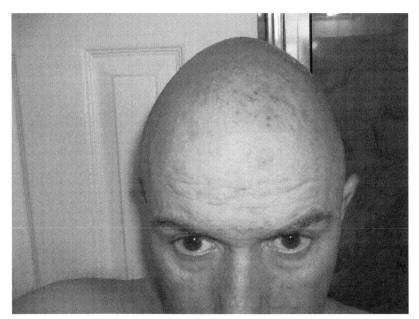

Rash on the top of my head from Erbitux (December 14, 2007).

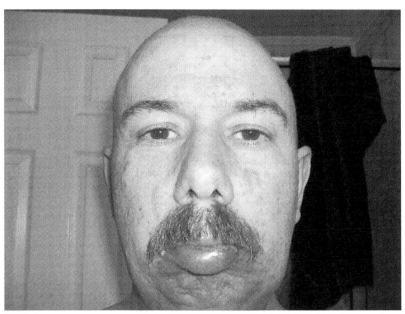

Rash on my face and sores on my lips from Erbitux (December 14, 2007).

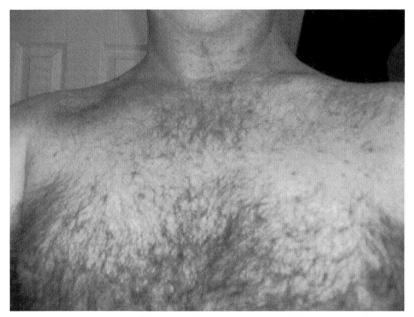

Rash on my chest from Erbitux (December 14, 2007).

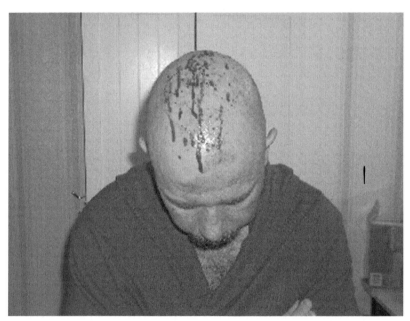

Blood flowing from my scalp after vomiting (December 16, 2007).

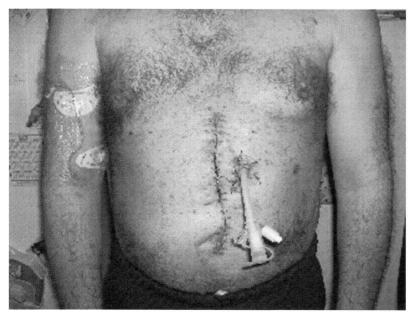

PICC Line and Feeding Tube Inserted (December 21, 2007).

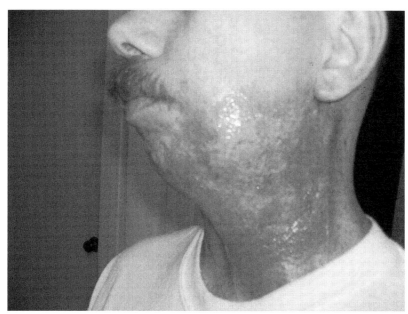

2nd and 3rd degree burns from radiation treatments (January 10, 2008).

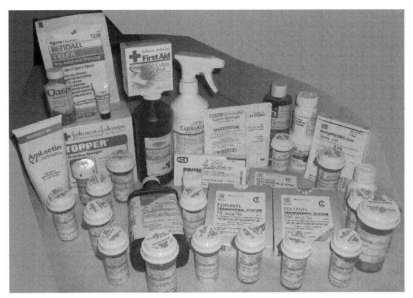

Some of the drugs I was on BEFORE I died – I haven't taken any of these since I was resurrected on February 16, 2008.

My second day back home after dying (February 27, 2008).

**[Note: For Full-Color Pictures please see the DVD titled:
Death, Heaven and Back: What If It's True?]**

9

Life After My Death

"Hear, O Lord, and be merciful to me; O Lord, be my help. You turned my wailing into dancing; you removed my sackcloth and clothed me with joy, that my heart may sing to you and not be silent. O LORD my God, I will give you thanks forever."
Psalms 30:10-11

As you've read from my wife's account, I died, and my prognosis, even after coming back to life (at least according to the medical physicians), was grim.

Well, as the good Lord (praise His Holy, Holy, Holy Name) would have it, the doctors were wrong all the way around. First and foremost, He answered the prayers of the many, many people who were praying for me to come back from being dead. Secondly, He really did heal me. Not only was I completely awake and cognizant in the next 4-5 days, I was out of the hospital in 10 days total. If you'll remember, I mentioned the state of my throat and mouth and how they were so damaged by the radiation and chemo treatments. Well, once I came back from Heaven, those were completely healed. I'm talking, COMPLETELY. Not only was I able to speak normally again but also I was able to eat any and everything that people put in front of me (and people put a LOT of stuff in front of me). In fact, the very first 'meal' I had after coming back to this life was given to me by Felicia H. and Kelly B. and it was pizza and candy-covered pretzels.

A follow-up swallow barium test proved to everyone, including my physicians, that I had been given, for all intents and purposes, a new throat and new tissue in my mouth and throat. Also, the Lord has given me a new taste for water. Water tastes like a malted-beverage to me now – kind of like a cream soda – which is wonderful since it's the only beverage I can find that is effective in alleviating (albeit temporarily) my dry mouth issues.

The first clear memory I have after coming back from Heaven is of waking up in a hospital bed not knowing why I was there but remembering, vaguely, of being intubated (a procedure in which a tube is inserted through the mouth down into the trachea – the large airway from the mouth to the lungs). I also remember noticing that I had a small, half-inch burn mark (something similar to a scab) on my lower chin, although I had no idea as to where it had originated. While I didn't know how the burn had gotten there, I do know that it concerned me. After making this discovery I became very tired and decided to nap a bit more. The very next memory I have is of waking up a couple of hours later, reopening the mirror installed in the tray used to set the meals I would later be brought, and noting, to my amazement, that the small burn mark was completely gone!

Without a doubt, I knew that God had performed a minor miracle on my face. What I didn't realize at the time was that this 'minor' miracle was part of a major set of miracles.

Short-Term Memory Loss

While the miracles God has brought about in my life have been mighty, dying did come with a price. For me, that price has been short-term memory loss. It's more than a bit interesting and disconcerting to wake up with amnesia. While I became fully cognizant of my surroundings on February 21, 2008, I didn't know it at the time but I had suffered tremendous memory loss.

The only two people I know for certain that I knew were my wife and her brother, Mark. Other than that, I was pretty clueless. In fact, when my doctor came in to check on me and asked if I knew his name, I said "*Yes,*" and pointed to the embroidered name on the chest of his white jacket. He smiled and asked if I knew what hospital I was in. I had no idea – even though I'd been going there for cancer treatments for the past three months.

As it stands today, I barely remember my brother, Jay, being at the hospital with me and I don't remember my Mom or my youngest sister, Gay, being there at all.

I also know that I didn't remember having children at the time. As the time in the hospital wore on, I began to ask questions about my life to try to reconstruct some semblance of memory. I've been told that during the first few days of my new life that I asked the same questions over and over: Which hospital was I in? How did I get there? What had happened? Who certain people were that had come to visit? Each time I was given an answer to one of these questions, I'd soon completely forget that I'd even asked the question.

Dawn, at my request, began to ask me questions to which, most of the time, I didn't have the answers. She also patiently worked to fill in the many holes in my memory. From what I understand, Dawn had to exhibit the patience of a saint (which she is – literally and figuratively) because I'd get very agitated and irritable at times. I cannot express in words the love I have for my wife or how wonderful she truly is to live with and to be loved by. I am honored that God has chosen to give me such an astonishing lady to have and to hold until death parts us (at least for a little while).

When my wife told me that we had two children, it *felt right* but I still had no concept of who they were, how old they were, or what they looked like. Then, slowly, the image of one of my two kids began to gel in my mind. I remembered Brance, my oldest child, but not Danielle. In fact, I didn't remember Danielle at all. Later, as we began to deduce the length of time that my amnesia went back, I came to realize why I didn't remember her. The amnesia I am afflicted with, for the most part, is limited to approximately the last four or five years of my life. Not everything was muddied, but certain aspects of my life were and are certainly unclear. One of those was my daughter, who was four years old at the time.

When my wife brought her to see me in the hospital room the first time she looked vaguely familiar. It seemed as though I *should* know the pretty little girl with the long, flowing locks of blonde hair and piercing blue eyes, but I didn't. Interestingly enough, I had an immediate sense of parental feelings for her yet I didn't remember her birth, any of her birthdays, carrying her on my shoulders, which, I'm told, I did quite often, or anything else about our relationship. To me, Danielle was a lovely little girl towards whom I felt a parental attachment but little else. This type of feeling continued for several weeks.

The memory loss I suffer from doesn't seem to have any rhyme or reason to it but, for the most part, it seems to be getting better. Of course, in this case, 'better' is a relative term. For instance, while I now remember most of my life with my children, I don't remember certain things such as the taste of Girl Scout® cookies. Other things I don't remember are getting my dog Pete (a cute Chihuahua), Christmas Day 2007, the death of our cat, birthday parties, approximately the last half of 2007 and the first quarter of 2008 and a whole slew of other things that might not seem important to anyone except for me but they make up part of who I am or, at least, who I was. So, while I've gotten better at utilizing words in sentences, I still struggle with memories that I feel are locked away in the recesses of my mind just beyond my grasp. However, the reality that I've had to face is that some of the memories I'd like to regain may simply be gone due to the massive trauma my brain sustained when I was dying.

On one hand, it's nice to get confirmation from my neuropsychologist who says it's 'unheard of' and a 'miracle' (her phrasing, not mine) that I'm able to remember an experience that took place during the time of the anoxic brain event, it's nevertheless very frustrating that entire blocks of my life seem to be completely gone.

So many times I look at my children and wonder what I've forgotten about them. Brance, my oldest, is sharp enough to realize that I'm often at a loss for a reference to whatever it is he's talking to me about and so he's gotten used to asking, *"Dad do you remember so and so…"* Again, while it's nice to have such a compassionate and caring child, it's exasperating to have to rely on such niceties.

Dawn hit the nail on the head when she asked me one morning, *"Do you sometimes feel like a stranger in our home?"* My answer was *"Yes."* She asked me how often and my reply was simply *"Often."* It's really scary to me that I've forgotten so many things about our life (such as how many years we've been married and our anniversary). It's even more disconcerting that I'm having trouble retaining new information for more than a day or two and that time seems to be all but a phantom to me – Monday through Sunday I have a difficult time remembering when it was, exactly, that I did something. In trying to explain this time discrepancy to people, I'll often tell them that if I meet with someone on Monday, by Wednesday, while I'll remember having a meeting with them, I won't recall exactly what day it was that the meeting occurred.

Admittedly, the loss of my memories is frustrating. Perhaps the best example of my memory loss is the fact that I don't remember preaching a single sermon at the church I planted (Deeper Life Fellowship East) or hosting Safe Harbor (a group I ran for teens). On the other hand, I recently went to a party celebrating the fifth anniversary of Deeper Life Fellowship Mobile, where I served as the Associate Pastor for a bit over three years, and I remember each and every one of the outreaches that were presented in a 30-minute video shown at the celebration. The memory loss I suffer from would seem to have very little rhyme or reason except for the fact that it seems to be engineered to protect me from mental and emotional trauma. I say this because I'm fully cognizant of the many outreaches that I've been a part of and while I remember being a T-Ball, Coach Pitch, and soccer coach for a local church, I have close to zero recollection of the 'bad' times during the past year or so. I don't mind having lost those memories.

Still, when one has amnesia of any type and for any length of time, it's disquieting because you actually lose part of your identity.

Something that is impossible for me to fully relate to anyone who has never experienced amnesia are the emotions one goes through as memories return. It's more than a little intriguing how the mind works in order to keep you from going insane as old memories suddenly reappear and have to be recategorized so that they blend with those you've recently created. For example, by the time I'd remembered my daughter, I had already created a new, workable profile for who she was and the relationship we'd had early on. Obviously, this was based on what I'd been told she was like by my wife and the relationship we currently had. So, once the actual memories of Danielle came back to me I immediately had two working profiles of my daughter – one assumed and the other reality. While this was disturbing to some degree, there was an almost instantaneous melding of the two sets of memories so that they overlapped incredibly well. Still, it's difficult to fully explain the fear, the depression, the disappointment, and the exhilaration that comes with amnesia and regaining what you lost.

Fear, depression, and disappointment often go hand-in-hand and when it comes to amnesia, these three are powerful adversaries to living a fulfilled life. Although the fear that I once had (that I would never be able to recapture the memories of my past) has significantly passed, I still undergo a great deal of emotional apprehension concerning the same. Depression is something I have to combat every single day. If I allow myself to dwell on what I don't remember and what I can't do instead of what I do remember and what I can now do that's different and better than in the past, then depression becomes a formidable foe. Disappointment is sneaky. It comes when and where you don't expect it. Even though I've come a long way since the day I died, if I don't consciously acknowledge this fact I'll become disappointed at my progress.

While my wife tries her best (and does a great job) to help alleviate anything that might send me into an emotional tailspin, I can honestly say that if it were not for my relationship with God that fear, depression, and disappointment would rule my life. As it is, I am able, through the strength He gives me, to overcome this unnatural and potentially crippling trinity.

Hyperbaric Chamber Treatments

Not long after I'd returned home, I received a call from Diane F., a woman who attended Deeper Life Fellowship Mobile. She left a message on our answering machine that a doctor for which she worked (Dr. Glen W., M.D.) had offered to allow me to use their hyperbaric chamber.

After doing a bit of research, I found that hyperbaric oxygen therapy (the medical use of oxygen at higher than atmospheric pressure) had been successfully used to treat patients who had suffered from strokes as well as for neuro-rehabiliation. Although I didn't know whether or not such a procedure would help, I decided to take the doctor up on his offer on the off chance that it would aid me in rehabilitating my faulty memory.

Dr. Glen was and is an extremely kind and considerate Christian man and, after examining me thoroughly, he led me to the room where the hyperbaric chamber waited. I clearly remember thinking that the chamber looked very similar to the Oscar Mayer® wiener that rides atop the Wienermobile™. Once I was comfortably inside the contraption, Dr. Glen turned it on and pressure began to build until I was breathing 100% oxygen at four times the atmospheric pressure of Earth.

Besides a slight popping of my eardrums I felt no discomfort and, in fact, fell asleep during my two hour stint in the chamber. Over the course of the next six weeks, I was allowed to visit Dr. Glen's office twice a week, two hours at a time. During this time, I experienced a remarkable amount of memory recovery. The first memory recovered was of my wonderful baby girl, Danielle. My memories of her came back to me in a rush on my second visit. I remember crying, profusely, when I realized how much I'd missed knowing her.

Oddly enough, one of the facts that I was having the hardest time recalling was my password for a popular online email service. I'd completely forgotten what it might be and I was very, very frustrated with the answers I'd received from the technicians who worked for the service. I'd tried to explain to the service techs my reasons for not being able to remember my password or the related password reminder questions and even though I provided them with several pieces of information verifying that I was indeed who I said I was, they refused to help. So, I was hopelessly stuck without access to very important information in my email account. Stuck, that is, until I visited Dr. Glen's office and was prayed over by him and Diane. Before I'd been in the hyperbaric chamber a full hour, my password came back to me! Praise God!

While a password may not seem like a 'big deal' to most people, it was to me because it marked the first time that I had a tangible hope of regaining much of who I had been.

10

I'm Not the Man I Once Was

"I will bless the LORD at all times; His praise shall continually be in my mouth.
My soul will make its boast in the LORD; The humble will hear it and rejoice.
O magnify the LORD with me, and let us exalt His name together. I sought
the LORD, and He answered me, and delivered me from all my fears."

Psalms 34:1-4

Since I've come back from stepping over to the side of eternity, I'm
different. I've changed. At least that's what Dawn tells me and, to tell
you the truth, I kind of feel that I have as well. Dawn assures me that
it's not all bad. For instance, my pastor, Mark Wyatt, recently told a
friend of mine that he enjoys being around me more because now I'm
'less intense.' The funny thing is, I don't have a clue as to what he's
talking about because I don't remember ever being any less or more
intense than I am today.

One way I do know that I've changed is that I'm less of a
conversationalist now. I remember that I used to be able to talk a blue
streak with people on just about any subject (be it a subject of
interesting content or one fraught with absurdities). Today, I find
myself being very laconic (concise) with people in my speech. Not
that my newfound brevity doesn't have an upside to it. I find that I
now tend to listen much more intently than I remember doing in the
past (perhaps this is what my pastor meant).

Another very annoying and embarrassing issue I had to come to
terms with is that until very recently I had trouble putting together
some sentences properly – at least when speaking. I simply didn't feel
comfortable speaking to others due to my inadequacy in coming up
with a stock of words to describe whatever it is I was attempting to
depict.

For instance, one Sunday night, at our church meeting, I began
teaching on the book of James. If you're familiar with the epistle, you
know that it's a fairly straightforward study. Unfortunately, while I
was very prepared mentally, I had such trouble putting together
sentences I knew were on the proverbial tip of my tongue that I believe
it was the worst lesson I've ever taught. I was completely mortified by
my ineptitude. In fact, it was so bad that I wasn't certain that I was

any longer cutout to be a pastor (at least not in the teaching department). Later, I was assured by several friends that it wasn't as bad as I thought it was but, still, I know there's a major difference between the me of yesteryear and the me of today.

But, I'm extremely blessed to have such a loving wife who can bring me up to speed about the memories I lack and who can comfort me about my lack of abilities and encourage me about newfound ones.

Speaking of my wife, not long ago, she remarked that she liked the way that I now enjoy rice and beans mixed together (something I supposedly used to despise, although I don't remember having such a dislike). My taste buds have definitely undergone a drastic change. For example, even the slightest amount of spice (such as you'd find in ketchup) causes me to wince in pain. And, while I used to like cookies and milk (my wife tells me that I used to regularly eat an entire sleeve of chocolate chip cookies in one sitting), now I can't taste either. Actually, that's not exactly true. I can taste both foods but they don't taste the same to me. This is especially true for cookies that have chocolate chips or cream filling in them. Most chocolate tastes terrible to me as the only flavor I can sense is the bitterness of it. As for cream fillings, they simply taste nasty to me. Milk and most other dairy products (ice cream, cottage cheese, cream cheese) simply taste extremely bland. I'm told that this has to do with the fact that my taste buds were changed due to a combination of the chemo and radiation I received. Whatever the reason, I don't savor the flavor of most foods like I used to. A caveat to this is that while most processed foods don't taste terrific to me, I've found a new love for fresh fruits and vegetables.

While my new love for a Mexican food side dish isn't apocalyptic in nature, it does serve to show, to a small extent, the change I've undergone. Not only have I changed physically (I'm now 48 pounds thinner than I was), I've also changed spiritually. This time, it's definitely for the better!

I find that despite everything I've gone through that I really do pursue and enjoy a great relationship with the Lord. I used to read the Bible and associated books with an 'ear' more toward the intellectual pursuit of knowledge. Since dying and coming back, I find myself just as interested in the intellectual side of Christianity but my interest is combined with a desire to know things on a more experiential level as well. The reason is simple: I no longer take miracles for granted and I am definitely more apt to grant their possibility and even their probability.

As a little boy, I used to dream of going fishing. There was a time that I was obsessed with the idea of fishing. I would sit around and try to imagine what it would be like to reel in a fish from cold blue waters. I tried to visualize what it would be like to bait a hook, to set the same when a fish struck my line, and to feel the pole straining in my hands as I fought to land my catch. The one problem with my imaginations was that I'd never actually been fishing. I was at a complete loss as to what it was like to fish until, one bright spring day, my brother took me fishing. At the point that I actually embarked on our fishing trip, everything changed for me. Prior to actually going fishing, even my vivid imagination could only take me so far in envisioning what the actual event would be like. Regardless of how many books I read on the subject, how often I talked with others about fishing, or how much I desired to know what it was like to actually fish, nothing could have prepared me for the actual event. But, once I'd actually gone fishing, everything I'd imagined was put to rest and I kept only that which was real. That's how I feel now that I've died and experienced a glimpse of Heaven. Practically everything that I once thought I knew about Heaven and God and how He works has been either tossed aside or steeled in my mind.

Prior to dying, I can honestly say that I didn't mind the idea of dying. Now that I've died and have seen the other side, I *really* don't fear death because I know that God has everything under control. My recognition that He really is in control also means that I've got to admit that He's not limited to my understanding (or misunderstanding as the case may be) of how He *should act*. Instead, I'm now more convinced than ever (and I used to be pretty convinced of this fact) that God works in our daily lives. He is the God of the Universe and whatever He wants to do in His universe should be okay with us. Even if it's not, I'll guarantee that He's going to continue to do whatever it is He plans to do anyway. It's just that you and I will be less embarrassed when He shows up if we're prepared for Him to show up beforehand. In any case, I now know with objective certainty that God heals and, as such, I'm going to pray for as many people as possible for both physical healing as well as for salvation. I also know that these are two things that every single Christian is called to pray for until the day they die.

Speaking of dying, on one level I'm not looking forward to leaving my family should that happen in the near future. But, that's simply the mortal part of me 'talking.' The greatest part of me is actually looking forward to being in Heaven again. In fact, it's hard for me to wait to go back. Of course, I wouldn't think of killing myself as this would be an affront to my Lord and Savior because He's sent me back with a purpose to fulfill. Still, I can honestly say that if I were to die today I'd be okay with it – more than okay, I'd be delighted!

As I said in my testimony about visiting Heaven, there isn't a day that goes by when I don't think about Heaven and all the glories I witnessed. There's also not a day that goes by when I'm not convinced that the glories I saw were only the minutest taste of what awaits every saint of God.

11

The Importance of Continuous Petitioning Prayer

"Do not be anxious about anything, but in everything, by prayer and petition, with thanksgiving, present your requests to God. And the peace of God, which transcends all understanding, will guard your hearts and your minds in Christ Jesus."
Philippians 4:6-7

While in Heaven, I was fully aware that people, my friends and family members, were praying that the Lord would allow me to return to them. As Brumbaugh stated, *"We were calling you forth from death much like Jesus did with Lazarus."*

The reason I bring this up is twofold: 1) To call attention to the fact that my friends and family, those who loved and cared for me, continuously petitioned the Lord for His grace towards them (as for me, the simple fact that I was in Heaven revealed His grace towards me); 2) To call attention to the fact that these same friends and family members were operating under the assumption that Jesus' words were true when He told us that His Kingdom was at hand.

As a person who grew up without much (practically zero) religious instruction, I didn't become aware of what I now think of as prayer-hesitation as far as beseeching prayer is concerned until I was around twenty-five years of age.

I believe that our hesitation comes from a general misunderstanding of what Jesus said in Matthew 6:7, *"And when you are praying, do not use meaningless repetition as the pagans do, for they suppose that they will be heard for their many words."*

The phrase 'meaningless repetitions' is the Greek word *battalogeo*. The verb <u>logeo</u> means 'to speak,' and the prefix <u>batta</u> isn't a word at all. Instead, it is a figure of speech (called an onomatopoeia in English) or, to be more exact, the vocal simulation of something by the supposed sound it makes. For instance, when children see a cow they'll often call out to it with a long 'mooo' or, in the case of a fly, we say that it goes buzzz. These are called onomatopoetic types of speech. Of course, these utterances mean nothing to either the animal or human who hears them because they don't correspond to any actual language. So, what Jesus is saying in Matthew 6:7 is, *"When you pray, don't say batta, batta, batta – which aren't intelligible, intelligent words but, rather, gibberish that means nothing at all."* Instead, we are to pray intelligently and with understanding. I can't help but believe that this is one of the primary reasons that Jesus then gives us a model for our prayers in Matthew 6:9-15.

All of this to say that we should learn how to be in continuous prayer for those things we seek from our Lord. Indeed, we are instructed to pray continuously in 1 Thessalonians 5:16-18, *"Rejoice always; pray without ceasing; in everything give thanks; for this is God's will for you in Christ Jesus."* Obviously, this verse isn't suggesting that we do nothing but pray and it isn't an admonition to simply repeat the same prayer over and over again but, rather, that we diligently pray for what it is we're seeking and to be thankful to God for whatever it is He's doing in our lives.

The diligent part of praying could and probably does include bringing our prayer list(s) before the Lord again and again. We know, for instance, that the Apostle Paul sought healing from the Lord concerning an affliction he called 'a thorn in the flesh' three times. While it's true that after beseeching the Lord to have this 'thorn' removed three times Paul was given an answer from the Lord concerning the same (*"My grace is sufficient for you."*), I don't believe that the Apostle mentions the number to set the specific amount of times we're allowed to pray for whatever it is we're seeking from Him. Instead, I believe that the lesson to be taken from this Scripture is that we should pray 'until we are given an answer from our Heavenly Father.' I believe a strong case could be made that had Paul not received an answer from God, he would have continued asking Him for relief from the 'thorn' he'd been given. I say this because we know that the same Apostle stated in Ephesians 1:17, *"I keep asking that the God of our Lord Jesus Christ, the glorious Father, may give you the Spirit of wisdom and revelation, so that you may know him better."* The phrase, 'I keep asking,' carries with it the connotation of continuous action. In other words, the Apostle didn't simply pray one time for the God of our Lord Jesus Christ to give us the Spirit of wisdom and revelation so that we might know Him better. Instead, he prayed and prayed and prayed with the same basic request. Should we do any less than an Apostle of our Lord? The obvious answer is NO – we should do at least as much, if not more.

So, is praying over and over again the same basic request a sign of weak faith or a lack of the same? I don't believe it is. For one, we don't know the mind or the will of God. What I mean is that we don't know how God is going to answer our prayers. For example, let's assume we pray for help with our finances. We don't know if the Lord will give us the opportunity of a great new job or if He is going to impress upon someone to send us money (when the need is temporary I've actually seen this happen time and time again) or even if He'll have someone give us a winning lottery ticket (this last one is much less likely, in my opinion, but it's still possible). We just don't know what God is going to do in any given situation or, even if we know 'what' He'll do, we don't know how He's going to go about doing it.

Whereas, we usually focus on the parts of life that pertain to or hold an interest to us, especially since we can't and don't see the depth and the breadth of how the pieces of life intertwine with one another to form a complete picture, God isn't limited in this manner. Thus, while our choices are, more often than not, based on this limited view of life (our lives specifically), the choices God makes aren't constrained in this way. So, God can base His decision as to how to interject His will into our lives from a myriad of choices that we can't even begin to comprehend. Our inability to know how God is going to act makes sense once we come to terms with the fact that while we do indeed 'see through a glass, darkly' (1 Corinthians 13:12), God clearly sees everything – from beginning to end and all the points in-between.

Again, if we ask God for something one time, thank Him for His decision on the matter, and then wait to hear from Him, is this a sign of weak faith or that we are not unceasingly in prayer to Him? I don't think so. I believe the Bible is clear on the fact that we should continually press-in to Him with our requests but, at the same time, we are to be listening for Him to answer our prayer requests. So, I think that we should pray until one of the following happens:

1) He answers our prayers (regardless of what His answer might be);

2) Our circumstances change (this could be an answer from Him);

3) He changes the emphasis of your heart by lifting the burden from you to pray for whatever it was you were seeking.

I do believe, however, that it is the height of audacity to believe that we should simply pray one time for something and then let it drop. Of course, there may be times when the Lord impresses upon you 'that is enough' because He is done or is doing whatever it is you've requested. When those times occur, we should be willing to let go of whatever it was we were praying for and simply wait to see how He answers.

I've heard it argued that because God knows everything we're going to say before we say it (Matthew 6:8) or even think it, for that matter, that we never need to repeat ourselves in prayer. This simply isn't true. If we followed that logic, then prayer itself would become inconsequential and unneeded since God does indeed know everything we need before we ask Him. If that's so, then why do we need to pray at all? The answer is simple: We pray because WE are the ones who NEED to know that God hears and answers us, not because God needs to hear our prayers before He can answer them. In other words, we don't pray to 'bring God up to date,' but, rather, so that we're reminded that we are completely dependent on Him in every situation of life. As we petition God for things time and time again, our mind, spirit, and heart become more accustomed to hearing from Him (if we're listening) and we're reminded of our need to rely on Him and Him alone. This is especially the case since, most often, our prayers are not immediately answered. Of course, this doesn't mean that God isn't working behind the scenes to give us an answer but, you've probably found as I have, sometimes we have to wait days, weeks, or even years before our prayers are answered.

My recent bout with cancer is a great case in point concerning the sovereignty of God and His timing.

As I've already stated, I was diagnosed with cancer of the head and neck in late 2007. This was after struggling with issues that led up to the diagnosis for four years. During this four-year time frame my wife and I, along with many of our friends and family, sought the Lord's direction and His grace concerning the health issues I was facing – specifically we entreated the Lord to take away the cause of the pain in my neck. As the symptoms I was experiencing worsened, our prayers to our most Gracious Heavenly Father intensified and more and more people joined in praying for me.

Unfortunately, or so it seemed at the time, things weren't getting any better. In fact, as my friend Brumbaugh says, "*I actually started getting mad at God because the more we prayed for Lonnie the worse he got.*" Brumbaugh's statement is actually an understatement because, as you can tell from the title of this book, I eventually wound up dead!

Thankfully, God's sovereign will was still in effect but the full effects of His will were seen only after I died and was brought back to life. Another one of my friends, David Easterbrooks, wisely told me, "*If the Lord had miraculously healed you of cancer, that would have made for a great testimony. As it is, since He not only healed you of the aftereffects of cancer and raised you from the dead, you've got an extraordinary testimony.*"

What David said is true – my testimony (both of miraculous healing and of resurrection) have gone out to many different areas of the world. I give God all the glory for this. Still, I have to thank those who prayed for me and continued to pray for me because I'm certain these prayers did not fall on deaf ears.

My wife, as an example, prayed and prayed and prayed some more for me to be healed. I did the same. When she was told that I had died she redoubled her efforts of calling on the Lord as did several people who knew me personally and wanted to continue to know me here on Earth. So, did this continual prayer show a lack of faith? On the contrary, I believe it showed a tremendous amount of faith. Have you ever noticed that, the more important something is to us, the more often and longer we pray about it? It's like another of my friends, Lee McDougald, who had Parkinson's disease. Notice that I said 'had' (in the past tense) Parkinson's disease. Lee no longer suffers from Parkinson's, even though it's incurable in the normal sense of the word (i.e., it's incurable by medicines but not by the Lord) because after years upon years of praying for him to be healed, God finally answered his and our prayers and healed him. I've known Lee now for a bit more than five years and I can vouch for his complete and miraculous healing!

Lee's story, in brief, is as follows:

12

Lee McDougald – Healed of Parkinson's Disease

"He was wounded for our transgressions, He was bruised for our iniquities, the chastisement of our peace was upon Him and with His stripes we are healed."
Isaiah 53:5

"**A**t the age of 22 in 1979, I was involved in an auto accident and suffered numerous internal injuries, a broken back and severe brain concussion. As a result of the injuries, I have suffered for the last 27 years physically. Thus far, I have been in the hospital over 45 times and had over 22 surgeries. In the mid-1980's I began having seizures and I was diagnosed as having epilepsy as a result of the head trauma suffered in the accident.

Years later, as the seizures subsided, I was diagnosed with Parkinson's disease as a result of the same accident. These years of illness have taken their toll on my family in the form of finances, relationships and quality of life. My wife has spent countless hours in doctors' waiting rooms, surgery and ICU waiting rooms, sometimes not knowing if I would live. Pain, slowness of movement, Parkinson's and general illness had become a way of life for me in the most recent years.

Sunday, February 26 – March 5, 2006

It was one of my better days as far as my health was concerned. With my cane clinched in my right hand, I hobbled into the Deeper Life Fellowship church building, taking short, steady steps with my head down and eyes fixed on the floor. I slowly progressed to my seat. I felt surprisingly good, other than dealing with the slow movement, tremors, loss of balance and unsteadiness as a result of the Parkinson's disease. At the age of 48, I had become a young victim of a progressive, degenerative neurological disease that had become a way of life for me. It was only 9:30 in the morning and I had already ingested 14 pills of various colors, shapes and sizes to kick off my medicated day. Only one more hour and it would be time for me to add three more pills to my already medicated body.

That day during the worship service, my pastor (Mark Wyatt) announced that he wanted to take me to Ft. Worth, Texas, to attend The Amber Rose Healing Conference to receive healing from the Parkinson's disease. He asked the church for prayer and help with the funds for us to make the trip. I was very excited about the possibility of going to the conference to be ministered to and to hear the great speakers.

That day, following the church service, my family and I went out for dinner. Only moments after eating my meal and departing the restaurant I felt a sharp pain in my abdomen. It felt as if someone had impaled a sword through my body. As each minute passed, the pain became more severe. With no relief, I was taken to the hospital only to have emergency surgery later that afternoon.

Awaking in the ICU the next morning, I felt defeated and any chance of going to the conference on healing had been smothered. In the days to come, I stated to my wife that I felt washed up… I was ready to die. In fact, I was crying out to God in my suffering and pain, *"God you've got to heal me. If not… kill me!"* It was obvious this was a direct attack by the enemy in an effort to keep me from traveling to Texas to attend the healing conference.

The church pressed in and continued to pray for me.

March 6 – 7

After coming home from the hospital, I was only able to eat very small amounts and take small sips of water, both of which caused me considerable pain. At this point, I had lost over 25 pounds in three weeks and was very weak. All of this, combined with the Parkinson's, made it extremely hard to move. My hopes to attend the Amber Rose Conference had grown dimmer.

The day before my pastor and I were to leave for Texas the pain grew more severe. I was in absolute agony. I called my pastor for prayer and my wife started the prayer wheels of our church and friends turning. Later in the day, the pain became even more intense with some signs of intestinal bleeding. I called my doctor's office that afternoon, knowing that by placing the call I would be immediately admitted to the hospital again. The nurse placed me on hold to summon the doctor. While on hold, I felt as if God was speaking to me, saying: *"Trust Me…Trust Me."* I immediately hung up the phone and began to pray. *"God heal me!! God allow me to go to the conference!"*

[After finally arriving at the conference, Lee continues...]

God Interrupts – March 8

After the praise and worship time was over, the first speaker of the conference was Jack Taylor. Jack first told how he loved everybody. He stated that since God loves everyone and Christ lives in him, he loved everyone. He then turned and looked at me from the pulpit, called out my name and reiterated what he had said earlier... *"Lee, I love you and God's going to touch you tonight."* After he made this statement in front of the crowd of conference attendees, an even greater sense of expectancy rose up inside of me. Suddenly, I felt the presence of the Holy Spirit come over me again as it had earlier. Tears welled up in my eyes. Although I was still in great pain and was very weak, I felt such a peace inside as if God had wrapped His arms around me to hug and caress me. Jack spoke about the Kingdom of God and the model prayer that Christ gave us to pray. During his message I began to pray: *"Thy Kingdom come NOW in my life! Come into my physical body!"* I cried out to God for Him to be glorified in my body! I wanted His kingdom and everything He had for me. I just had to have it! Just as I had prayed a few days earlier, I declared: *"Lord, heal me or kill me!"* It was as if I had grabbed hold of God and I was not going to let go of Him until He did something for me.

The next speaker was Bill Johnson. He also spoke about the Kingdom of God and His power to heal. Only a few minutes into his message he abruptly stopped and stated: *"There is someone here experiencing severe pain in their abdomen and God wants to take that away from you right now."* I said to myself *"Hey, that's me!"* I immediately pushed my hand into the air. At that point he asked Jack and Randy Clark to pray for me. He had the entire crowd to point their hands toward me and pray. Jack Taylor placed his hands on my stomach and Randy placed his hands on my head. Both of them spoke softly and lovingly. Jack prayed for a healing touch from God as Randy spoke against the pain and the root cause with authority and commanded it to leave. As they prayed I felt a warmth and slight burning sensation in my abdomen. They prayed for about four minutes and then asked me how I felt. I realized that the pain was gone! Gone! No more pain! God was so good. I felt so much better.

He had touched me. Little ole me!

Everyone rejoiced with shouts and applause that I had been healed from this tormenting pain. The conference had only just begun and a loving God had already showed up and demonstrated His love and power in a mighty way. As I sat there in my seat, I rejoiced and thanked the Lord for what He had done. Then I remembered the original reason we had come to the conference. I reflected back to the Sunday when my pastor announced to the church that he was bringing me to the conference to receive healing from Parkinson's disease. *"Oh, yeah,"* I thought. As it turned out, the abdominal surgery and constant pain I had experienced was just an attack by the enemy to keep me from receiving from God. It was a filthy ploy and an evil distraction. But now it was gone! Now I could freely receive from God what he had for me. I resumed praying, *"Thy Kingdom come NOW in my life! Thy Kingdom come NOW in my body! Increase Your Kingdom in me oh Lord!"*

Bill resumed speaking and after a few minutes was interrupted again by the Lord. He stopped and made a statement that sometimes people are involved in accidents and receive injuries and a spirit of infirmity takes over their body and they will continually suffer for many years. At that point, my pastor, who was sitting next to me and who knew my background and history, leaned over and tapped Jack on the shoulder. With a tone of excitement he tells him that Bill is talking about me. Jack stands up and calls out to Bill and exclaims with his distinct Texas accent: *"Bill, that would be this man sitting right here."* Then he points to me. As a hush fell on the crowd, every eye in the building looking at me, Bill Johnson inquires from the podium of my condition. My pastor, Mark Wyatt, immediately stands and with a hurried and excited high-pitched voice gives 27 years of medical history to Bill and the entire conference attendees in 30 seconds. He explained how after a serious auto accident, I had been in the hospital countless times with multiple surgeries and was suffering from the progression of Parkinson's disease. I then said to myself: *"Now it's time to get down to business! This is why I'm here!"*

Randy Clark turns and leans over and begins to whisper into my ear. He tells me of a lady he saw who was in the last stages of Parkinson's who could not even raise her hand off the mattress of her bed. He told of how God healed and delivered her completely. My faith was

Death, Heaven and Back

90

increased greatly by this. I continued to inwardly cry out to God in desperation for Him to heal me! At this point Bill Johnson asked the crowd to point their hands toward me and agree in prayer for God to deliver me from the infirmity in my body and for me to be healed. Once again, Jack Taylor and Randy Clark laid their hands on me and softly began to pray. Jack prayed for healing and an increase in God's Spirit in me and for increase of His Kingdom in my whole being. Simultaneously, Randy Clark places his hands on my head and begins to command, in the name of Jesus, a spirit of infirmity to leave my body. Then he prays for God to regenerate the cells in my brain and to restore my entire neurological system. Suddenly, I felt heat in my head that began to burn. Then the burning sensation proceeded to move through my head down my neck through my body and down my legs. As it proceeded through me, it intensified as if it were a hot fire burning inside of me. I felt as if my entire body was on fire but, at the same time, it was peaceful and soothing. Again, the presence of the Holy Spirit came over me just as before and then a great peaceful heaviness fell on me. I was unable to stand up any longer and fell back into my seat. Randy, Jack and my pastor continued to pray for me. After a few moments the burning sensation subsided. My clothes were saturated with sweat although the building was crisp and cool. Then I realized that I was holding my head straight up. I was no longer looking at the floor! My whole body felt as light as a feather. I immediately stood to my feet and felt a steadiness that I had not felt in years. Was this it? Did I get it? Oh, my God! Yes! Yes! It happened!

Pastor Mark then stated that I was taller by at least 3 inches. Again, the crowd praised God for what he had done.

As everyone was still standing, Bill Johnson continued to talk. After a few moments, he asks the people to be seated so he can continue. Then I looked down at the cane still clinched in my right hand. I said to myself: *"But I still have my cane."* As I spoke those words to myself, it was if God hit me in the chest with a sledgehammer and His voice rang through me: *"Lee... THAT IS NOT <u>YOUR</u> CANE! Get rid of it!"*

I realized at that point that I had taken ownership not only in my cane but also of the Parkinson's disease and all the sickness I had suffered over the years. Oh...I get it! I'm a child of God. God did not give me that stuff. I was not to have ownership in anything that was not of God. I immediately pushed my pastor out of the way and told him I had to get rid of my cane. As people were seated all around me, I walked upright (something I had not been able to do before) to the front and center of the worship center. I threw the cane down as hard as I could in front of the podium where Bill Johnson was standing, then turned and proceeded back to my seat. Upon seeing this, there was yet another interruption by God in the service and Bill pointed to me as I walked away and declared: *"It is finished! It is over! It is done!"*

I returned to the second row only to collapse in my pastor's arms, and I began weeping uncontrollably. It was as if 27 years of pain, hurt and sickness were now leaving my body. I was tearing up the deed to all the things I had taken ownership of that was not from God.

Oh, God is an AWESOME GOD! His mercy, grace and love are indescribable. Glory to the Most High God!

Being Restored – March 9

It was the second day of the conference as I walked in to the worship center without that cane and standing in a straight and upright position. The tremors were gone from my hands and body. I had no limp when I walked. I took normal steps instead of the short choppy steps I had become accustomed to over the last few years. Many people greeted me with excitement and joy as they saw me. Several people stated that I looked twenty years younger than I did the day before. All I could do was alternate from crying to laughing that day. All of a sudden, I realized I felt the same way Jack Taylor stated he did the day before. I just loved everybody! And most of all, I loved my God of Grace!

In the second session of the conference that day, I began to think about my wife and all she had endured over the years. I was saddened at the thought of the countless hours she spent in hospital ICU and surgery waiting rooms. I thought of all of the thousands upon thousands of dollars spent on medication and doctors' bills over the years. I thought of how my daughters had missed out on the best years of my life. My heart became so broken as I remembered these things that I began to weep. Then that same feeling I had experienced the day before when I was healed came over me. Here was a loving God visiting me once again through His Holy Spirit. God wrapped His arms around me and spoke to my heart as a loving father would. He said: *"Lee, I am going to rewrite your history. Everything that the enemy has stolen from you the last 27 years, I'm going to return to you sevenfold! Any ground he has taken in your relationships with your wife, your children and ministry will be restored! You will be restored financially, emotionally, spiritually and physically! It will be as if none of these things had ever happened!"* He said He would rewrite my history. WOW! What an Awesome God!'

Then I was reminded of a verse in the Old Testament I had not looked at in years. I believe the Holy Spirit gave me recall of this verse to seal the deal God had started: (Joel 2:25-26)

"I will restore to you the years that the swarming locust has eaten, the crawling locust, the consuming locust, and the chewing locust, my great army which I sent among you. You shall eat in plenty and be satisfied, and praise the name of the Lord your God, who has dealt wondrously with you."

Lord… let Thy Kingdom come! In my spirit, in my soul and in my physical body!"

[End of Lee's Story]

Pray, Pray, and Pray Some More

Did you notice the common theme throughout Lee's story? It was prayer. Continuous prayer. For years.

So, I beg of you, never underestimate the power of continued petitioning of God for whatever it is you're seeking.

By the way, I count myself lucky to personally know Lee, The Healed Guy. Why? It's because I knew him before he was healed and now I know, without a doubt, that he is completely healed. Regardless of what anyone thinks of my story about going to Heaven, there are two things that can't be denied: 1) The FACT that I was miraculously healed of some life-altering problems with my throat and possibly deforming burns on my face; and 2) the FACT that Lee was and is healed (completely) of Parkinson's. It's a matter of fact that neither Parkinson's nor a burned throat and face simply disappear because of some psychosomatic belief. So, if anyone has a problem with the fact that I went to Heaven, I can deal with that. But, let no one doubt that our God is an Awesome God who can and does still heal.

If you'd like to read Lee McDougald's testimony for yourself, in its entirety, you can visit his website at: **www.TheHealedGuy.com**.

One last point I'd like to make concerning petitioning prayer is this: We should go to our Heavenly Father as if we were children because children have a tremendous amount of faith that isn't dulled by the 'realities' of life. If you have children, you know what I mean. Children have a capacity for faith in others, but especially their own parents, that is unparalleled. For instance, when my children were much smaller than they are today, I used to have them run across a picnic table and jump into my arms. They didn't realize that I am a small man and that, if I had missed, they could have been seriously injured (I didn't actually think much about that fact at the time or I probably wouldn't have done it). What they *knew*, without a doubt, was that I WOULD catch them. So, they ran and jumped, ran and jumped, and ran and jumped into my arms time and time again – until I finally said it was time to stop.

If our children place this kind of trust in us, then when we consider our Heavenly Father, who is All-Powerful, All-Knowing, and All-Loving (in other words, He doesn't do stupid stuff like we sometimes do and He not only has our best interests at heart but He has the ability to make certain of these interests come true)… how much more should we be willing to go to Him in faith?

My son, Brance, who was 8 years old at the time of my death, had faith in our Heavenly Father. I know because of what I've been told he did the day I died. If you remember, I had fallen asleep in Brance's bed the night of my death and my wife woke him as she tried to revive me. Once he had dialed 911 and given them our address, he went and sat on our couch as paramedics and our neighbors arrived. Jenny P., one of our neighbors, asked Brance if he wanted to go next door to her house to wait until another of our friends, Alicia B., came to pick his little sister and him up to take them both to her house. His response was one that still, to this day, brings tears of joy to my eyes. He said, *"I think that I need to pray for my dad."* At that point, my son, a giant in my eyes, turned over, buried his head in his hands behind a couch pillow and began praying that God would bring me back and that I'd be okay. Talk about FAITH!

To this day, Brance isn't traumatized by the events that took place on that early February morning and it's because he believed what it says in Mark 11:24, "*Whatever you ask for in prayer, believe that you have received it, and it will be yours.*" Notice that the verse doesn't say, 'Believe that you might receive it' or 'Believe that you will receive it.' No. Instead it says, "*Believe that you <u>have</u> received it and it will be yours.*" This verse is like saying, "*God I believe you can do it; I know you will do it; so, in my heart of hearts, I'm going to take for granted that it's already done.*" Now that's childlike faith and it's exactly this type of faith our Lord and Savior demands of us. In fact, He said as much when He stated in Matthew 18:1-4, "*At that time the disciples came to Jesus and asked, 'Who is the greatest in the kingdom of Heaven?' He called a little child and had him stand among them. And He said: 'I tell you the truth, unless you change and become like little children, you will never enter the kingdom of Heaven. Therefore, whoever humbles himself like this child is the greatest in the kingdom of Heaven.'*"

The point our Lord was trying to make is that children are humble in that they think less of themselves and more of those around them – especially adults (the authority figures in their lives). So, just as my son knew that he couldn't rely on himself or anyone else to help me and, instead, went to the Father, we should do the same!

Having said all of the above, here is what I would suggest you do concerning petitioning prayer. Simply make certain that what you're asking for lines up with His will and pray, pray, pray. Remember, the part you play in prayer is that you are to pray passionately, from the bottom of your heart, and truthfully, taking your most genuine concerns to Him. His part is to pay attention to your prayers and to kindly answer you in His own time according to His will. If we do our part, God will not fail to do His.

13

Living With the Fear of the Recurrence of Cancer

"The LORD is my shepherd, I shall not be in want. He makes me lie down in green pastures, he leads me beside quiet waters, he restores my soul. He guides me in paths of righteousness for his name's sake. Even though I walk through the valley of the shadow of death, I will fear no evil, for you are with me; your rod and your staff, they comfort me. You prepare a table before me in the presence of my enemies. You anoint my head with oil; my cup overflows. Surely goodness and love will follow me all the days of my life, and I will dwell in the house of the LORD forever."

Psalms 23:1-6

Unless you've ever suffered from a disease that is as devastating as cancer (one that can be 'cured' and yet crop-up again at any given time), it's impossible to fully understand the fear that those of us who have must deal with. I'm convinced that the only ones who haven't personally suffered from such a disease who can possibly know this type of fear are our caregivers.

For the most part, I don't think about getting cancer again. But, every now and then, especially around the anniversary of when I was first diagnosed with the demonic disease or when the date of a scheduled checkup grows closer, fear grips me with a fury that's unmatched by any other I've ever encountered.

Part of the fear I experience is wondering how the people in my life will be affected if I get sick again. This is a special fear for me as it concerns my children, but I also worry about how others will be affected as well. One of the reasons for my apprehension is because people begin to treat you differently the further out from the disease that you get timewise. This is both comforting and aggravating at the same time. It's comforting in that you want to be treated as if you're normal and yet it's aggravating because people have a tendency to forget that you aren't normal. For instance, people I've known for a long time, even my close friends, often treat me as if I'm absolutely and completely fine while I feel that I have a time bomb inside of me and it's just waiting to explode. But, I never want to confront these people because they are my friends and they've stuck with my family and me throughout this ordeal. I live with the fear that if I tell them how I really feel (frustrated, scared, angry and calm, protected, sad and happy all at the same time), they'll either have one of two reactions:

1) They'll pity me and treat me as if I'm frail and feeble; or

2) They'll get angry with me for not being stronger.

Part of me *needs* to be well (free from cancer) because I need my friends to see me as triumphant over the disease. Of course, this is pure nonsensical hogwash because both they and I know that it's not me who defeated the cancer in the first place any more than I caused it to appear inside my body. Still, there's a big part of who I am that wants to be a hero for everyone involved in my recovery. I'd imagine that many people who've suffered from a curable disease and are in remission feel this way.

Having spoken to many people who've gone through cancer treatments and came out on the other end alive I can tell you that your family and friends (those whom you know love you) often say things that are completely insensitive. For instance, I recently had someone with the best of intentions tell me, *"I feel badly that I didn't contact you sooner because I know so much about natural health and nutrition. The reason I feel bad is because so many people are so naïve about what actually causes cancer and how to get rid of it naturally. I know you chose to take the medical route, to have an operation to remove some of the cancer that had invaded your body and then to have radiation and chemotherapy to kill the rest of it, and it isn't and wasn't necessary. But, I understand that people get scared and don't know of any other alternatives."*

I can't tell you how offensive this type of well-meaning comment is to someone who has been through any type of cancer treatment. Honestly, it's infuriating that someone would have the audacity to not think through such comments. In essence, what I was being told is that I had failed to consider all the alternatives at my disposal before subjecting myself to debilitating and disfiguring surgery and subsequent treatments for the cancer I was afflicted with. Still, since I know the heart of the person who said this to me, I can't really get too offended by the comment because I know it was said with the best of intentions.

A word of advice I'd like to give anyone who knows someone with a life-threatening illness is to be less sympathetic and more empathetic to the person you're dealing with. In counseling, one learns that to be sympathetic is to *'maintain a distance from another's feelings'* while to be empathetic means to *'understand or imagine the depth of a person's feelings.'* Almost no one likes sympathy but almost everyone craves empathy because it means to have feelings *with* a person rather than feeling sorry *for* a person. In essence, when someone is being empathetic towards me, it means they are willing to *walk a mile in my shoes.* Honestly, I've not met all that many empathetic people in my life – especially as it concerns health issues. Those who are, such as my wife, seem to be able to cut through the garbage of life and go right to the heart of the matter at hand. They are the ones who you'll see at AIDS clinics, cancer centers, heart hospitals, and other places actually interacting with patients, their caregivers, and their families instead of just doing *stuff* that helps but that isn't really healing. Please don't get me wrong. I know that people have different gifts and strengths and that some are better suited for one-on-one interactions than others are. I used to be one of those people (shy, introverted). I wanted to do more for people in need but I simply had not learned how. So, I LOVE it when anyone reaches out on whatever level they're able to. If the only way you know how to reach out to someone is by mowing their lawn, doing dishes, cleaning up their homes, emptying out bedpans, or any number of other chores, I pray that God will bless you richly! But, I sincerely hope that one of the ways He blesses you is by introducing you to a deeper level of outreach, an outreach that becomes in-reaching and therefore enriching for both you and those you come in contact with. However, I can promise you that in order for you to become effective in such a ministry you'll need to press yourself inward and towards those you see who need your help.

By all means, serve on outreach teams so that you can reach out to the community at large. But, while doing so, be open to the possibility of praying for others or, if they aren't 'into prayer' be willing to sit with them and just chat. I can't tell you how important talking with people is – especially for the patient. Believe me, I never expected anyone to fully understand what I was going through when I had cancer and was undergoing treatments for the same. Still, it was fantastic when someone who wasn't sick showed me enough kindness to simply sit down and talk to me. I encourage you to not be all that concerned with how the conversation is going to go. You aren't going to be expected to give any life-changing advice and, normally, the conversation you'll have won't even be all that morbid. In fact, most of the conversations I had with people who were willing to talk with me were very life giving. I've found that the majority of people who are faced with life-threatening disease aren't all that wrapped-up into discussing death or even the afterlife. What we all want is to feel normal and part of normalcy is to talk about things that interest us. For me that meant that most of my conversations revolved around religion, cooking, and family. Others like to speak about sports, friends, hobbies, and a host of other topics that aren't related to death but, rather, to life.

So, if you're willing to enter into the life of someone else (especially those who are ill) here's a few crib notes to remember:

1) Pray, pray and pray some more. Pray before you go, pray when and if they ask you to and pray after you've left them. Don't worry if you're asked to pray for them that they're expecting some great oration. Use simple words and just talk to God. When you pray, you need to believe that God has the power to heal them but you should also be willing to accept it if He doesn't. Believe me when I tell you that prayer really does move God.

2) Smile. A lot.

3) Be patient with those of us who are patients.

4) If you're nervous about speaking to someone, bring along something to do with your hands such as a book (non-religious is best unless you know the person very well), a deck of playing cards, a checkerboard, gum, etc. so you don't fidget.

5) It's important to eliminate distractions such as music, television programs, rowdy children, etc., so that you and the person who is ill can have real, meaningful conversations. However, this doesn't mean that you should chitchat just for the sake of avoiding silence. Remember that silence is okay and that often just making yourself available to the person is enough support.

6) Respect that the person you're trying to communicate with will probably have differing levels of energy at different times (I know, based on the notes I took, that this was definitely the case in my situation). As such, you should allow them to dictate the length of time you visit and converse. Ask them to let you know if they need to rest and be alert to visual signs that they are getting tired.

7) Allow the person you're speaking with to express their feelings (even if these feelings include guilt, depression, anger, or fear). Always keep in mind that these feelings aren't caused by you even if they are directed at you. Also remember that your 'job' is to listen and empathize with the person. They aren't really looking for someone to give them answers, they just need a friendly shoulder to cry on and someone they can trust not to get offended if their behavior seems a tad abnormal.

8) Don't be afraid to ask the person about their recovery or treatment options. We like to talk about the options we have. Of course, if the person doesn't want to talk about their options, don't pursue the matter.

9) As you get to know the person or if you feel led by the Lord, ask the person you're speaking with if they need or want to contact anyone to tell them what's going on. This can be an especially helpful offer since some people put off contacting friends or family until it's too late. Having you make an offer to be a go-between can not only challenge the person to be honest about who he or she needs or wants to contact but it can also alleviate much of the stress of them having to make the initial contact.

10) Ask about their life, what they've done thus far and what they plan to do in the future. In other words, get them to reminisce and to imagine a future. Don't be shocked if this type of talk brings one or both of you to tears – and don't be afraid to cry in front of them!

11) And last, but not least, don't smoke around a person who is ill!

14

Rediscovering and Reinventing Myself

"A new command I give you: Love one another. As I have loved you, so you must love one another. By this all men will know that you are my disciples, if you love one another."
John 13:34-35

Knowing who I was and yet having to rediscover who I was and am is trying. The fact that I face each and every single day is that I'm not the man I used to be. While the greatest part of me is okay with who I am now there is still a significant part of me who desires to be the man I once was. Of course, having been to Heaven removes this possibility as the man I am now knows something to be true that the man I once was only held as a cherished hope. Having also survived an advanced stage of cancer has also changed me as well. As it stands, I simply have to accept that changes have occurred in my life that have greatly impacted the man I am and the man I will become and commit all these changes to my Lord and Savior whom I know is in control. As long as I can keep the fact that He is in control at the forefront of my mind, I'll be okay.

With this in mind I've set about rediscovering who I am and reinventing whom I choose to be. In many, many ways this is incredibly freeing. My wife tells me that some of the 'bad' habits I once had are gone and that I've developed new 'better' habits. I've discovered that I'm now doing things that I would probably have never attempted before, such as developing a party company (called FunFxMobile.com) for kids. I've also begun learning new skills and adapting latent abilities to help me compensate to my new life in ways that astound me. For instance, I used to be able to speak quickly and forcefully and I used this as a tool to hide a lack of self-assurance. Today, I'm learning how to accept the fact that I have a speech impediment (namely that part of my tongue was removed and that having no salivary glands causes me to have to drink water repeatedly throughout any conversation) and to both be and speak more confidently. While I may never again be able to give a hard-hitting, fire-and-brimstone sermon (not that this was ever my style), I know that I can still present the gospel in an effective manner as long as I follow the leading of the Lord. And, while I may be less intense than I once was during conversations, I know for a fact that I have a much more intense and private prayer life. All in all, I think I'm doing a good job of handling things, but only time (and those I love) will tell for certain.

Honestly, the amount of healing I've undergone has been nothing short of miraculous.

I've regained all of the strength and more that I had before I developed cancer. I've gone from having to ride around on the little 'scooters' provided by many supermarkets to being able to work out on a bike for an hour at a time at level 6 and 7 (out of 10). Plus, whereas I wasn't even able to use resistance bands (the large rubber bands used in aerobics) when I first came home, I'm now lifting in excess of 80 – 100 pounds on a universal weight machine for reps at a time.

I'm maintaining my weight, my blood pressure is normal and, as I've stated before, I take no drugs whatsoever for pain, depression, or hypertension – all of which I'd been taking while undergoing chemo and radiation.

One of the most exciting aspects of my life since I returned from Heaven is that the Lord has given me a renewed vision and heart for helping those who are having a hard time making it financially.

Specifically, the Lord has me working to develop both food pantries and *soup kitchens* in the Alabama areas. I've italicized soup kitchens due to the fact that the kitchens I'm helping develop do much more than cook and hand out soup. The fact is that we're developing menus for the people who visit to actually order from. Helping people retain and maintain a sense of self-worth is a very important aspect of our ministry. One of the ways I've found to help others do this is to give them choices, even if they're minor ones. With that in mind, the soup kitchens are to be run like mini-restaurants where the people who need food are seated at tables and served by the volunteers. The food pantries, which are designed to facilitate the distribution of groceries (canned and pre-packaged foods) and other essentials (soap, toothpaste, toilet paper, etc.) to individuals and families who can't make ends meet, fill an entirely different need.

Together, the soup kitchens and the food pantries provide a way to minister to a variety of needs and people from virtually every walk of life. People who honestly care about the needs of others get a chance to minister to those in need. Conversely, those ministering to others find that they themselves receive far beyond their own capacity to give. It really is a win-win situation and I'm so happy the Lord has seen fit to allow me to be a part of such an undertaking. This is how I feel we can all fulfill the command given to us in John 13:34-35.

So, for now, I find that I'm content to concentrate on loving those who are around me and doing what the Lord has sent me back to do, which is to tell people about His Kingdom.

15

The Kingdom – Here But Not Yet Here!?

"From that time on Jesus began to preach, 'Repent, for the kingdom of heaven is near.'"
Matthew 4:17

That the kingdom of God is already here and yet is not fully manifest (has not come in its fullness – and will not until Christ returns) is a certainty. We can see the kingdom is 'at hand' by the fact that God still works, through nature and miracles, today. Divine healing, fruitful evangelism, missionary works and the manifestation of the gifts of the Holy Spirit are all proofs that His kingdom is active in the present day. Of course, due to the fact that God's kingdom isn't yet present in the fullest sense, we still suffer under the burdens brought about by the sinful fall of man. So, while Christians (those who have chosen Jesus Christ as their personal Savior) have eternal life, our earthly bodies still wither and die. While we have been freed from the bondage of sin and stand forgiven of sin (past, present, and future), we are still beset by the temptation to sin and by sin itself. Obviously, if the kingdom of God weren't active in the present day the problem of sin would be much more rampant. As it is, there is a Restrainer of sin and that is the person of the Holy Spirit (2 Thessalonians 2:6-8).

So, while warfare, scarcity of food and finances, sinfulness, illness and death continue in the present, there is still a manifest presence of God's kingdom in our midst as can be seen by the many miracles performed by God through many different agents as well as by Himself alone (as in the case of my resurrection) today.

Knowing that the kingdom of God is both here and not yet here, my question is: Why do most Bible-believing Christians fall into the group of believers who adhere to a 'not yet' instead of a 'here' mentality?

I believe that one of the primary reasons we fail to observe more of the presence of His kingdom is because we don't ask to see the same manifested. Or, rather, we ask but with very little faith that what we ask for 'will be done on Earth as it is in Heaven.'

This attitude towards prayer should seem strange to anyone who is a mature believer. Why? Simply because we are told that whatever we pray in faith, not doubting that God can do what we ask Him to do (Mark 11:24; James 1:6-8), that is in accordance with His will (1 John 5:14,15), when we keep His commandments and do what we know we're to do (1 John 3:22) and when we pray in His name (John 14:13-14) it <u>will</u> be done!

If I may, I'd like to comment on the phrase *'in His name'* as it concerns petitioning God. While many people simply tack on the phrase, 'in Jesus' name' or 'in the name of Jesus' or whatever, at the end of a prayer (as if 'in His name' is the equivalent of abrakadabra), this isn't what Jesus is talking about. Rather than being a magical formula, Jesus uses the phrase to mean that when we ask for something 'in His name' that we do so fully understanding (or with as much understanding as is possible on this side of eternity) who He is. In the Bible, a person's name represented his will and his influence or authority. As it is, we pray 'in Jesus' name' because He is the one mediator between God and man, our High Priest (1 Timothy 2:5; Hebrews 4:14-16). Thus, we pray *in His name* because it is *through His authority* that God can hear us and *by His authority* that God acts.

What Is The Kingdom of God?

Technically, the Kingdom of God is anywhere and everywhere that God is King. This means that with few exceptions (in the heart of those who have not accepted His Son as their Savior, Hell, and in the lives of demons and satan himself, etc.) the Kingdom of God is *everywhere.* While some theologians and many more lay people treat the term 'Kingdom of God' as if it were *only* an alternative term for 'Heaven,' Jesus Himself taught that God's Kingdom was both 'at hand' and 'here' as well as 'to come.' The Kingdom of God and the way the term is used by none other than our Lord makes it one of the paradoxes of Scripture's simultaneous teachings on those things that are present and not yet at the same time (the presence of Jesus, salvation, eternal life, righteousness, Christians being kings, princes and rulers, etc.). Of course, it's more than appropriate to use the terms Kingdom of God and Kingdom of Heaven interchangeably as long as one understands what the terms do and don't mean. As it stands, even a cursory reading of the Scriptures will reveal that it was (and is) the belief of the Lord that His Kingdom (i.e., the Kingdom of God) was and is in our midst on Earth. Further, He demonstrated this truth by casting out demons (Matthew 12:28), healing people (Matthew 4:23) and even raising people from the dead (Matthew 10:7-8) and by telling those who followed Him to do the same things.

When Jesus spoke of the Kingdom of Heaven, He was not normally talking about going to Heaven when you die. Obviously, the Kingdom of Heaven includes the intermediate Heaven (the one where all believers go today when they die – the one I was blessed to have visited) as well as the future Heaven where the New Earth will be and where God Himself will reside with us eternally, but it also includes life in the 'here and now.' So, less technically but possibly more specifically, the Kingdom of God is any place where Jesus is the King; it is His government; it is an invisible, spiritual kingdom that isn't restricted to a specific location and whose power is able to manifest itself in numerous ways.

What Are The Dynamics Found In His Kingdom?

In the Book of Romans (14:17), the Apostle Paul tells us that the Kingdom of God is "...*righteousness, peace and joy in the Holy Spirit.*" So, we know that if the Kingdom of God is manifesting itself in a person's life (i.e., if the person in question is being ruled by God), then they will be happy, at peace with their circumstances, and they will be righteous in their actions. This doesn't mean that Christians will never fall into depression or despair or that they will never act in an unrighteous manner but these should be exceptions to the rule.

Further, love, justice, mercy, favor, and blessings will follow when the Kingdom is manifested in the lives of people. All of these come about when His people exhibit faithfulness to Him. Conversely, when faithfulness to God isn't found, the opposites are manifested (hate, injustice, cruelty or animosity, curses, and unrighteous intolerance).

Directly or indirectly, the often *less sensational* signs and wonders of love, justice, mercy, favor, and blessings are responsible for the more overt signs and wonders (healings, exorcisms, resurrections, tongues, etc.) that we see throughout the Bible. To be certain, the Apostle Paul was correct when he stated in 1 Corinthians 13 that the greatest gift of all is love. So, directly, without a love for God and one's neighbor, the likelihood of your praying for any good thing for others is nil. It just won't happen – at least not without an ulterior motive. Indirectly, then, the reason is simple: Without a true love for and belief in God, we are dead in our sins and are unable to please God or show true love (which is always Christ-like) to anyone. Therefore, since genuine, Godly love must be manifested before we are willing to bestow genuine, Godly justice, mercy, favor, and blessings upon anyone, it's obvious that the same must be present before the other signs and wonders will be manifested.

What Happens When the Kingdom of God Manifests Itself on Earth?

Having said all of the above, I'd like to propose that when the Kingdom of God manifests itself in our world, we see miracles and signs and wonders happening much like we see in the Gospels and the book of Acts.

What does this mean on a practical level? It means that we should expect to see people healed of all types of disease when we pray for them; we should expect demons to be revealed and cast out in the Name of Jesus; and we should expect to see people raised from the dead (just as I was).

Sickness, demonic possession or oppression, sin and death are all a result of the breakdown in the created order of God. Certainly we'll not have complete deliverance from these things until God Himself rules and reigns personally on the New Earth but, since Jesus Himself told us that the Kingdom of God was 'at hand' we should go into prayer with expectation that His will shall be done on Earth just as it is in Heaven.

Take just a moment and imagine how you'd begin to live if you really and truly believed that the power of God was available to you as a Saint? How would you live your life? Would you be more inclined to give more generously to those in need? Would you be more apt to take chances with your life if you honestly believed that God was truly in control? How would you pray for people who had diseases or disorders such as cancer, HIV, AIDS, diabetes, eye problems, amputations, or any other number of issues if you REALLY believed that God was 'still in the healing business?' Would you treat others with more respect if you KNEW in your heart of hearts that they really were valued by Almighty God? What would you do or how would you act when you were faced with a naturally insurmountable problem if you recognized that the grace of God was truly sufficient for you in all circumstances? How would your feelings of inadequacy change if you understood how much God loves YOU?

I know how living in this manner has influenced me and my walk with Him. I know how living in this manner has affected those in my church and those who knew me before and after I died and came back from Heaven. Living with this type of knowledge... knowing that God is in control and that He's given you (as His Son or Daughter) access to His Kingdom right now, here on Earth, is empowering.

I encourage you, regardless of whether or not you believe that I actually died, went to Heaven, and came back, to follow the Apostle Paul's advice when he told us in 1 Corinthians 11:1 to *"Imitate me, just as I also imitate Christ."* If you'll do this one thing, I promise you it will change your life and you'll begin to impact the lives of others tremendously.

16

When We Are at Our Weakest, God Is at His Strongest!

"And He said to me, "My grace is sufficient for you, for My strength is made perfect in weakness." Therefore most gladly I will rather boast in my infirmities, that the power of Christ may rest upon me."
2 Corinthians 12:9,10

The emails that follow this section provide a level of detail about what I went through and how I handled the stress of the treatments that I simply couldn't put into novel form. I've left the details in the accounts as pristine as possible (changing or deleting only a few names at the person's request). What you're about to read will give you an idea of what I was going through, how I handled all the stress, and what I chose to do throughout my treatments. You'll read emails from me, to me and about me and the subjects will range from the theological to the mundane. As you'll probably gather, I began the process of dealing with the cancer in my body with a fairly positive attitude. Only as I began to become sicker and sicker did the mood of my emails change. Obviously, I had zero idea as to what God ultimately had in store for me (a trip into Heaven) until the fateful day in February.

Throughout the comments of my friends you'll notice that the theme of 'Lonnie's Battle' recurs over and over again. Honestly, I don't think I ever thought of the ordeal I went through as a battle. It was simply something that I had to deal with and the only way I knew I'd survive it was by relying on the strength of God and His will for me. As it stands today, the 'battle' everyone speaks of turned out to be the greatest blessing of my entire life – thus far. It seems that the Lord had a greater purpose in my life other than simply surviving cancer. Instead, I was to be given a vision, an actual experience in Heaven, which I am to share with as many others as possible.

My wife and I have been asked by a couple of people if we're planning on suing the doctor who overdosed me and ultimately caused not only my death but the suffering I've had to endure. My response to this question hasn't changed: *"No. Why in the world would I sue him when he gave me the greatest opportunity of my life – to personally see Heaven?*" In all honesty, I don't think it was my doctor's fault but, rather, God's. He allowed me to die and to visit His realm. For that, regardless of whose 'fault' it was, I'll be eternally grateful.

If I can encourage you with just one message, it would be that when we are at our weakest, God is at His strongest! My wife and I are living proof of this fact. There is rarely a day that goes by when we aren't reminded of our complete dependence on God. Whether that dependence is due to a financial need, or our family's health or some other spiritual or physical need He manifests Himself in our lives in such a way that neither of us could or would deny His strength. If I could persuade you to do two simple things in your life (after accepting His Son as your Lord and Savior) that I believe would revolutionize the way you live as well as your ability to live, they would be:

1) Spend time with God, one-on-one, in expectant prayer. What I mean is that when you talk to God, *expect* Him to answer you and look for those answers. Don't be deceived by satan that just because you don't audibly hear from God or notice an immediate change because of your prayer that God either hasn't heard you or isn't going to answer you. Remember that even here on Earth, parents often answer their children in ways that are subtle but they answer them nonetheless. I know this is true in my life. For instance, if my son asks me for a drink of water I happen to be enjoying at the time, I might: A) Audibly say, "*Okay, here you go,*" and hand the water to him; or B) I might simply nod my head "*Yes*" in confirmation that it's okay that he take the water and drink it; or C) I might simply gesture towards the water as a confirmation that I've indeed heard his request and am granting it. No one who witnessed any of these three ways of answering my son's request would deny that I have, without a doubt, answered him. Certainly he might prefer that I answer in a specific manner but, still, if he receives an answer from me, then it's his duty to be aware of my answer and acknowledge it. The same goes for us as God's children. God may choose to answer us in a myriad of ways and, if we are wise, we'll be aware of this fact and look for His answer and then acknowledge the same.

2) Praise God regardless of your circumstances. In speaking to people, I've found that this is one of the most difficult things to do

because it seems that when we're suffering our natural tendency is to turn inward or outward instead of upward. Believe me when I say that I know what it's like to suffer. Certainly I haven't and don't suffer anywhere near what some of you who may be reading this are suffering. But, from being physically ill to being financially broke to losing a parent to watching my wife struggle to come to terms with having a husband who isn't the same man she married, I know what suffering is. As such, I can tell you that, once you begin praising the Lord in every circumstance of your life, He will undergird you with a strength that is beyond human imagination.

It is my prayer that, as you read through these emails, you'll find in them some of the encouragement and strength that our most gracious Lord gave to me.

[**Note:** The weeks are date-based, sequential weeks based on when I actually wrote them. So, you may find certain weeks deleted (such as when the emails go from Week 1 to Week 3. This isn't a mistake.]

17
The Emails

"For God did not appoint us to suffer wrath but to receive salvation through our
Lord Jesus Christ. He died for us so that, whether we are awake or asleep,
we may live together with him. Therefore encourage one another and build
each other up, just as in fact you are doing."
1 Thessalonians 5:9-11

Week 1

[Note: This is the first email I have where I mentioned the lump(s) in
my neck that would eventually be diagnosed as cancer. Also, our
church at this time was only about a month old.)

8-12-07 From: Lonnie Honeycutt

Subject: Gas Buy-Down…

Gas Buy-Down on the Eastern Shore by Deeper Life Fellowship

Continuing our ongoing commitment to servant evangelism, Deeper
Life Fellowship Eastern Shore hosted a gas buy-down at Murphy's gas
station on Hwy 98 in Daphne, Alabama. This station gets a lot of
traffic because it's directly connected to the local Wal-Mart super
center.

To be quite honest, we didn't know if this evangelism project was
going to come to pass. I had already contacted a couple of gas stations
in the area and, as of yesterday, had not gotten a response.

On a whim (or the leading of the Holy Spirit), my wife, Dawn,
decided to call the Murphy's station and to ask if we could give away
gas. Her initial phone call was met with surprise but not a negative
answer. Justin, the person on duty, had to call his manager (Cynthia)
who, in turn had to contact the district manager for the Murphy gas
stations in Daphne and Mobile Alabama. To make a long story short,
after a couple of clarifying conversations (they wanted to make certain
we weren't planning on badgering anyone who didn't happen to agree
with our particular religious views), we got permission to do the event.

I found out later that getting this permission from a district manager
was akin to witnessing a miracle. To put it plainly, due to the potential
problems people have with others participating in any kind of religious

activity in the public arena, it's simply easier and usually less likely to involve legal questions, to *'just say No.'* Frankly, I think this was God-ordained. Maybe it wasn't, but I figure I'll give Him the credit until He tells me otherwise.

Anyway, it was great. One of our new members, David M. – a former army sergeant – joined Dawn and me as we gave away gas. Our tag line was simple: *"We know you need gas, so we'd like to buy you $5 worth for free – no strings attached."* When asked why we were doing this, our response was simple, *"To show the love of God in a practical way."*

The response to this outreach was overwhelmingly positive. When my wife told one lady that we were going to buy her $5 of gas she threw open her car door, jumped out, and gave Dawn a bear hug. This shocked me because by this time Dawn, David, and I were soaking wet with sweat (the heat index was already topping 100 degrees). Another lady bought us bottled water just to say 'thanks for being so kind to everyone' and many people marveled that people would be taking time out of their day to buy something for people they didn't even know. David was able to assist a gentleman whose car needed a jump – I don't think the engine ever started but just the fact that David was there to help him was a major blessing.

Have you ever wondered about what a small world this really is? We met two people who knew about our outreaches with Deeper Life Fellowship Mobile and one of the two (Randy) had actually put the Sheetrock up in the Mobile DLF. Those two encounters were pretty neat.

Only two people refused to let us buy them gas. One gentleman begged off by stating that there were other people who could probably use it more than he could (a perfectly honorable response) while the other was just too suspicious. After being given a Wal-Mart gift card, he mulled our proposition over 'Free Gas – No Strings Attached' and finally gave it back saying, *"Nah, nothing's free. There's gotta be a catch."*

The first thing I thought and what I still believe is that this man has been hurt – probably often. He's one of the ones that Christians need to be on the lookout for to show him that some things really are free – such as love, etc. Actually, people are correct when they say the things we do on outreaches aren't really free. They do cost someone something, just not them. We who do outreaches and those who support us are the ones paying the cost so that the people we meet can receive something with zero strings. Sounds familiar, doesn't it? That's what happens in our exchange with Jesus – He gives us His righteousness which He paid an infinite price for. But, we get to call it 'Free.' Kind of neat, isn't it? Through outreach to our neighbors, to people we don't know and may never meet again, we get to taste a very small sample of what Jesus did for us – we give of ourselves, of what we have worked for, without any guarantee that what we're offering will be accepted.

Judging A Book By Its Cover

Okay, here's a confession... I, like many others, often judge a book by its cover. Fortunately, I don't often allow my initial judgment to jade me one way or the other – good or bad – because I know that my surface judgment needs to be balanced by a deeper inspection of the person or situation.

Today a gentleman pulled up to the pumps driving a rather beat-up older red car (a car whose 21"+ rims probably cost more than the entire vehicle). The driver had very long dreadlocks and the stereo was blasting rap. My first thought was (and I'm being very honest here), "*Sigh, I don't want to waste the gas card on this guy.*" That was what my 'flesh' thought. Then, the Holy Spirit convicted me and my spirit immediately rejoiced and I thought, "*I'm so glad this man has come here today! This might be the last day he's not a Christian!*"

Even though my flesh was weak, my thoughts were taken captive by the spirit of Christ and I was able to approach this man, whose exterior presented someone rough and tough and potentially dangerous, with a heart of compassion and friendliness. I said our tag line to him and his entire demeanor changed. Where he had not been smiling, he smiled. Where he and I at one time might not have ever exchanged pleasantries, we did.

I don't have to wonder what Jesus' response to me would have been had I not served this gentleman. He wouldn't have been pleased. As such, I wouldn't have been pleased with myself. Frankly, I don't know what this man's story is. Perhaps he was and is a Christian who simply chose to listen to music that I didn't listen to (I don't always listen to Christian music). And what about his car – so what if I don't have the same taste in vehicles (or maybe the car wasn't even his – he might have borrowed it). My point is this: This man, just like you and me, are made in the image of the Almighty God. He is loved by God, Jesus died for him, and the Holy Spirit wants him to become His child (if he's not already). So, if I'm going to be a true ambassador for King Jesus, if I'm going to try to do His will on Earth, then I have to be willing not to jump to conclusions. Actually, that's not true. ALL Christians should immediately jump to a conclusion. That conclusion: Every person we meet deserves our respect because they are made in the image of Our God and Father and He wants us to treat others the way He treats us – with love.

Thanks so much to those who made this outreach possible. Blessings upon you! Please pray that the Lord brings us more members so that we can spread the glory of His name far and wide.

Rev. Lonnie Honeycutt (RevLon) Deeper Life Fellowship East

PS: I'll be going into the doc's office in a few days to have the lump or lumps in my neck checked into. Please pray that everything is okay.

Week 3

[Note: The following is one of the very few emails I have where my wife asked for prayers for me specifically. Not that she didn't ask people to pray for me whenever I was ill, but this is simply one of the only ones that referenced the headaches that had become a normal part of my life at that time. They were a portend to what would eventually be found.]

9-1-07 From: Dawn Honeycutt

Subject: Pray for Lonnie

Libby, Could you ask everyone to pray for Lonnie? He's been really sick today with a migraine. He doesn't usually have this type.

Thanks, Dawn Honeycutt

Week 5

9-10-07 From: Garland B.

Subject: Lonnie's Mass

Lonnie just left the hospital. Apparently they stuck a tube down his nose and discovered not 1 but 2 masses in his neck. One is pressing against the carotid artery, the other against the jugular vein. Obviously, both of these are a big problem, but add to it that they mentioned lymphoma as a possibility and he really needs some prayer.

He is returning home, but he is in a lot of pain. He needs healing and pain relief immediately. Please pass along this prayer request for our brother and former associate pastor. Garland

9-10-07 From: Lonnie Honeycutt

Subject: The masses in my neck…

Hi Guys and Gals! Seriously, I'm doing okay. I can honestly say that I'm not worried one iota about the things in my neck – heck, maybe I should change Deeper Life Fellowship East to Catholic Services now that I've observed a mass – ha ha ha ha, you know on the scan – (ok, okay, I hear the groans).

Gotta tell you though, the images from the CT Scan were pretty awesome. Being able to look inside your own body gives you a definite sense of the awesomeness of God – not that I'm all that awesome but you know what I mean.

Anyway, let's remember to remember Pam P. (breast and lymph cancer) and Ramona O. (foot surgery) in our prayers and in practical application of the Kingdom of God. Love all of you! Lonnie (RevLon)

9-11-07 From: Lonnie Honeycutt

Subject: From Lonnie to Everyone

Hi one and all. Thanks for your calls and emails. I really appreciate them. My neck is still really sore from the 'procedures' yesterday and I didn't get much sleep last night but, all-in-all, not too bad.

Guys and gals, I've got to tell you... if you haven't yet volunteered at the food bank, you should really think about doing so. I went there this morning because they needed some help and spent about 3 1/2 hours ministering to people. I loaded food, carried food, filled out paperwork, and got to pray for a BUNCH of people. It was awesome – tiring but awesome.

I spoke to Ramona this afternoon and she's doing better. The pain is less and she's not having to take her pain medication very often. Also, she said to say THANKS to those who have taken her food. Please keep her in prayer as she's already bored and wants to get up and around (who wouldn't, right?).

As for Pam P., her surgery is on Friday at 10 AM so please pray for her and that the docs get everything that needs to be gotten surgically.

Also, thanks for the heads-up some of you've given me about possible sales on X-Boxes. I haven't found what I need in the price range I'm looking for but as long as there are good leads, I'll check 'em out.

Ok, I'm sure there's something else but that's about it so far.

Love all of you! Rev. Lonnie Honeycutt (RevLon)

9-13-07 From: Lonnie Honeycutt

Subject: From Lonnie to Alan and Alessandra

Hi guys! We really miss seeing you each week. Thanks for your phone call. The latest news, as you may already know, is that I have two masses in my neck instead of one. Currently my neck is pretty swollen but there's not a lot of discomfort. While the doc in charge of my case (we've gone through 3 physicians so far) wanted me to wait until next Tuesday to talk about options I made a call and convinced them to meet with me tomorrow morning.

There's still a possibility that whatever is going on with my neck is cancer but I think the possibility is fairly remote (based on what all three doctors have told me thus far). Only a biopsy of the entire section will tell for certain.

In any case, I'm not letting this slow me down.

Guys, thanks SO VERY much for checking up on me. I REALLY appreciate it. The three of you are very special to me. By the way, how is Alessandra's dad? In Christ, Lonnie.

9-13-07 From: Dawn Honeycutt

Subject: Lonnie is having surgery

Lonnie had biopsies done on the masses in his neck this week. The results came back inconclusive because they did not get enough cells in the biopsy. We just got back from seeing the surgeon.

Lonnie is scheduled for surgery on Monday, Sept. 24th. They will remove 3 masses in his neck and possibly the jugular vein. One of the masses is close to the carotid artery and he doesn't know what will be required there until he gets inside. They said he will have nerve damage to his ear and possibly to his shoulder and arm. After they remove the masses they will test them to see if they are cancerous or not. He will need to lay low for about a week after the surgery.

Please pray for complete healing before the surgery. We believe that our God heals!! Let this be an awesome witness to our Lord's incredible mercy. Thank you all for your calls and prayers. Dawn

9-14-07 From: Lonnie Honeycutt

Subject: Neurogenic Tumors

Hi everyone! Okay, here's the scoop about what's going to be happening.

While I could be wrong (and probably am since I'm not an otolaryngologist) the masses they've found in my neck are being classified, for now, as neurogenic tumors. They might be malignant, they might not (whew – that's conclusive isn't it – it's like saying 'we absolutely will, maybe'). Anyway, the exact type of tumors I have won't be known until they are surgically removed, dissected, and tested six ways to Sunday. After that we will definitely know... maybe. ☺

If the tumors happen to be cancerous then I'll start treatment to combat that disorder. If not, I'll just heal from a very invasive neck surgery.

Without being too graphic... the surgeon(s) will slice my neck from just behind my ear down to my throat, open me up and begin removing tumors. A couple of the tumors are slightly larger than a golf ball in diameter although they aren't shaped the same (more elongated).

Here's where some of the potential problems come in. One of the tumors is compressing my jugular vein but that won't continue to be an issue because the surgeon has flatly stated he's going to remove the vein completely (well, at least the part that's in my neck). He believes that this will be necessary because of the damage he thinks has already been done to it (don't want the jugular vein to start spurting right in the middle of a sermon). It's possible he'll try to place a splint where the jugular vein once was but it's improbable due to the fact that there will be nerve and muscle damage during the surgery. The good thing is that I've got an extra jugular vein on the right side of my neck and the body (praise be to God) will probably, eventually, develop secondary transporting veins into my brain.

During the removal of the tumors I've been told that they'll have to remove some amount of muscle from my neck (don't know how much) and that I'll be left somewhat paralyzed on my left side up to and possibly including my ear. Frankly, I'm not really worried about the paralyzation because, it'll probably just be a loss of feeling more than a loss of movement due to the fact that the incision will be behind my ear rather than in front of it. What I am concerned about is that my eardrum will be paralyzed. If that happens I'll be going in for a hearing aid immediately because I'll need to control the volume of the sounds that I come in contact with. If that happens I'm going to see if they've come out with a Bluetooth hearing aid so I can answer my phone without anyone knowing how I'm doing it – ha ha.

I've got to tell you that the surgeon who will be performing the operation on my neck is a man of many talents. Not only does he do plastic surgery (he's promised I won't be too deformed), and ENT (ear, nose, and throat) surgery but he's also an oncologist (cancer doc). Plus, and if there's one thing that'd give me confidence in him treating me it's this... he's got a degree in Zoology!!!! Oh, Yeah – I've got a ENT doctor who even knows his way around the nose of a giraffe!

All joking aside, this surgery has a LOT of probably's, possibly's, and maybe's in it. The reality is that because of my medical history, the invasiveness of the surgery, and a few other factors, this is going to be a serious procedure. As my physician said, *"This isn't an overwhelmingly dangerous procedure, but it's not extraordinarily safe either."* Hopefully everything goes very smoothly and I'll be out the day after I'm sliced on.

After the surgery I'll be down and out for about 7 days – there goes our trip to Texas for awhile (you know, one of these days I'm actually going to get a vacation – ha ha). So, if you can recommend any good movies on DVD, let me know – just nothing that'll make me laugh or cry – just dull kind of stuff like *'Jacques Cousteau Teaches Underwater Basket Weaving'* or *'The Life of a Fruit Fly in Slow Motion.'*

Besides healing the one thing I'd like prayer for is this: In the next week I'll be writing letters to both of my children just in case the surgery ends up being fatal. I'm not trying to be morbid, just realistic. The prospect of writing these letters is already taking an emotional toll on me for what should be obvious reasons. So, pray that this is done with ease.

Thanks a bunch for your prayers.

Okay, now for some GREAT news!

DLF Eastern Shore is going to be having our first two baptisms this weekend! We're doing it in the 'Bay of the Holy Spirit' in Fairhope. Please pray that we don't get 'lightninged' out (I'm not worried about rain since we'll all be wet anyway)!

Plus, the Take Charge! forum for women's health is coming together good – I've already got confirmed an M.D., a registered dietician, an RN, an LMT, and a few others. If you know any women who will be around on the 22nd, let 'em know about this. Love all of you!
Rev. Lonnie Honeycutt (RevLon)

Week 7

9-23-07 From: Lonnie Honeycutt

Subject: Surgery Tomorrow Morning

Hi everyone! Ok, tomorrow at 10 AM I'm going in for surgery (unless the Lord heals me overnight). I'll be arriving at the hospital at around 9:30 AM because I want to have an outreach for those who are in the waiting area at the hospital.

My recovery time shouldn't be too bad... about a week. Please keep my family in your prayers. I love all of you! Lonnie (RevLon)

9-23-07 From: Lonnie Honeycutt

Subject: To PJ from Pastor Lonnie

Hey PJ – I would have sent this directly to you but I can't, try as I might, find your personal email address.

Anyway, I wanted to personally apologize for not being able to get together with you. I had planned on inviting you to see a new movie with me but almost this entire week I've had massive headaches.

Anyway, just know that I didn't blow you off on purpose.

I'll be in surgery tomorrow and I'd appreciate it if you'd take a moment to pray for me. I know you said you had reservations about God and all but I'd still like you on my side.

Tell Sarah I said Hi and I'll see y'all later. Lonnie (RevLon)

[Note: The day after I died, it was announced that BOTH PJ and Sarah gave their lives to the Lord!]

9-26-07 From: Lonnie Honeycutt

Subject: Two Days After My Surgery

Hi Everyone! I'm writing this from the most comfortable hospital bed I've had the honor to lay in. Seriously, these hospital beds are pretty darned comfy – of course it could feel so nice because I'm on pain meds (haha).

As you've probably guessed, since I'm writing this at 6:10 AM on Wednesday, this isn't coming to you posthumously. Before I start I want to apologize to you if you called or came by and I don't remember. I've had some amazing hallucinations and I'm still trying to decipher what actually happened and what I imagined over the past couple of days. For instance, while David B. was holding a bucket for me to vomit in (yeah – he's a true friend), I was carrying on a conversation with my son, Brance, who wasn't actually in the room. And, when Suzi R. and Barbara B. were both in my room, I thought, for what I think was just a couple of minutes, that I was watching a film of the two of them talking about me while I lay there looking at them in a daze. Anyway, please forgive whatever my memory has forgotten or fabricated.

Two days ago when I went into surgery I thought I had some idea of what I was facing. Today, as I begin my recovery, I know how little I actually knew.

Upon entering my neck cavity my ENT specialist discovered that the masses that had grown in my neck were more extensive and more invasive than originally thought. While the MRI had helped the surgeon to accurately gage the density and even the size of the tumors, it didn't show how 'rooted' they were. As it was explained to me, one of the masses extended so far into my chest cavity that he almost had to remove my left clavicle bone (he didn't) to reach it (instead he was able to pull and tug until my jugular vein was stretched enough to cut –

sounds like all kinds of fun, doesn't it?). Another of the masses extended into my skull almost 2 inches (my wife says that my big head finally came in handy since the surgeon had room to maneuver – hahaha). All in all, the entire surgery lasted a few hours (up from the 1.5 hours they'd expected).

It was also determined that I definitely have cancer. What type of cancer they don't know yet. The tumors that were removed have been sent to one of the pathology centers of the AFI (Air Force Institute) – they're the ones who diagnose all the weird things that normal pathology centers can't. We're hoping to know within just a couple of days what type of cancer we're going to be dealing with.

Many of you have called to ask what my physical limitations are going to be. Well, for the next 3 or so weeks my overall movement will be somewhat limited due to three factors: 1) The invasiveness of the operation – I've got staples that extend from behind my left ear to my esophagus in an artsy sort of curve; 2) It'll take a little while before my body adjusts to no longer having a jugular vein on the left side of my head (blood flow will eventually return to a normal rate, it'll just take a bit – most of the returning blood flow will be 'up and running' by the end of this week; 3) The surgeon had to remove some amount of muscle from my neck as well as a nerve. Gotta tell you, the nerve thing is the most aggravating right now. Each time I extend my arm it feels as though my 'funny bone' is being hit – not really fun but I'll get used to it over time. The extraction of the nerve has also left part of the left side of my face numb (paralyzed) though not completely. I can still feel pressure and my smile hasn't been diminished. My left ear, however, feels as though it's made out of wood – thanks be to God that my hearing doesn't seem to have been affected.

What all of this means is that I'm going to have to force myself to slow down a bit – not too much, just a little.

Okay, enough about me. Now I want to talk about YOU.

First and foremost I want to apologize that this letter has to be generic in nature since, quite frankly, I don't have the energy to write dozens of individual thank you notes – please know that I would really like to do so but because I wanted to get this out to you today it's a limitation. Secondly, THANK YOU for praying for my family and me. It is a GREAT honor to be surrounded by such a tremendous gathering of brothers and sisters in Christ. Next, my thanks go out to each and everyone of you who have so generously given towards the ministry God has started on the Eastern Shore. Your financial gifts mean so much – probably more than you'll ever know on this side of eternity – to a new and budding church. Each day has to be lived in faith that God will provide and the knowledge that He provides through people such as you. When something like this occurs (my being hospitalized and my body being attacked), the undergirding of the provision you've made possible takes on whole new levels of meaning. The first couple of years of a new church are always tremendously difficult when the pastor is well – when he/she is undergoing physical trials – well, you can just imagine.

Finally, I'd like to simply share a few thoughts with you.

Lest anyone think that I'm not sober about what I am facing personally or what my family is facing individually, let me assure that I am. I know that it's possible for the biopsies to be returned as demonstrating an aggressive malignancy that is terminal. I also know that life itself is terminal – none of us are going to get out of life alive unless Christ returns for us before we die. That being said, we also know that He is in control. I personally know people who have 'rebounded' from terminal cases of stage 3 and stage 4 cancers to become cancer free. In one case, the cancer simply 'went away' (the doctors call it a fluke, I'd call it a miracle – in either case, God gets the glory because the medical profession has no clue as to what caused it to disappear). Another case involves a stage 4 brain cancer that was supposed to be terminal in 6 months – that was nearly 9 years ago and the lady (who is a sister in Christ) is still going strong and is in total remission. One of her doctors I spoke with years ago said, "*Go figure.*" I corrected him. I said, "*Go God.*"

[Okay, fast forward several hours – I'm home from the hospital now.]

The fact of the matter is that I don't know how long the Lord has given me to live on this side of Heaven. None of us do. And, it really doesn't matter. What does matter is how I choose to live during the time I am allotted. While I want to see my children reach adulthood and for Dawn and I to spend our twilight years together, what matters more than these good things is for me to be focused on the good things of the Lord – His work. It is also my responsibility, as both a Christian and a pastor, to help others realize this same truth. OUR responsibility, as the corporate and individual body of Christ, is to 'be about the Father's work.' What is that work? It's loving each other and it's being an ambassador of Christ to people who might otherwise never know what a true disciple of Christ is or to people who simply have a distorted view of the Lordship of Jesus.

You know, we all speak about the Kingdom of God being 'at hand.' The great news is that it IS at hand. The troubling news is that while God's kingdom is active in the present, so many in God's kingdom just don't understand that they have all the privileges, freedoms, and responsibilities that come from being kingdom citizens. Far too many of us don't truly live out the truth that we are children of the Most High. Oh, we proclaim this truth and we love the idea of this truth but we don't really 'live the truth.' Folks, we MUST be walkers and not just talkers when it comes to who we are in Christ Jesus. It's great to be edified (built up) by going to conferences and church events and prayer meetings and by seeing demonstrations of the power of God. It's most excellent when the Lord allows us to witness His unbridled mercy and compassion on people such as Lee McDougald (who has been completely cured of Parkinson's) and on sister Ann Wolfe (Brother Fred Wolfe's wife) who has been relieved of terrible pain after suffering from the same for a couple of decades. But, if we aren't committed to going forth and making disciples, we haven't allowed ourselves to become a true disciple of His.

It thrills my heart to know people such as you who have a heart for introducing people to the love of God – no strings attached. Thank you so much for choosing to follow God to the best of your ability. It is so comforting to know that I have an army of brothers and sisters behind, before, and beside me as I go through this life crisis. It makes the crisis seem so much less of a crisis and much more like an opportunity. Who else, in all the world, besides Christians can rejoice at whatever life brings? No one. Only Christians can say that to live is Christ and to die is gain. Whichever we do, we win!

Before I sign off and rest, I'd like to thank those of you who were able to join with me on the day of my surgery and who kindly gave out gift bags to those in the waiting room. Your prayers for those in that room came to my attention on Tuesday. I tell you this because I want you to know that God was glorified by your kindness. It also gave me the opportunity to pray for many of the nurses who attended to me while I was hospitalized. It's pretty neat to know that even while you're bedridden that you can still be extending the love of God to others. Finally, I am absolutely beside myself about how well the Angel Food ministries that God has allowed Deeper Life Fellowship of Eastern Shore to begin is going. We've gotten so many phone calls from people who need this type of help – without one bit of advertisement. The Lord is wonderful!!!

Okay, that's it for now. I'm extremely tired and need to get a lot of rest.

Sorry if I've rambled but thanks for your being loving enough to allow me to do so. In Christ, Rev. Lonnie Honeycutt (RevLon)

9-26-07 From: Libby B.

Subject: Re: Two Days After My Surgery

Oh Lonnie, I feel like we just had a long visit. Melvin and I want to come out to see you as soon as your company leaves and you are up to it. We just need to see you and hug whatever part of you that is not sore.

We are fervently praying and fighting for you because God threw the mold away when He made you. We feel like all of us have been in a train wreck getting such a report from your doctor, but we are depending on God Who has the Last Word "*You were healed by the stripes of Jesus.*"

Hope to see you in the next few days. Love you Bunches!! Libby and Melvin

(My reply to Libby – several hours later) Libby, thank you so much for your kind words, thoughts and prayers. It's been a pretty rough night. I've only been able to sleep soundly for a couple of hours because the pain meds I have to take make me hallucinate a bit and my dreams are incredibly vivid – so much so that I can't distinguish them from reality until I've been awake for awhile and had time to process them.

I look forward to seeing the two of you in the next couple of days. ☺ Love you both! Lonnie

9-27-07 From: Lonnie Honeycutt

Subject: Prayer Needed

Hey guys and gals, the physical strain Dawn is under right now is incredible. Not only is she trying to take care of me (I'm pretty much a lump), but Danielle is now sick at her stomach. Please pray that this passes quickly. Dawn needs more rest than she's getting – my family is SOOOOOO very blessed to have her in our lives.

As an ending note, thanks for all the food and well wishes!

To the glory of God! Lonnie

9-28-07 From: Lonnie Honeycutt

Subject: A Word of Thanks and a Picture

Hi everyone! I'm finally out of bed for a few minutes (probably going to get back under the covers in a little while) so I wanted to write a short note of thanks!

I just read the email Dawn sent out not too long ago and she's right, today is BAD. Oh well, it could be worse. But, what definitely makes it better is knowing how awesome you (my brothers and sisters) are. The food and cards I've been receiving are both very uplifting and filling in different ways. I'm so sorry that I haven't been able to have visitors but I simply haven't been up to it physically. Hopefully that'll change soon.

For those of you who are wondering what I look like, I'm attaching a picture that was snapped of me today after the tubes in my chest were removed – yeah, that was fun. As the picture shows, I haven't changed much – with the exception of having a bunch of chest hair shaven and what looks to be a small train track on the outside of my neck.

Well, that's it for now. I love all of you! Rev. Lonnie (RevLon)

Week 8

9-30-07 From: Lonnie Honeycutt

Subject: God Is In Control!

Hi guys and gals! It's been a couple of days since I've been able to communicate effectively (thank the pain pills and the pain they were combating for that) so I thought I'd write a short update to everyone who has taken my family into their prayer before the Father.

First and foremost and always – THANKS! I wish that you could peer into my heart and know all the emotion and sentiment and understanding that I'm placing on that simple six-letter word. While 'thanks' in the context of a note seems and is extremely limited, please know that it abounds with meaning in my heart.

Folks, I can't adequately express my gratitude that you've taken up my cause even though I know you have 'stuff' going on in your own lives. The fact that some of you reading this don't know me at all but are dutifully and without hesitation praying to God Almighty for a speedy and comfortable recovery on my behalf speaks volumes about your Christ-like heart.

When the Apostle Paul was imprisoned he wrote to fellow saints the following: "*Have no anxiety at all, but in everything, by prayer and petition, with thanksgiving, make your requests known to God.*" I mention this to you as an encouragement. Not only does God want us to bring our needs to Him (as well as the needs of others) but He wants us to do so free of anxiety. It's not often hard to bring our requests to God but it is sometimes hard to do so without anxiety. The Greek word for anxious or anxiety in Philippians 4 is the same as found in Matthew 6 (merimnao) and the context of both mean simply 'don't worry about it because God's in control.'

I can't help but believe, based on Scripture and the happenings within my own life, that the reason God wants us to bring everything to Him is not so things will get done, but so that we're in a constant state of 'remembrance.' In other words, if we consistently bring needs to Him (ours and others) we're doing so not to get His attention but to 'keep our attention on Him.' This is an important distinction since, while we (as Christians) know that God is in control, we're also pretty apt to overlook this fact as the days and years and circumstances wear-on. Simply stated, the awesomeness of the fact that God IS in control can lose its wonder if we allow ourselves to be distracted by the ordinary.

Secondly (yeah, I know that was a pretty long first point), in his letter to the Philippians, our brother Paul reminds us that we are all saints. What an absolutely AWE-INSPIRING thing to remember! Not only does God want to hear from you and me, but He also considers us to be '*one who is consecrated, holy, and sacred to God*' – a Saint! I've said it before and I'll say it again and again, we are who we are because of our faith in Jesus Christ and through His grace we've become children of the Most High. I don't know about you but I think that's just absolutely jaw-droppingly amazing!

Okay, enough with the minor sermon.

The reason I'm writing today is to express my gratitude to you for allowing God to use you to bless us. When people are going through hard times, it's completely appropriate to remind them that 'God will provide.' What we sometimes forget is that, more often than not, we're the instruments of the provision that God provides. What a fantastic honor!

This last week (of which I can clearly remember 2 days) has been such a blessing to me. While it's true that I've pretty much been bed-bound because of severe headaches, nausea, and just pain in general, I've also been able to beseech God and inquire of Him about several different issues in my life, in the life of our new church, and in the life of others I've found out are hurting. The uninterrupted time I've been able to spend with Him has honestly refreshed me. The fact that I've been in so much pain has also enabled me to focus solely on Him, which has resulted in some answers that I may not have been aware of without this time of recovery. All-in-all, I'd rather not have had to go through this period of trial and tribulation, but, since I have to, I'm really genuinely glad to have had His company.

My friends, I can say, without fear of contradiction, that YOU have been a great source of release and refreshing for me. I've gotten lots and lots of snail mail and email notes, cards, and pictures (some from as far away as overseas), many from people I don't know. The correspondence I've received have expressed words of comfort and concern for my family's well-being and me spiritually, naturally, and financially. I've read stories of recovery and struggle and hope from people I currently know and from some I'll probably not meet on this side of eternity. My family has also been blessed by food – lots and lots of food. My kids probably think we've turned into some kind of restaurant. The food has been SUCH a blessing, it's hard to overstate my thanks!

Knowing that Dawn hasn't had to worry about fixing meals for our family while I'm laid up (I usually do the cooking) has really allowed me to rest easier. I know from talking to her that your kindness has been a major blessing to her – it's great to be able to just whip something into the microwave and 'voila' it's done.

But, one of the kindest gestures I've experienced thus far, happened today...

Two of my sisters-in-Christ delivered some foodstuffs to our home and took the time to pray for our situation. I was able to join them in this prayer and it was delightful (they said I really looked good with the exception that my throat seemed to have been on the losing side of a gang war). After they left I noticed two small gift bags on the counter. Thinking they were for me, I peeked. They weren't for me. They were for my children, Brance and Danielle! My heart leapt. I was speechless. I don't know whom they came from and it doesn't matter. The very fact that someone thought about my kids during all of this has made me nearly giddy.

My son, who wasn't in the room at the time, found the bags a few minutes later. His squeal of delight and that of his sister's told me they were joyous about the contents. Brance ran into my room not long afterwards and told me, breathlessly, that someone had brought them gifts. Via the prompting of God I took the time to inquire as to why he thought that was important. This is what he said, almost verbatim...

"Because somebody thought of Danielle and me. They knew that maybe we'd be sad because of you being sick and they thought about how to make us happier too. That's what Christians are supposed to do, think of everybody, right?"

Too cool, eh?

Again, my thanks goes out to whomever sent these gifts to Brance and Danielle. This has been a very hard week for them. While they see my scar (Danielle was too scared to sit in my lap for the first couple of days) and they know I don't feel good, they still don't understand the implications of all that's going on. Knowing that someone took the time to consider every part of my family makes me feel closer to every single one of my brothers and sisters in Christ (You). It also makes me proud to be a part of your family.

Well, that's it for now. I need to rest. Oh, one last thing, the Angel Food ministries we just started (where people can get around $70 of food for $25) is going GREAT. If you're in the Alabama area, tell everyone about it.

I'll let you know more about what's going on tomorrow after I talk with my physician. For now, please keep me informed as to who needs prayer – I've got lots of time and I'd love to spend it praying for people like Gary and Pam and Cathy and Corkie and Mark and Anne, and whomever else I can petition the Father for! Praise be to God! Rev. Lonnie (RevLon)

10-2-07 From: Lonnie Honeycutt

Subject: PET Scan, Treatment, and Pain

Whew! What a tiring day…

Okay folks, for those of you who are interested, here's what's happening – or going to happen.

Dawn and I spoke to the oncologist today (well, one of the oncologists). Here's what he said (paraphrased):

I have to wait three weeks to have a PET scan due to the fact that my healing neck would register a false positive (PET scans show brighter in areas that use a lot of glucose – such as cancers – and, because the body uses the same substance to help heal itself… well, you get the idea – my neck would light up like the fourth of July.)

Once the PET scan is done, the MINIMUM therapy will include both localized radiation and chemotherapy. The type of cancer we're trying to fight will determine what type of chemo drug is used. By the way, he did tell me that I had an aggressive malignant (not benign) form of cancer. Sheesh!

Since the existing cancer is in the far recesses of my tongue (back behind the uvula – the little piece of skin that hangs down at the back of your throat – you can see it when you say 'ahhhhh') the radiation may be localized to that region. Here's the real bummer: in all probability my throat will become extremely sore and aggravated – so much so that there's a possibility that I'll have to have a feeding tube inserted in my body (yum, yum – nothing like eating puréed steak). I'll virtually lose all sensation of taste and what does remain will be highly altered. Plus, (yes, there's always a 'plus') I'm going to lose my voice starting within a week or so of the beginning of the treatment because my salivary glands are going to quit working and my throat is going to swell. The 'upside' is that there's going to be a limited amount of radiation treatments. The downside is that I'm going to have one treatment 5 days a week for 8 weeks. The upside is that I won't be bed-ridden. The downside is that I was told, point-blank, that I should expect to be disabled for about 6 months.

I may be missing something in there but, if I am, you can bet it's not delightful.

Honestly, I'm pretty concerned about all this. It's not really the physical aspect of the pain etc. that I'm concerned about (though the prospect of trying to swallow through a tube of raw nerves and cardboard doesn't thrill me), but how Dawn and the kids are going to handle everything. I know my body and I know how it normally reacts to inflammation – which will definitely be a part of the treatment. In short, I'm going to run fevers and I'm going to feel as though I've been hit by a bus (without the nicety of being knocked out by a steel bumper). While I may be given pain meds, Dawn is going to have to go through the winter months with two little kids and a sick husband. I've got to tell you, I feel pretty darned miserable about that alone – it's a lot to ask of anyone. So, please pray for them (Dawn especially).

As for what this means at the present: Well, for one it means that Dawn and I have a lot of decisions to make. I've got to figure out what I can do for work that doesn't require either talking or a lot of energy – yeah, right. We've also got to meet with the members of DLF Eastern Shore and go over the possibility of closing the doors – of course before this decision takes place there will be a LOT of prayers to the One who asked me to open them in the first place. We have to figure out medical coverage (Garland and Alicia, if you're reading this – thank you, thank you, thank you for having your engineering firm and BC/BS) and the limits thereof.

California Bound

Mark Wyatt (Pastor of Deeper Life Fellowship of Mobile) and I talked today and I'm going to be traveling to California to Bill Johnson's church to be prayed for over the course of a couple of days. I don't know who it is that offered me this opportunity but I want you to know that I cherish your Christ-like heart. I wish I could say more about this gesture but words utterly fail me. I think I'll be leaving for Bill's church sometime next week.

A Theological Issue

Opinions about healing vary from person to person and I've been asked a bunch about my stance on the subject – especially as it concerns me. Since this subject will require many more words than would constitute a short note, you can find my thoughts on the subject at the following link:

[Note: My comments on this subject can be found in a forthcoming book titled: ***Does God Send Sickness*** by Rev. Lonnie Honeycutt.]

If you want to find out what I believe you can read what I wrote. If not, you can skip it. Either way, I hope it'll suffice. If you have questions or comments about the statements I make in the book, please feel free to ask.

A 'Yay God' Moment

I gotta tell you folks, God allows us to minister in all the right places. Today as Dawn and I were waiting to see the one of my attending oncologists, she (Dawn) began a conversation with two people and ministered to both of them. For the sake of brevity I'll only tell you about one of the conversations she had. Dawn began talking to an older lady (80ish) and engaged her in what began as a light conversation but which eventually allowed us to learn the following:

Ellie is wheelchair-bound and a dialysis and cancer patient. She graduated from Alabama and worked for 40 years as an RN – she used to help treat people who had problems similar to those she's facing today. Her children live around the area but they don't visit very often. She visits the clinic we were at 4 times a week and knows all the doctors and nurses by name.

Learning that she paid a friend to bring her to the clinic, Dawn kindly offered to do errands for or with her and mentioned that we were members of a body of believers called 'Deeper Life Fellowship.' In short, Dawn immediately sensed that this lady was lonely and needed help – even though she was fiercely independent (if you'd heard the conversation you'd know what I mean). While I was filling out paperwork, our sister-in-Christ was ministering to what the world would call a 'rank stranger.' The real testimony isn't that Ellie was ministered to by someone she hadn't known an hour before but that the people in the waiting room, the nurses, and the receptionists all took note of the ministry. What a multi-fold blessing. Yay God for providing such an opportunity and Yay Dawn for seizing it.

My Apologies

I know that I don't need to apologize for the following, but I'd like to anyway. I apologize for those I haven't been able to call back and talk

to personally. I've just been haggard (but not Merled –
hahahahahahahahaa – get it, Merle... Haggard – oh well, must be the
drugs)!! Seriously, I feel bad that I haven't been able to respond to
everyone. Please know that I love all of you and appreciate you more
than I can say (even though I try to say it often). Have a Great Night!
Rev. Lonnie Honeycutt (RevLon)

10-04-07 From: Mark Wyatt

Subject: Prayer In Redding

Hey Lonnie and Dawn, I emailed Bill Johnson's church about your
receiving prayer and this is what they recommended:

*"If you will send them over the weekend, it would best.....they can get
prayer at the Friday night service, Saturday morning in the Healing
Rooms at 9 and then again at the services on Sunday. They would
then get soaked for three days. We also have the Alabaster House
available for them to just go and soak in....it is our prayer house that is
open 24/7."*

We are ready to send you whenever you want to go. I suggest next
weekend. I also STRONGLY encourage both of you to go. Let Mike
and Patti keep the kids, and you guys do this together. Please trust me,
money is not an object for this! Do not take that into account.
Blessings, Mark

10-05-07 From: Dawn Honeycutt

Subject: Re: Prayer in Redding

Mark, this sounds wonderful. Lonnie and I have talked it over and
we would both like to go. We were thinking though the next weekend,
the weekend of the 20th. There are a few reasons, the most important
being that Lonnie will have a little more time to recover for the trip.
We also have Angel Food distribution next weekend that neither one
of us want to miss if possible. We also checked Bill Johnson's
itinerary and it looks like he may actually be back in town that
weekend.

So, if that sounds okay, what do you need from us to make the plans?

Mark, to whomever is providing this, please send our love and
endless appreciation. This is more than we could have hoped for.

Love you and thank you for all the support. Dawn

Week 9

10-07-07 From: Lonnie Honeycutt

Subject: Time for some braggin'

Hello one and all. Hope you're having a GREAT weekend.

It's time for another update (hopefully shorter than the last several but we'll see – I never know how much I'm going to type).

First Things First... I'm Going To Brag a Little!

God tells us that Christians will be rewarded in Heaven. We're also told that it's okay to work towards the goal of finishing the race (life as a Christian) well and for receiving these rewards. The Apostle Paul says, "*I have fought a good fight, I have finished my course, I have kept the faith: Henceforth there is laid up for me a crown of righteousness, which the Lord, the righteous judge, shall give me at that day: and not to me only, but unto all them also that love his appearing*" (2 Tim. 4:7-8).

I bring this up because I was sincerely impressed this week by the gestures of kindness my family and I have experienced during this time of trial – gestures that might not seem that grand on this side of Heaven but, I'm convinced, will be rewarded in Heaven.

People have brought food to our home. I can't begin to tell you what kind of blessing that is. I mention this simple act of kindness because I've made lots and lots of food and taken it to people over the years. Quite frankly, I like to cook so doing this never seemed like that much of a big deal. But, as one who hasn't felt much like standing in front of a stove (this applies to Dawn as well), having ready-made meals we can just pop in the microwave, heat and eat is a tremendous blessing. By the way, if you've never had food delivered to your home I'll tell you this – every meal is a bit like 'Deal or No Deal' because you never know what you're going to get. So, since I like all kinds of food, every meal is kind of a treat.

I've gotten cards and letters (email and snail mail) from people all over the place – many from those I've never met. I just received a 4 x 6 handmade card from a Christian school which had the signatures of about a dozen or so children – written in everything from pencil and crayon to what I swear looks like eye-shadow (not that I'm an expert on eye-shadow or anything). I've got that card (and others) on my wall. The personal notes on these cards and emails mean the world to me. The very fact that someone took the time to sign a card or type a message to me is INCREDIBLY uplifting.

This last week, one of my neighbors, a dear, dear man by the name of Bob P. took the time out of his day to come and mow grass for me. This may not sound like a big deal to you, but it is to me. Bob has vision problems – bad vision problems: so please remember him as you make your request to our Father – and he's retired (so he's not a spring chicken any more). Still, he knew that I was having a pretty hard time of it this week (more on that later) so he hopped on his mower and mowed the grass. He didn't stop by to shake my hand to make sure I knew what he'd done. He didn't call. He just showed up and left. Awesome!

One more...

I was out this week at AutoZone (it was one of three places I've been able to get to this week by myself – well, Danielle was with me but I did all the driving) and I met an elderly woman – she reminded me of the lady in the 'Where's the Beef' commercials only she was black and not white.

Hazel is probably about 90 and she was at AutoZone to pickup some oil for a car that I'm pretty sure was older than I am. She and I arrived about the same time so I took my time getting out of my truck so I could hold the door open for her. She slowly climbed out of her front seat, opened the backdoor, took out a walker, and made her way to the entrance. After she'd gotten inside I went around the store looking for some transmission fluid (I was hoping low transmission fluid was the reason my Rodeo wasn't going into gear but it wasn't). She and I checked out at the same time so I hoisted a half dozen quarts of oil she had purchased with my good arm and opened the door for her again. As I walked her to her car I asked if she wanted me to check the oil for her (at this point some of you who know me already know I was almost in over my head – checking oil is about as far as my mechanical expertise goes). She popped the hood of her car, I checked the oil and added a little of the same. As I slammed the hood she asked me how long I'd worked at AutoZone because she wanted to tell my manager how nice of an employee I was. Once I'd explained that I wasn't an employee but a pastor of a semi-local church, a 15-minute conversation ensued. During the conversation I found out that her husband had died 5 years ago, two of her children had died a couple of years before, and that she'd outlived some kind of exotic bird she'd gotten as a pet in the 1950's (it died a few months ago). I also came to know that she was on a fixed income, that she and Mayor Sam Jones (the Mayor of Mobile, Alabama) were cousins, and that her favorite flavor of ice cream is cherry – don't ask me how that came up but it did. As we closed our conversation I took her hand and prayed with her. Then I handed her a few coupons for free Chic-Fil-A chicken sandwiches and explained to her what they were. Here's the cool part: she refused them. She said, "*Honey, I appreciate this but there are a lot of other folks who need them more than me. Why don't you save 'em for those folks. Me and the Lord do all right. Here, when you find somebody who is hungry I want you to give them this.*"

This little lady who was twice my age living on a few hundred dollars a month, handed me a five dollar bill. I was floored. We hugged and parted ways. An hour later I'd found a hungry person and they walked away with prayer, chicken coupons, and a major financial blessing.

I'm telling you guys and gals... as Christians we should all be bragging about people like that.

My Week In a Nutshell

I saw my medical oncologist (cancer doctor) this week and the news wasn't any more encouraging or less frightening. I'm not worried about dying but I sure don't like to think about having a throat that's so blistered that I may have to be hospitalized or fed through a tube.

I got hold of my pathology report and I was amazed. I kind of knew how large the tumors were that they took from my body but it didn't really register until I read the report. Two of the tumors were larger in diameter than a golf ball but one was about 3 inches long and the other was as large as a good-sized pickle (that was the one going down into my chest). After reading the report I now understand some of why I still don't feel all that great.

The left side of my face feels like it's been scalded. It hurts 24-7. What's weird is that part of my skin is numb and the other part is hyper-sensitive. What this means is that if I hold a phone up to my left ear I can't feel the actual phone but it hurts terribly. Plus, when I sleep I can't be on my back or my left side because it hurts too much. Even my beard hurts – I mean really hurts. AND, if that's not enough, periodically I get what I can only describe as 'explosions' under my jaw line that are so painful I wince. With all that's happening to my face and back (same as above only more intense), I hardly notice that it hurts to extend my left arm completely.

Heck, with a heart condition, no spleen, and cancer, I may qualify to get a handicapped sticker tattooed on my forehead – hahaha.

Aside from the physical stuff, weird stuff's been going on with our house (I think the roof is leaking a bit so if you know of a good (but cheap) handy man (or woman), please let me know), our truck (the transmission is slipping), and with our furniture – one of our creditors from when we had to file bankruptcy (long story but we had no choice) has decided to 'repossess' our couch and loveseat (why they'd want 6-year old furniture is beyond me). Heck, I guess if the roof really does start leaking we can just move the T.V. and have an indoor swimming pool – haha.

Still, all-in-all, it's not been a terribly bad week. I'm finally getting up and around (I have a few hours of 'good time' just as long as I don't push it), my wife is tremendously supportive and my kids are back to driving me crazy (definitely a good sign since I know this means they realize the worst is over).

Okay, it's time for me to get to bed. While my internal clock is still kind of loopy, I know I must be tired so I'm going to lie down and stare into the darkness for a bit. I'll write more later.

Do Me a Favor...

One last thing, I'd like you to do me a favor. If there's someone you know whom you haven't contacted in a long while, take a few minutes to earnestly pray for them. Then, if you can, drop them a quick note (or a phone call or email) just to say Hi. It doesn't have to be a long note and it doesn't even have to mention that you prayed for them – just that they were on your mind. Even if they never reply, they'll be blessed and you'll have done something that Jesus would be (and will be) proud of. Love Y'all. RevLon

10-08-07 From: Libby B.

Subject: Re: Time for some braggin'

We loved being with y'all yesterday, just hope we didn't do you both in with our extended stay. I felt right at home. I am still so blessed by your song writing and singing. You are packed with talents for sure! Love you, Libby

10-08-07 From: Lonnie Honeycutt

Subject: To Melvin and Libby

Libby and Melvin – Thank you so much. Melvin, I just figured out that you filled up our car with gas yesterday while you were out and about. I can't tell you how much that touched my heart. I know that you know you didn't have to do such a thing and that's what makes it such a special gift. When I realized that the car was full and that neither Dawn nor I had filled it... well, let's just say while tears filled my eyes, joy filled my heart. Love you both! Lonnie

10-09-07 From: Lonnie Honeycutt

Subject: Church Update from Lonnie

Hi everyone! As you probably remember, I was going to have a meeting to decide the fate of Deeper Life Fellowship Eastern Shore. Well, the meeting never happened because I'm positive God hasn't released me from the responsibility and privilege of pastoring it. The fact that we have people who are committed to serving in DLF East already is further confirmation that God really is starting something wonderful.

So, if satan wants me out of the church, he'll witness me kicking, screaming, and praying all the while. I don't know what God is going to do with DLF East but whatever it is it's going to be His decision as to what happens. I said 'no' to planting a church about 4 years ago and I paid for not honoring what He had called me to do then. I'm not going to make the same mistake again. So, if we run out of money, if everyone leaves or if the church just isn't effective after a year then I'll take that as a sign that God is giving me permission to close the doors. Until then, it's full steam ahead.

On that note I've got to tell you that I'm very, very excited about some of the things that are happening. Not only is the Angel Food ministry going exceedingly well but we're about a week away from starting a major outreach to the Hispanic population on the Eastern Shore and possibly even in Mobile. Plus, Safe Harbor is moving to

Saturdays in the afternoon and if Thursday nights were any indication, that'll be a blast.

So, keep praying that God provides people who really want to get plugged into something terrific and that the finances required to keep a new church afloat come in regularly. The question of what's going to happen if I become incapable of preaching, teaching and serving for 3 - 6 months keeps coming up. Believe me, that's one of the questions on the forefront of my mind. Frankly, I don't know exactly what's going to happen. I do know that Mike and Patti Woods are more than capable of leading and that others are ministers as far as it concerns relationships and church functionality. Another question concerns the financial health of DLF East. Currently we're in good financial health – we've made every effort to be extremely good stewards of the money we've saved and been given by others. As I've always said, God provides through people so it's up to Him to place people in our congregation who grab hold of the vision He gave me. All I can do is to follow the vision He's given me and make certain that the words He gives me are taught with passion and accuracy. Without a doubt, this new church start will give God a chance to shine.

Lastly, I can tell you without reservation that this church plant as well as the development of cancer in my body has definitely increased my ability to 'walk by faith.' Thanks for all your support – physically, spiritually, emotionally, and financially. I'll write more later. Lonnie (RevLon)

10-10-07   From: Eddie Honeycutt (Mom)

Subject: What you said…

Good morning! I don't know what it was that upset me when we talked yesterday. Being a mother it doesn't take much to upset me when it is about one of my kids, so don't let it worry you. It's just another one of my habits.

A lady was picking through the frozen turkeys at the store, but couldn't find one big enough for her family. She asked the stock boy, *"Do these turkeys get any bigger?"*

The boy replied, *"No ma'am, they're dead. "*

Have a good day and don't worry about me, I am okay.

Love, Mother

(My reply to my Mom, Eddie)

Hahahhaha – Yeah, I completely understand what you mean about being a parent and it not taking much to upset you when it comes to your kids. I know I've been brought to tears before at just a thought about my own children.

Seriously, though, I really am doing very well – mentally, emotionally, spiritually and physically. Mom, one of the things I learned from you growing up is that we all have stuff to go through. Your constant reassurance that I could do things regardless of my physical issues has really paid off. I know my limitations but I've learned, with the grace of God, to harness those same limitations and use them for ministry. I can't express in words how much I appreciate your example as a strong but sensitive person.

While I'm thanking you for stuff, here's something else: You may not even remember testifying to me about Jesus but I do. Frankly, I don't know if I'd be a Christian today if it had not been for you telling me of your belief in and commitment to Him. Certainly, I wouldn't have the assurance that while we're miles apart today that we'll be able to 'get to know each other' and enjoy one another for eternity to come had you not given me your testimony. I can't tell you how much more secure I am in this life because of you. It's GREAT to know your mom is a Christian because that means we won't lose each other even in physical death. I wish I had the same confidence with Dad but I don't. If he ever accepted Jesus as his Savior there was never any outward manifestation of a change in his nature – he failed to show any fruit. This saddens me to no end. However, I take an immense amount of comfort in knowing that you are saved because, without question, you are one of the great heroes in my life. If I turn out to be half the person you are, I'll be happy.

Well, that's it for now. I've got to get a couple of chores done and drive out to the church to get it setup for Saturday. Love you, Lonnie

Week 10

10-18-07 From: Lonnie Honeycutt

Subject: From Lonnie to April Rush

Hey Dudette! How's it going? I'm still recovering from my surgery but, all in all, things have been progressing fairly well. I realized that my ear still has a way to go this morning when my dog (Pete) leapt up and starting gnawing on it (playfully) and I didn't feel anything.

Your mom said you might be interested in helping me translate some stuff for our website? If so, that'd be great. If not, that's okay too.

Well, I'll wait for you to reply to make certain I've got the correct email. I'm going to take a nap pretty soon – gotta fly to California tomorrow. RevLon

10-18-07 From: Lonnie Honeycutt

Subject: Update Requested by Libby

From Libby: Lonnie, your friends would like to hear from you before you leave. How are you feeling? How do you want us to pray and pray we will!

(My reply to Libby) Hi everyone! For those of you who have been waiting for an update from me, I want to apologize for not sending one until now. Honestly, I don't think I'd be doing so tonight if it weren't for the request made by my friend Libby. The reason is two-fold: 1) I'm concerned that my updates might be a bit much for some and 2) I haven't sent an update because I had to 'mentally check-out' a bit this week just to keep it together (sometimes reality isn't all it's cracked up to be).

With that being said, here goes...

I've been asked how I feel. Well, that depends on the hour of the day. Thankfully, I'm now up to feeling pretty good (sometimes really good) for four or five hours at a time. Believe me, when I'm feeling good I try to take advantage of it. For instance, this Tuesday morning I was able to volunteer for about 4 hours at the Prodisee Pantry (a food pantry that gives out meals to those who simply can't afford it). If you live in the Mobile/Daphne area and would like to do something fun and rewarding, the Prodisee Pantry is a good place to start. I was able to pray with a number of people who came through the doors and DLF East was actually able to bless a few of them because you've been so generous in helping us get diapers (that's a BIG need) and the like.

Unfortunately, once my 'energy spurt' is over, it's over. I nosedive like a one-way roller coaster.

While the left side of my face really, really hurts (24/7 – it feels as though there is acid beneath the skin), probably the most irritating thing is that I'm 'well' enough to realize just how incapacitated I am. For instance, carrying the trash out is a struggle as is picking up my baby girl and even reaching for things in the cabinet (all because of the amount of muscle and the nerve that was removed). Turning my head is still a struggle. But, on the bright side, I'm now able to talk non-stop for several minutes (for those of you who know how much I like to talk, you know how much of a good thing this accomplishment is). Another good thing is that my ear is no longer so painful that I can't sleep on it – it just feels like a piece of wood (no 'blockhead' jokes, please – haha). Shaving has also become a bit weird – not being able to feel the blade but having your whiskers hurt would seem like a physical contradiction, but that's what's happening (was that too many contractions?).

Tonight I was trying to cleanup the house and I reached for a piece of paper – that was the wrong thing to do. The act of slightly over-extending my left arm caused so much pain that I thought I'd actually torn something. Fortunately, I didn't. I'm probably just a complainer at heart but it really bothers me that I'm not doing better than I am – especially when I consider what the months ahead hold if the Lord doesn't heal me completely. But, I'm not going to dwell on that.

As for what you can pray for...

As it concerns me, I'd like you to pray that I'll try my hardest to be a good husband, father, pastor, and friend. I don't want to become self-centered. I want to be a good steward of the blessings God has given me and allowed me to partake in. Physically, I'm really not that worried about things as far as pain is concerned – with the exception that pain sometimes manifests as irritation towards others (I don't want that to happen). Someone asked me about how much pain medication I'm taking. The answer to that is 'as little as possible.' I was given enough pain medication for about two weeks but I decided to make it last as long as possible by taking as little as possible and only when I really needed it – not just for the sake of comfort. I'm happy to report that what I have will probably last a month or more at the rate I'm taking it – I am certainly not going to become dependent on it (plus, I don't want to be loopy – can you imagine the results if a pastor were to come up with a sermon while on pain pills? I think that's how cults get started isn't it? Haha).

If I can bother you to also pray for my emotional stability I'd appreciate that. I'm not morbid about what I'm facing but the one time I began to seriously contemplate having to help my children prepare for the worst-case scenario was extremely hard emotionally. It's also tough because, as a minister, I really want to 'be there' for people (including my family). Having a 'good sermon' is important but, as my friend Mark Wyatt says, *"As Christians we get our position by trying to 'out serve' on another."* So, as a pastor, it's my job to lead the way in serving others. That's the example Christ walked, talked, and taught. So, having to slow down has been very tough for me. By the way, I do realize that it's okay for me to slow down and rest and that doing so was also taught and demonstrated by Jesus.

All-in-all, this has been an interesting couple of weeks. From creditors and hospital bills (whew – those mount fast) to transmission problems and our oven going out, to a wonderful opportunity to serve others through Angel Food ministries and being blessed by someone who is paying our way to Bill Johnson's church.

Okay, enough said about me. Before I sign off I'd like to again thank all of you who have helped or offered to help my family. There are too many of you for me to name individually but please know that I appreciate everything. Please, please, please, pray for someone tonight (or today depending on when you get this). Knowing that people are really praying for us has helped me to focus on praying for others even more – it really is important.

I'd also like to publicly acknowledge my wife (she gets these emails too – that way she can tell me I've written too much or that I sound like a dork or that I did a good job in expressing my thoughts):

Dawn, you are AWESOME! How you can teach the kids, help run a business, take care of me and our children, schedule meetings, appointments, and juggle a dozen other projects while not going insane, is beyond me. Thanks for putting up with my insecurities, frailties, and faults. Thanks for helping me be a better man, for supporting me even when we disagree, for being my friend, for all the hugs and kisses, and for being such a Christ-centered lady. Sweetheart, I'll never be able to adequately thank you for all the love you show me but I'm sure going to give it a shot.

Blessings, blessings, and more blessings to everyone! Love you! RevLon

PS: My Pet Scan is due to be conducted on Wednesday (next week).

Week 11

10-24-07 From: Lonnie Honeycutt

Subject: After California…

After California…

Folks, if you ever get the chance to visit Bethel church in Redding, California, you should. The school of Supernatural Ministry, if the students are any indication, is awesome. Dawn and I had the honor and privilege of speaking to a number of students – two of whom prayed for me and demanded that cancer, both now and in the future, be banned from my body.

On Sunday morning, we attended a packed-out worship service – around 500 people were in the main sanctuary at 8:30 AM. I don't know how many people were in the 10:30 AM service but it looked to be a little more crowded. In any case, I was prayed for by two staff members (as well as the aforementioned students) and we visited the Bethel bookstore (we also took numerous notes as to what we could immediately integrate into DLF East and what we believed the Lord was/is leading us to do differently).

Bill Johnson's sermon was moving, practical, and Biblically insightful (what else should we expect from a pastor, right?) He touched upon the distinctives found in different denominations of Christianity and stated emphatically that we should all want to enjoy all the fullness of God's Kingdom that's possible in the here and now rather than simply waiting for the 'sweet by and by. ' I couldn't agree with him more. Regardless of what our eschatological view is (pre, post, mid, or a-millennial), we must be about the Lord's work as is clearly defined in the Bible – we should definitely pray for clarification on those parts that aren't apparent and clear, but we shouldn't let our own prejudices or lack of understanding prevent us from doing that which is plain (worshipping the one true God, teaching about the Kingdom of God, telling others about Jesus, bringing others to an understanding of salvation, imploring them to 'seek and find, ' healing the sick, visiting the infirmed, taking care of widows, baptizing those who have accepted Christ, and all the other commands given to us – regardless of how imposing they seem).

Bill also spoke at length concerning the Kingdom of God – what it is and what it isn't. He made it clear that healing, specifically physical healing, was only one part of the manifested Kingdom (the same, he said, was true of tongues and other spiritual gifts). I've got to admit, Bill's admission that he was often frustrated when, time after time, physical healing did NOT come about even after he and others fervently prayed, was spiritually uplifting in that such an acknowledgement takes away the fear of 'not having enough faith for your healing' (an unfortunate but very common assumption in certain Christian circles). As you may or may not know, Bill's son (who also spoke on Sunday morning) is severely hearing impaired – he's nearly deaf and has to wear very strong hearing aids in order to function. It was also a joyous occasion to me to see several people, members of Bethel's congregation, who were in wheelchairs or who hobbled into service on crutches or walkers. The fact that they were impaired wasn't joyous. No. Heaven forbid that we should ever glory over infirmity for the sake of infirmity itself. Rather, the very fact that these people were able to 'press into the Lord' and exhibit joy because of their relationship with the Lord and His children (other Christians) despite their infirmities gave me joy. It also gave me confidence in their level of maturity. They continuously sought the Lord's mercy for healing but didn't waver in continuing to praise and serve Him even when their healing didn't come about in the time or manner they desired.

Before he left to go across town, Bill announced that he'd just received the first shipment of *Here Comes Heaven*, the children's version of his book titled, *When Heaven Invades Earth*. He gave three copies to three single moms in the audience. Dawn and I later purchased a copy and it's a really good book for kids. Bill said, "*It's my first children's book and I didn't even write it*" (it was edited by people who work with kids and understand their language).

At the end of the service, I received prayer in my stand against cancer and I received another word about a gift that the person praying for me felt he'd been told I had. At this time I feel the need to keep the exact gift noted to myself so that I can test to see whether or not it is from the Lord. I hope it is but I need to assess the validity of the word.

Lunch Time Surprise

When we were worshipping at Bethel that Sunday morning the one thing I kept telling God was that as nice as the weekend had been, the one thing that would make it perfect for me was if we could meet someone to bless and minister to.

This is a story of God's kindness.

After church, Dawn and I spent about an hour in the bookstore at Bethel and were able to pick-up some goodies – books, etc. (of course, the books I consider 'goodies' might seem as dry as sandpaper in the Sahara to others). I only mention the time we spent because of what happened about 30 minutes later. After leaving Bethel we traveled to Marie Calendar's restaurant (if you've never had a freshly baked chicken pot pie from them – not the frozen stuff – you owe it to your taste buds to have one). Upon arriving we were seated and I immediately felt the need to go to the bathroom (yeah, I know, too much information – but it really does play into what happened).

As I approached the host counter, which was positioned just before the men's bathroom, I noticed a very tall African American lady standing in line. I immediately recognized her as one of the single mothers who had been given the *Here Comes Heaven* book. The fact I remembered her startled me because I had only casually glanced at her out of the corner of my eye when the books were distributed. Still, I was certain it was her.

Without hesitating I strode up to her and said something akin to: *"Hi! Hey, are you waiting for someone or are you by yourself?"*

"No, I'm here by myself."

"Well, would you like to eat with my wife and I?"

"Sure."

I escorted her from the waiting line to our table.

Okay... take a breather for a second and let me explain how weird this really could have seemed.

It's important to remember that this lady did NOT know me – she had NOT seen me at Bethel even though I'd seen her (I know this for a fact because, after an hour of talking, we finally approached this subject).

So, there I was, a little, white, bald guy walking directly up to a very tall (around 6' 3"), nice looking, African American lady (about 10 years younger that me) – a rank stranger – and asking her if she was dining alone.

On any other day the smart thing would have been for her to beat a hasty retreat (or to beat me off with her purse). Instead, she looked down at me (way down), smiled a smile that I recognized (on the way to the table) as one that said, *"Hmmm, I must know him because he obviously knows me – too bad I can't place his face,"* and actually followed me to a table at which I seated her with another perfect stranger – my wife.

To top off everything, just before I offered her a seat at our table, I politely asked her name (it's Alia – pronounced 'uh-lee-uh'), told her mine and, told her my wife's name. By the way, Dawn, was in the middle of ordering our drinks and gave me a look that I've become very familiar with – it's the one that instantly conveys the questions and the message...

"Okay, what are you doing? Who is this? You are a very strange man." And... *"I guess this is perfectly normal in your weird little mind."*

After Alia was seated with my wife, I immediately left to continue my quest for the restroom.

To set your mind at ease, Dawn is pretty quick on her feet and by the time I returned to the table, she had Alia comfortably engaged in conversation.

Now for the summation of this wonderful event.

I'm convinced that this was a providential meeting because of what Alia told us. Paraphrased, this is what we learned: Alia had JUST finished a 40-day fast and this lunch was to be her first meal (she always goes to Marie Calendar's and has their onion soup after a fast). She'd arrived at the restaurant approximately 15 minutes before Dawn and I and had sat in her car listening to a couple of worship songs. Even though she was very eager to go inside to eat she said that the Lord told her a couple of times – *"No, not yet."* Alia made it clear that while she didn't understand the reason she wasn't being allowed to go inside, she felt compelled to continue worshipping. Finally, she went inside just as I was going to the bathroom.

Folks, do you realize that had the timing of all these events not been perfect – had I not glanced at the young lady (one woman out of hundreds) during Bill's monologue and had I not been prompted to go to the bathroom when I was (once I got there I found that I really didn't have a physical need to 'go') and had Alia not waited to come into the restaurant – our meeting wouldn't have happened. As it was, we met a wonderful Sister-in-Christ, were able to fellowship with and pray for each other (and her seven year old daughter), and we went away with a new friend.

Honestly, I don't know exactly why I shared the story about Alia with you but I hope it blesses someone who reads it.

The Kind of Witness We Don't Want To Be

You never know when the opportunity to be a witness for Jesus is going to arise. I mention this because on the way back to Alabama I had the opportunity to listen-in on a conversation between two men that, for awhile, centered around Christ. While the plane we were on in Dallas sat on the tarmac (runway) until a storm over Louisiana cleared, the two guys sitting in front of us (Greg and Dale) began talking, rather loudly, about their experiences in AA (Alcoholics Anonymous). It wasn't long until one of them (Dale) brought up the question of the 'higher power' mentioned in the 12-step program. Dale openly questioned why so many people he met at the meetings he'd attended thought of the 'higher power' as being Jesus. Greg casually affirmed that he too believed that Jesus was the higher power in question. Incredulously, Dale asked, "*You mean you actually pray to Jesus as God?*" When Greg answered "*Yes*" the conversation began in earnest.

Greg told Dale that he was raised Catholic and that he believed Jesus was God, the Bible was true, and that we (mankind) had a responsibility to recognize this. Dale was full of questions about the Catholic faith specifically and about Christianity in general. Patiently, Greg articulated his understanding of certain practices peculiar to Catholics as well as the doctrines of Christianity (Catholic and Protestant). Honestly he did a great job. Even though I didn't (and don't) agree with everything he said as it pertained to the Catholic faith, he was, at the very least, being an honorable defender of Christianity and theism (inasmuch as this term denotes a belief in God), and he seemed to be getting through to Dale by answering the questions with 'gentleness and respect' (1 Peter 3:15).

Then... everything came crashing down.

Just as Dale seemed to be enjoying the conversation (he had some really good questions and was responding very positively), the pilot announced that we'd be unable to take off for another half hour. Personally, while I wasn't looking forward to being delayed from getting home, I thought this was a terrific opportunity for Greg to continue ministering to Dale. Unfortunately, that didn't happen.

After the announcement, Greg called someone on his cell phone and said (paraphrased), *"We're in the (bleep) plane on the (bleep, bleep) runway because of a (major BLEEP) storm. We may not be able to get to Mississippi until (bleep) tomorrow. I hate this (bleep, bleep)."*

In case you haven't guessed, the 'bleeps' were foul language.

Immediately after Greg's phone call (and I mean the very next sentence), Dale said, *"Yeah, you know the AA manual has a section for agnostics. I read it and THAT WAS WRITTEN FOR ME exactly."*

From that moment on Dale didn't ask another question about religion and Greg couldn't find a way to get the conversation going again. Why? He'd lost all credibility. I'm sure that in Dale's mind Greg was a guy who 'talked the talk' but didn't 'walk the walk.'

This was a reminder to me that people really are watching those of us who claim to be Christians and that we are held to a higher level of accountability (as it should be) because we not only claim an allegiance to God but a relationship with Him. Sobering, isn't it?

Just In Case You're Wondering What the AA Manual Says to Agnostics
(If you don't want to know just skip the following section.)

Page 44 of We Agnostics from Alcoholics Anonymous...

"Much to our relief, we discovered we did not need to consider another's conception of God. Our own conception, however inadequate, was sufficient to make the approach and to affect a contact with Him. As soon as we admitted the possible existence of a Creative Intelligence, a Spirit of the Universe underlying the totality of things, we began to be possessed of a new sense of power and direction, provided we took other simple steps. We found that God does not make too hard terms with those who seek Him. To us, the Realm of Spirit is broad, roomy, all-inclusive; never exclusive or forbidding to those who earnestly seek. It is open, we believe, to all men. When, therefore, we speak to you of God, we mean your own conception of God."

The very last line is what Dale clung to: *"When, therefore, we speak to you of God, we mean your own conception of God."*

This is such an open-ended ('all inclusive, never exclusive') non-definition of 'god' that it allows people like Dale to simply develop their own personal deity – regardless of what that deity is (just as long as the 'god' in question doesn't demand to be known as the one and only true God – as the God of the Bible does).

My PET Scan and Simulation Experience

Today (October 24, 2007), I went in for my PET Scan. The PET scan will be coupled with other diagnostic tools to determine if my body still contains any cancer cells. 'Simulation' is simply the term used for what is, essentially, a 'dry-run' – they do everything they need in order to get ready for radiation treatments without actually administering the radiation.

If you've never had a PET Scan or a Simulation for the treatment of cancer of the head and neck, let me tell you about my experience.

First, you can't eat anything but protein for about a day prior to the PET Scan and then you have to stop eating altogether. As far as the timeframe is concerned, how many hours of fasting prior to the procedure is hotly debated by medical professionals – some say 4 hours, others 6 hours, and others are somewhere in-between. I can't tell you how much this lack of agreement irritates me. When going in for this type of diagnostic test you've already got enough to think about. The least they could do is tell you exactly when to stop eating. If they don't know, just do a 'rule of thumb' and say 6 hours or whatever – just give the poor patient a standardized timeframe.

My first stop was at the radiation clinic. It was here that the technicians designed a mask for me that is used to hold your head securely in place for radiation treatments. I use the term 'designed' very loosely. What they actually did is place a warm, wet, very dense, funky smelling plastic net over my entire head. This was done while I was strapped to a table in a very unnatural manner.

If you want to get an idea of what this felt like, get three sets of panty hose and pull them over your head (yes, I've had a pair of panty hose over my head before – no, it wasn't for a crime spree, it was for a skit in school).

The mask was uncomfortable. Not only did it squish my nose and press against my mouth (forget about doing anything but mumbling), it was also difficult to blink. While there were plenty of breathing holes it didn't matter, my neck was tweaked so that it seemed difficult for me to get enough air. There's no way anyone who is claustrophobic could handle that mask. I can't imagine having to be inside that mask everyday for 8 weeks. Yuck.

On the upside... I was able to convince one of the technicians to take a couple of pictures of me in the mask. Not only did I want to know what I looked like, I figured it'd be a good visual for all of you who endure my incredibly long emails. I've attached two pictures of me in the mask (eat your heart out, Hannibal).

Once the mask was created I left for my PET scan. After arriving at the diagnostic center (which is about 600 feet from my primary oncologist's office), I was asked to fill out paperwork that included my medical history. This is another aspect of our health care system that irritates me and I've said as much to those in charge. The paperwork I filled out was EXACTLY the same as the other 4 sets (count 'em – FOUR) of paperwork at the SAME hospital in the SAME central location. Haven't these people ever heard of a wonderful invention called a computer? It's even more irritating when you actually read the 'agreement' you sign. It says, explicitly, that you give the medical office permission to share the information they gather about you with other physicians. I've signed the same form all four times. If they want to make hospital visits a bit less stressful, they should adopt some 21st century technology. Heck, most of us have cell phones that could transmit this type of information. Hmmm, maybe the medical offices are in cahoots with pharmaceutical companies that produce high blood pressure medicine and this is just a sly way of selling more of the same? Is it just me or does anyone else wonder how much we should trust 'professionals' who can't grasp the simplicity of email? Sheesh!

Okay, once the paperwork was completed (and the co-payment paid), I was taken back to a station where they pumped about $600 of radioactive isotopes into my veins (with all the x-rays, MRI's and radiation pretty soon I'm going to be a human night light). After this, they led me to a room with a recliner in it. This was part of the procedure I hadn't been told about. Seriously, the only things in the room were a recliner that I swear felt like it had a sheet of plywood underneath the cushions (La-Z-Boy furniture needs to give these guys a call), a couple of sheets to cover-up with, and a closed-circuit camera (to observe you). Oh, I almost forgot about the cold air. There was PLENTY of that. I'm one of those guys who don't get cold very easily (partly due to the 'fur jacket' the Lord blessed me with) but this room was so chilly that even fully clothed and with two sheets over me, my toes almost went numb (okay, maybe not 'numb' but they were definitely c-o-l-d). Once I was seated in the recliner I expected that someone was going to come in and chat with me about what was going to happen. But, no! The nurse said, *"I'll see you in about an hour."* Then he shut the door!

There I was in a cold, dark room with nothing to do but think. Guys and gals, I've got to tell you... being left alone with your thoughts when you don't know exactly what's going to be happening isn't good. I have to admit, having radiation coursing through my body and knowing I was going to have my entire body scanned for cancer didn't do much for my disposition. I had nothing to read, I couldn't make phone calls, there was no music – it was just cold and dark. So, I did what most people would do... I started worrying and praying. I worried that I hadn't been praying enough and then I prayed about worrying too much. Vicious cycle. Then I had to pee but I had 45 minutes to go (in a cold room, mind you).

My hour in purgatory was finally up and I was taken to the PET Scan machine where I was strapped onto a very hard table and had the aforementioned face mask secured to my head. One thing that medical professionals should know is this: When someone is facing a battle with cancer (or any potentially life-threatening disorder), it's not a good idea for the patient's mental health to put them in any contraption that resembles the inside of a casket. They could at least put some decorations on the inside of those machines (or paint them with colorful, non-reactive enamel) – anything to make them a bit more festive. As it was, I had my head torqued backwards so that my chin was abnormally raised and my shoulders were pinned to the backboard like I was on the wrong end of a wrestling match with Hulk Hogan. Even though my lower back and my butt kept wanting to flex upwards I was told to *"hold perfectly still and try to relax."* This kind of command is as silly as someone telling a person facing a firing squad to *"just breathe normally."*

I was also told, in a very kind tone, *"This will go pretty fast. We'll be done in about 20 minutes."* Okay, that's another pretty stupid comment to make. There's no 'we' when you're having a PET scan done. While I had to be content with going in an out of a machine that was shooting electromagnet waves through my body, they were in another room, telling jokes, talking about family, eating Baked Lay's potato chips and drinking Pepsi (yeah, I noticed all of that – I was hungry, remember). So, using the majestic plural 'we' doesn't cut it. It's just annoying.

After the procedure was done, the nurse told me that 'sometime next week' the doctor will look over the results and we'll be able to schedule your treatment plan. Again… Sheesh!

Is it part of the medical code that a physician isn't allowed to tell a patient anything until they've gone through a weekend of wondering?

So, that's where we are as of today. I've had an incredibly bad headache since this morning (actually yesterday morning now – it's about 2 AM on Thursday) and my sleep patterns have been about as unpredictable as a case of hiccups. As far as my neck is concerned, it's healing well. However, the simulation and PET scan aggravated it and I'm really hurting right now. Also, shaving is incredibly painful – I didn't expect that but it is.

Folks, I can't thank you enough for sending me emails and notes. I know full and well that you've got 'stuff' in your lives that rival or surpass what I'm going through. This makes your kindness even more meaningful. Thank you so much! With love, Lonnie (RevLon)

Week 12

10-31-07 From: Lonnie Honeycutt

Subject: Cancer Is Still Present

Hi Folks! Okay, here's the scoop. The results of the PET Scan came back and I still have cancer at the base of my tongue (waaaay down deep – not the oral part – not the part I speak with). It has also spread to my lymph nodes!

So, I have some choices to talk over with my oncologist. Personally, I'd rather have a doc remove the remaining cancer surgically. That's what I'm going to suggest and ask for. I won't know until I actually get an appointment with him if that's possible – it could be so deeply embedded that the surgery would leave me permanently impaired. The other choice is chemo and radiation. I'd really rather not undergo that since there is a GREAT chance that I'll be permanently impaired to some extent by the radiation therapy. I'm not too worried about the chemo even though it won't be fun. So, if you'd like to pray for me, pray that surgery is a viable option. If it isn't, then I'm still looking at about 40 radiation treatments plus chemo and that'll put me on the disabled list for quite some time. They'll probably push for this type of treatment plan because the affected area is so close to the brain and because they want to be very aggressive to make certain the cancer is eradicated. If we go that way, Christmas day is going to be the pits.

I'll tell you one thing – it's good to know 'something' instead of being 'in the dark. ' Okay, that's it for now. Love all of you, Lonnie Honeycutt (RevLon)

PS: Thanks for all of the food you've brought that we were able to heat in the microwave. That's been a blessing because I'm still pretty tired and because our oven is on the fritz. Y'all are SOOOO great.

11-03-07 From: Lonnie Honeycutt

Subject: The Cancer Verdict

The Cancer Verdict

Just so you know upfront, the following email is going to be brutally frank. While I've still got a good attitude about this trial, what you're going to read isn't easy to write.

As you know, I recently went in for a PET Scan to determine whether or not I had cancer and, if so, where the cancer was. I'm sorry it's taken me so long to get this out to you but to be quite honest, I've needed the time to process the verdict and to put it in perspective.

The Good, the Bad and the Ugly.

I don't know if I mentioned this in my other updates, but the cancer that had invaded my body was found in 9 out of 14 of my lymph nodes (not good). These nodes, as well as a nerve, a jugular vein, part of my tongue and some (about 6 inches) muscle tissue were all removed. The recovery from this highly invasive surgery hasn't been fun but I've gotten through it with your prayers, help with food, and kind calls. I'm still in the rehabilitation stage of my arm (I'm beginning to be able to extend it again without much trouble – just a lot of pain). Regrettably, the hearing in my left ear is being affected – I'm beginning not to be able to distinguish sounds due to inflamed tissues pressing on certain nerves and muscles. My face still hurts quite a lot too but I'm pretty used to that now.

The good news is that while the cancer had spread past its point of origin (never a good thing), it is now located in one major spot (the base of my tongue – behind or below the uvula and several lymph nodes). So, as I just stated, I still have cancer. Another piece of somewhat moderated good news is that it's treatable (at least it is to some degree). None of the oncologists I've spoken with are willing to state emphatically (with assurance) that the type of cancer I've been stricken with is curable but they are saying that they've seen more cures than fatalities.

Now for the bad and the ugly – and there's a lot of both.

What Kind of Cancer Is It?

The cancer in my body has been classified as Stage IVa squamous cell carcinoma (also known as oropharyngeal cancer). If you're aware of how cancer is staged you know this is almost as bad as it gets. There's only one higher grade and I'm on the fringes of that. Also, a lump or fatty mass (tumor) was found in the left lobe of my lung. Upon seeing it, one of the cancer doctors said, and I quote… *"Huh! I've never seen anything like that."*

I gotta tell ya folks, I'm getting pretty tired of being an oddity. ☺

Out of about 40,000 cancers like the one in my body that were diagnosed last year (2006), over 11,000 people have died from the same. I don't care who you are, that's a pretty sobering statistic especially considering that most of them were around my age.

Surgery isn't an option at this point because it would almost certainly result in my being mute or severely vocally impaired (while I don't plan on entering any yodeling contests in the near future, being able to talk is an aspect of my life I'm not ready to part with at the moment – though I'm sure Dawn sometimes wishes that I'd be quieter).

So, starting November 13, 2007, I'll begin treatment. The treatment is going to consist of simultaneous radiation and chemotherapy for about 8 weeks.

According to the information that I've been directed to by the doctors and the American Cancer Society, even after successful definitive therapy (such as I'll be undergoing), *'head and neck cancer patients face tremendous impacts on quality of life'* (isn't this the news everyone wants to hear?) and *'some patients have significant functional deficits'* (oh, joy!).

As for what the survival rate is like, the clinical data presents the following answer: *'Survival advantages provided by new treatment modalities have been <u>undermined</u> by the <u>significant percentage</u> of patients cured of head and neck squamous cell carcinoma (HNSCC) <u>who subsequently develop second primary tumors.</u>'* In short, the treatment I'll be getting (called field cancerization) often actually <u>creates other cancers</u> that are, in their words, a *'major threat to long-term survival after successful therapy of early-stage head and neck squamous cell cancer.'*

This almost sounds like the cure is as bad as the disorder.

Besides nausea and vomiting, the radiation I'll be treated with can affect my digestive system, cause dificulty in swallowing (which can lead to choking), lead to a reduction of vital fluids, reduce my ability to breathe due to lumps, internal swelling, open sores, and bleeding in my throat and can create an electrolyte imbalance that can negatively affect the functioning of my heart (just what I need since I have two holes in my heart already).

Again, apart from the radiation I'll be treated with a chemotherapy drug called Cis-diamminedichloroplatinum (commonly known as Cisplatinum or Cisplatin). This drug is used to intentionally damage your DNA in hopes that the crosslinking that occurs will initiate a repair protocol by the body. Let's hope so. Unfortunately, Cisplatin has a number of potential side-effects such as kidney damage, nerve damage, nausea and vomiting (a double whammy), hearing loss (there isn't a treatment for this as of yet and the loss can be severe), and hair loss (at least this one I don't have to worry about – haha). As such I'll be undergoing lab work each and every week (sometimes twice a week – anyone else thinking 'human pin-cushion?').

What I'm Concerned About Right Now

As with any major illness, of which I've had a few (congenital heart defect, diaphragmatic herniation, meningitis, endocarditis, and some other 'itises'), the cost, even with insurance, can be and is becoming daunting.

While I've been able to work, I haven't been able to do what I usually do. Due to the fact that my energy level ebbs and flows dramatically and my sleep patterns are so out of whack (and this is before starting treatment), my ability to effectively run a business is next to nonexistent. Fortunately, our ministry with Deeper Life Fellowship over in Daphne hasn't suffered – at least I don't think it has. Opportunities to serve others are always presenting themselves. Unfortunately, our congregation isn't large enough at present to afford me the luxury of drawing a salary and the income I'm currently receiving by the grace and love of our sister church (Deeper Life Fellowship of Mobile) is diminishing and will probably stop altogether as of the first of the year.

Knowing that I'm about to become even more disabled and less able to provide for my wife and children doesn't exactly thrill me. Still, my wife is gainfully employed and I'm confident that the Lord will provide a way to keep my family safe (He's already shown us how many wonderful brothers and sisters we have in His family). We are also blessed in that despite the financial hardships we've come under, the Angel Food ministry we've become affiliated with has helped our family to reduce in-home food costs by around $50 a week (now if we could only find an Angel Heating and Angel Gasoline ministry – hahahaaha).

Besides the financial crunch, what I'm most worried about is becoming a burden on my family or letting down the Lord in my ability to do the work He's given me to carry out. Further, I don't like the idea of not being able to play with my kids the way they need me to, of not being able to enjoy food, of having the ministry of DLF East falter, and of becoming a complainer. I'm also somewhat concerned about the bouts of depression I've been facing. While I 'put on a good face' and am usually genuinely at peace with what's going on, I am finding myself getting more and more depressed. Of course, when that happens, I pray more – so maybe depression isn't such a bad thing.

What I'm Joyous About

First and foremost I'm happy that I'm alive and one of God's cherished children. Secondly, I'm joyous about having a wonderful wife, two great children (my daughter just turned 4 on November 1st), and an abundance of friends. I'm head over heels overjoyed that Safe Harbor (our ministry to teens) is seeing such growth – we had a LOT of kids show up today (Saturday) and most of them don't attend church regularly or at all. How great is that? We get a chance to show them God's love while making smokebombs (non-explosive but really cool)!!! Too awesome! Finally, I'm happy that you are willing to pray for me.

In summary, things seem very dark in the 'natural.' However, spiritually, I'm doing great. I'm convinced that God will make a way for me to do His will even if it's not in the exact way I'd like to be able to do it. Love you! Rev. Lonnie Honeycutt (RevLon)

Week 13

11-05-07 From: Lonnie Honeycutt

Subject: Goat Herding, Donkey Wrangling, and Pig Petting

From the Subject heading you might think this was an email about farm exploits. But, no, it was just another normal Sunday for those of us at DLF East.

Well, okay, goats, donkeys and pigs aren't normally part of our Sunday but serving each other definitely is and this time they were involved.

Here's the story...

Two of our members, Shannon and Anna (Mother and Daughter), own Rosemary Petting Zoo and they had the opportunity to set-up at Jubilee Baptist Church over on the Eastern Shore. Hearing about this and what it entailed, several of us 'jumped right in' and offered to help with set-up, clean-up, whatever.

So, after eating lunch, we made our way over to Jubilee Baptist church and began to get our hands dirty (along with our fronts, backs, bottoms and a few other places).

Not long after arriving we had three or four chickens and ducks moved into a round-a-bout pen along with a HUGE turkey – unlike the other turkeys I've seen (and I'm not talking about co-workers or people who work for the IRS) this bird was beautiful. After all the fowl came three earless goats (yep 'earless') known as La Mancha (as in, 'The Man from...') gopher-eared goats and a couple of white/pink baby pigs. Up to this point, everything was fine and going smoothly.

Then came Walkerina. Walkerina is a friendly young burro whose apparent fear of open doors would soon cause massive chaos (well, 'massive chaos' on a petting zoo scale – which is about the same level of chaos that normally ensues when one tries to care for a house full of sugared-up boys all afflicted with raging ADD).

I (Lonnie) and my daughter (Danielle) were inside the pen peaceably walking around, clucking at chickens and petting pigs (just like all pastors and their children in Alabama do on Sunday afternoons) while Dawn (my wife) and Shannon were gently guiding Walkerina towards the then closed Petting Pen door. No problem thus far.

Then, horror of horrors to the donkey, someone had the audacity to *open* the 'door to oblivion' and all motion ceased. With her ears pinned back, her legs as rigid as frozen pistons, and the rope around her neck pulled taut, Walkerina was determined not to enter in the pen. Unfortunately, at the same time that Walkerina decided that the door was the portal to perdition, the goats I'd been trying to help Danielle pet were envisioning it as the entrance to gopher-eared goat nirvana and they made a trot for it.

The dutiful but altogether inept shepherd in me suddenly came to the surface and I hastened towards the open gate to prevent the animals from escaping. That was the wrong thing to do. The goats spooked and darted out of the door directly towards Dawn and Walkerina who, upon seeing what she must have thought were four-legged, ear-challenged demons coming from the pen, decided that the best place to be at the moment was anywhere else. Walkerina pulled back against the harness Dawn was holding as she tried to back away from the pen. Instinctively, Dawn gripped the rope as if it were a lifeline and, being a couple of hundred pounds lighter and much less stable than the donkey she was attempting to control, she succumbed to the laws of physics. Down to the ground she went.

As I watched the goats leave the pen I saw my wife fall to her knees and be pulled, unceremoniously, onto her back where, for a brief moment, she flopped around like a hooked fish out of water. As the donkey pulled her to earth I had time to note that Dawn was looking at me as if I'd suddenly donned a bright red suit, grown horns, and was wielding a pitchfork. Of course, nothing could have been further from the truth. I simply happened to be in the wrong place at the wrong time with a four-year-old clinging to my leg as if she were a growth so that my 'mad dash' to help my wife was more like a 'moseying limp.' Still, as my wife was lying on the ground clinging to a spooked donkey, the goats, who were obviously ignorant to the fact that as a minister I am, by default, a shepherd to whom they should have been subservient, leapt graciously over her dust-covered form and headed for freedom.

I quickly evaluated the situation. I could either hang around to help my wife, who I'm fairly certain was uttering things under her breath that a pastor's wife just shouldn't utter (especially *about* the innocent pastor), or I could choose to go on a merry goat chase with a screaming little girl who had adhered herself to my body. I chose the goat chase.

Long story short... we corralled the goats, got them back to the pen, and I attempted to make amends to my wife by allowing everyone who had seen the entire incident to wonder aloud, over and over again, why I had chosen to chase the goats out of the pen in the first place. Sigh!

Once the goats were penned, Walkerina, who had won a brief reprieve and had used her respite to leisurely search for grass or hay or whatever it is that a donkey likes to munch on, still had to be gotten into the enclosure.

Dawn, Shannon, and Anna pulled, tugged, called, begged, and did everything short of calling Dr. Phil to persuade the donkey to go through the archway. Nothing doing. It wasn't going to happen. There were no mule whisperers around. That's when Regis B. Sr. and Regis B. Jr. stepped up.

Taking a firm grip on the rope that held Walkerina, the two Regis' began to tug. So did Walkerina. If you've never seen two guys trying to move an unwilling donkey, you should make every effort to do so. It is a site to behold. In a surprising feat of strength, Regis and Regis began to pull Walkerina towards the pen door. The burro had so locked her legs that, as she was moved, twin ruts formed along the ground. But, as soon as her head made it past the doorway all resistance ended and Walkerina happily strode into the pen, over to a small stack of barley, and began eating as if all was right in the world. It was like watching a child who, in the throws of a tantrum caused by their not wanting to try a spoonful of 'white glop,' suddenly realizes that the glop their parent has forced between their lips is ice cream. Getting Walkerina out of the pen was the reverse of the above.

The rest of the evening went quite well. My son (Brance) ran around the pen like a boy possessed, intent on catching and petting every chicken, duck, and pig in the pen (to his credit, after around an hour he'd succeeded in achieving his goals). Danielle got to hold the piglets and Jacob B. befriended a very fluffy bunny whose fur was so long, light, and soft it seemed more like a toy than a live animal. By the way, little piglets, while extremely cute (if you consider hair that's so coarse you could use it to clean a BBQ grill and a nose so flat and runny it could substitute as a grease gun 'cute'), are also very, very, very loud. We're talking decibels in the range of an air raid siren. I tried to record it with my cell phone but I was too close and the microphone kept scrambling out of sync – it sounded more like a hiccupping screech than a piggy squeal. Still, once they were in your arms, Bitsy an Betsy were quite content to snooze.

Before I Sign Off

Lots more happened at the Fall Festival held by Jubilee Baptist but those stories will wait. I'd like to say 'thanks' to those who gave of their Sunday afternoon to show love for a single mom and her daughter, both precious ladies, and to help those visiting Jubilee Baptist have a good time. It was fun.

Well, that's it for now. Hope you enjoyed the retelling of our adventures as much as I enjoyed living them. Love y'all! Rev. Lonnie (RevLon)

11-08-07 From: Lonnie Honeycutt

Subject: To Libby from Lonnie – Personal

Hi Libby, I hope you don't mind but I need to 'talk.'

Before I begin, I'd like to say that the appreciation I feel for you and Melvin goes beyond any possible explanation – verbal or otherwise. You two are truly salt of the earth and I am majorly blessed to know the two of you. That God would have allowed me to experience your friendship is beyond my comprehension because I've done nothing to deserve such an honor.

Libby, I am feeling completely overwhelmed at the moment. Dawn and I just had a conversation that set me back emotionally. It concerns finances. I am completely aware that our lives are in the hands of the Lord but, as the Psalmists often did, I am crying out to Him in earnest frustration and desperation. I know you know that I have faith so I'll stop trying to defend my spiritual maturity at this point. I just need to vent if you don't mind.

Knowing that I'm about to start chemo and radiation next Tuesday is impacting me on at least two different levels. First, I'm not looking forward to the pain and discomfort that I'm certain is coming. Secondly, since I haven't been able to work for the past 5+ weeks, I'm utterly depressed that the next 3+ months (possibly as much as 6) will bring a level of disability that I'm not at all prepared for. The fact that Dawn is having to take on the responsibility of caring for me while also running the house and paying the bills is pressing on me so much that it feels like I'm being crushed. The very fact that I'm feeling sorry for myself because of all this when I know what she and my kids are going to go through (having a husband and a father who is sick) makes me feel like a complete loser. Further, knowing that the David and Jody A. are experiencing a sickness in their family and that I should be able to minister to them more fully makes me feel like a heel. But, the reality is that I'm concerned about my family and I am feeling angry about all of this. Today was the first day in 5 weeks that I felt like my old self. I so much wanted to contact all of my business clients to ask for work (and I did contact a number of them) in hopes that I'll experience a few more of these days so that I can bring some income in for Christmas, the mortgage, food, etc. At the same time, I'm conflicted about working on days like this because I want to be able to spend my 'good days' with my family. I've got to tell you, today was TERRIFIC because I got to play with Danielle and Brance like I haven't been able to do in weeks (maybe months – the headaches I'd experienced prior to the cancer surgery haven't been bothering me) AND I was able to do a bunch of housework (which helps take stress off Dawn) and I actually cooked a meal for my family. I cannot express how worthwhile today made me feel. Being able to dig in the dirt with Danielle and build a fire with Brance... that was priceless.

Libby, I am so sick of being sick and I know that more is still to come. I want to provide for my family. I want to be there for them. I want them to have a dad and a husband who is more than just a medical mystery waiting to happen. I want to be a great pastor who works diligently for the Lord whom I love dearly. I want to be a friend who gives instead of needs. Sister, it feels as though I'm failing on all of these accounts.

So... Please pray for me that I'm able to feel good enough to provide for my family and for the congregation I'm responsible for.

Thanks for letting me 'cry on your virtual shoulder.'

With much love, Your Brother in Christ, Lonnie

11-08-07 From: Libby B.

Subject: Re: To Libby from Lonnie – Personal

Dear Lonnie, I am so honored to have your trust and respect. Most of all that you feel close enough to be gut-wrenchingly honest.

Get my poem I wrote you and read it again.

I understand as much as possible how you feel, but, Lonnie, you are so much more than a provider. God promises to provide and I have knowledge that I am not to give yet that provision is coming and it is coming from Jesus through His people.

You will be astonished as you just rest in the arms of your Daddy God in Heaven how He is going to provide for your family. Many of your friends are having meetings and making plans. I wouldn't tell you this if I didn't think you needed to know right now.

That old saying... *"If it is to be it's up to me"* is straight from the Pit. If it is to be it is up to God, who took full responsibility for you from your birth and new birth and assumed all your needs in advance and has already provided for them all.

First, we know that God knows your heart and He is a Heart God and grieves with you. Second, your friends know your heart and the word Loser would never enter our mind. If God is for you, who dares to be against you? I know from Melvin that men get a lot of their self worth from their work. Maybe God made y'all that way. But when all the outward stuff is shut down for a while, who are you really? An awesome spirit being of magnificent worth! His life, death and resurrection says you have great value or He wouldn't have paid such a high price to purchase you. I know you probably wish I could shut up and just listen... but the Mama that I am has to encourage you.

I remember that Dudley Hall sent out a tape one time called *Dryness, Despair and Depression*. One of the things Dudley said was that we were to 'expose the absurd and then remember His past faithfulness.' No way do I believe God brought you this far, equipped you for ministry and it's over. I believe it's part of preparing you for greater ministry. Don't let my intentions of affirming and building you up keep you from being honest and talking anytime. Lonnie, you are a great man of God and you have a balcony full of people cheering you on because we love you!!!!

Thanks again for sharing your heart and letting me share mine. I love you and Dawn more than you know. Libby

11-8-07 From: Lonnie Honeycutt

Subject: From Lonnie to Bob

Hi Bob! I'm Lonnie Honeycutt and Brenda forwarded me your email address.

I'm about to undergo treatment for Stage IVa cancer of the Head and Neck. From reading the description you gave it sounds as though ours were nearly exact as per the location. I had surgery about 5 weeks ago (removed 5 lymph nodes, muscle tissue, a nerve, and the jugular vein from my left side).

Since I'm a pastor I'm VERY concerned about losing my voice and the effect that the radiation will have on my salivary glands. How has your voice been affected?

I'm also praying fervently that I don't have to have a feeding tube inserted although that may be a foregone conclusion.

In any case, I'd appreciate knowing what it is that you've experienced to date.

In your email you asked Brenda how old I was. I am 42. I have 2 children (one boy, one girl – 8 & 4 respectively) and a wonderful wife.

I look forward to chatting with you. Rev. Lonnie Honeycutt (RevLon)

11-09-07 From: Robert (Bob) T.

Subject: Re: From Lonnie to Bob

Lonnie: I asked and asked what stage I was in and finally the surgeon said between II and III. At first they talked about doing the surgery immediately. Then they decided to do the treatments (radiation and chemo) in order to reduce or eliminate the cancer. My primary was at the base and left rear of my tongue. They had to use a scope to find it. Then they CT scanned and PET scanned me looking for any primary source of the cancer. They finally decided that it was at the back and base of my tongue. I went through thirty-three (33) radiations, every day, excluding Saturdays and Sundays. At the same time, I had six (6) 24-hour chemos. I sat all day getting the chemo drip at the doctor's office and then they sent me home with a pump. I had it unattached the next morning.

I had a mask similar to yours. Brenda sent me two (2) pictures of you. The radiation will make your throat sore, eventually. Mine got sore about halfway through the treatments. At about that same time, nothing had any taste anymore. So, I began to use the feeding tube. I used it exclusively for about eight (8) weeks. I still use it now, although I try to eat through my mouth as much as I can. The problem with eating right now, is nothing has much of a taste and it is still slightly hard to chew and swallow. Basically, I force myself to do it. Food has no appeal and I do not get hungry. I only keep the calories going down to help my throat heal. I am healing very slowly, according to my radiation oncologist. The dry mouth really bothers me. My treatments ended just before Labor Day and I have not had any saliva since about a month before that. Then there's the mucous mouth. I guess it's something your body does to protect your throat from the radiation. It can get really thick, foamy and nasty. I have less of it now, but I still have it. They say it will get better.

I have been able to talk all the way through this ordeal. My voice got raspy about halfway through the radiation and chemo. It sounds funny to me, but everyone says I sound like my old self. The voice will get better. I had surgery to remove lymph nodes and whatever was left of the cancer on Monday, 10/08/2007. I am still healing from that. The surgeon said he was pleased how the treatments had reduced the cancer. As I understand it, he took lymph nodes and a speck of what was left of the cancer. The whole team (Surgeon, Radiation and Chemo) thought it was a success. I have my next appointments in mid-January. I will get a CT scan and a PET scan and some other tests at that time.

What else can I tell you. I assume you did the surgery first? I ran into some that did it that way. I have a contact that has helped me because he is about eight (8) months ahead of me. He told me his saliva has come back and his taste too. They say that takes a while to come back. The saliva as long as three (3) to six (6) months. The taste can come back quicker. Others have said it was a whole year before they felt anywhere near normal again. I took medicine (2 shots) everyday before the radiation that was supposed to protect my kidneys and saliva glands. They said it could make my saliva come back anywhere from 70% to 80% of what it was. The shots occasionally made me sick. I took nausea medicine to combat the chemo and radiation shots making me sick. I sort of got used to throwing up. It became no big deal.

Ask away. I'll tell you whatever I can. I wish you the best. Have a good support group around you. I am single but tons of people supported me and thought about me and called me and prayed for me. I felt their good thoughts and prayers. It all helped.

I'll put you in my thoughts and prayers. Hang in there. A lot of this thing is in your head. Think positive. It will help. Bob T.

Week 14

11-12-07 From: Arlen J.

Subject: Christmas With the Honeycutts

Dear Rev. Lon, my heart and Prayers go out to you and your precious family. Your email update of Nov. 3 2007 found it's way to me last week, I was totally unaware of this attack against you.

I took the liberty of sending your email to my employer Chuck M., he is the owner of our company (GCAH). Every Christmas the employees of GCAH adopt a family for Christmas. This year the Honeycutts are our Family!

Lonnie, it will be a joy for us to be a part of your Christmas. Please let me know of specific needs so we can best help you and your family.

In HIS love, Arlen

11-13-07 From: Lonnie Honeycutt

Subject: Re: Christmas With the Honeycutts

Hi Arlen! Wow! My brother, I am completely blown away by this generous offer. Honestly, it's an answer to prayer and so appreciated. My wife and I were having a discussion last week about finances when she told me, "*If you want me to be perfectly frank, we have nothing.*" Whew, I can't tell you what a blow that was. When something like this (in my case, cancer, surgery, and treatment) comes up and you're faced with the task of getting through the ordeal while also trying to survive financially, the emotional toll is enormous. To have it happen around Christmas with a 4 and 8 year old... you can just imagine.

In any case, while I sincerely appreciate the offer of your company and its employees to sponsor us, I don't have a clue as to how this works. So, can you give me some guidelines? As for specific needs, prayer would be GREAT! Also, if anyone has any Ensure or Boost coupons that'd be helpful as well since I'm probably going to end up with a feeding tube in the not too distant future (Yum, yum, Thanksgiving turkey through a tube).

Thanks again! Rev. Lonnie Honeycutt (RevLon)

11-11-07 From: Robert (Bob) T.

Subject: Re: From Lonnie to Bob

Lonnie, are you doing okay? Let me know if my message helped any? Bob T.

(My reply to Bob) Hi Bob! Sorry I haven't written sooner. I've just been incredibly busy. Since I don't know how soon the radiation and chemo is going to start affecting my physical or emotional ability to function well (I don't have a spleen and I have a heart condition so I'm more susceptible to energy ebbs), I've been cramming in as much stuff as possible. The day after tomorrow is my last 'free' day so it's going to be packed.

Yes, you did help me by giving me a heads-up as to what to expect. Your experiences seem to mimic those I've read about on Medline etc. I've been doing quite a bit of research as to what types of medicines might help to protect my salivary glands and throat and I'll be discussing those with my radiation oncologist tomorrow.

Knowing someone who is several months into the process is also helpful because I've been able to prepare myself, at least a bit, for the long haul. Gotta tell you, like everyone else, I'm dreading these treatments. Both sides of my neck are going to be treated and I've been told by a couple of people that it'll be brutal about the time Christmas rolls around.

Ah well, what's a year or two of healing if I get another 20? Lonnie

11-15-07 From: Lonnie Honeycutt

Subject: First Day of Cancer Treatment… Whew!

Hi everyone! Yesterday was an experience.

Waking up at 7 AM to go have poisons pumped into my body and my head, neck, and chest cooked with radiation isn't my idea of the start of a good day. But, like many things in life that initially don't seem so great, this may turn out to be one of those.

When I arrived at my first cancer appointment, the room was about 3/4 full. I immediately noted that I was the youngest of the crowd by about 20 years – I also had the least amount of hair (for now) and I was the only one with two pimples on my nose. You know, I gotta tell ya, it just doesn't seem fair that I should have cancer AND pimples. Sigh! ☺

I had to watch a short video that did nothing for me personally except make me antsy. It kept talking about how you needed to be 'okay' with needing time for yourself, taking care of yourself, saying no to things you might otherwise say yes to and on and on and on. Professionally and rationally I know what the film is saying is right. Emotionally and personally it just rubs me the wrong way. I may need some prayer about that.

I was one of the first to be actually hooked up to the IV pumps so I had the opportunity to greet everyone who came in. For the most part people were putting on good faces as their treatment began but, as I talked with them, there was a real presence of fear that permeated all but one of them. Harold and Jerry were both being treated with chemo daily for lung cancer while Hazel and Jo Anne were there for breast cancer (these two ladies are also with me when I go for radiation treatment). I got to talk to all of them for about 4 hours and I found out how they were doing, who had been through treatment before, what they did or used to do for a living and what some of their needs were. Another man, whose name (Greg) I picked up only because I overheard the nurses talking, was in a different room so I didn't get to know him at all – maybe next time.

In any case, after talking to them for quite some time I remembered that I had some 'outreach bags' in the truck (never leave home without 'em) and I somehow convinced the charge nurse to allow me to take my IV bags with me into the parking lot. I promised her that I wouldn't steal the IV contraption and assured her that if I tried I was pretty certain the police would notice the poles hanging out of the window as I made my escape. After about 10 minutes of pretty constant pestering she allowed me to go to my truck (mind you, she had no idea as to why it was so important to me to go outside since I couldn't whisper my plans without being overheard and I wanted it to be a surprise). You know, I just realized that I may not have even told Dawn about this part of my treatment.

Returning from outside I garnered quite a bit of attention as I had gifts in my arms and one hanging from the IV pole – something I'm quite sure isn't on the safety or health protocols for some governmental control agency. Entering into the treatment room I began handing out the gifts to all the patients (I even eventually got one back to Greg with the help of a nurse) as well as the nurses. I explained, as we always do, that this was just a practical way to show the love of God.

Well, I have to tell you that opened up the spiritual realm. I was able to pray for all four patients and two nurses – one of whom was eyeing me extremely suspiciously – as if the candy I was giving out was somehow going to thwart their treatment protocol (of course, once she saw that we had placed Reisen's dark chocolate in her bag all suspicion went away).

Life For Me Right Now

While I previously had an understanding of what cancers do to the body, until now the effects I 'understood' were merely intellectual. Now they are experiential and all too real. Supposedly chemo patients don't usually experience major side effects such as raging nausea and vomiting until after 6 to 8 weeks after beginning treatment with Cisplatin. Well, I am the exception (what's new, right?). My side effects started about 4 hours after treatment and continued for hours. So, yesterday and this morning were pretty tough. I vomited so much that I had to go in and have I.V. fluids administered. One of the worst things for me would be to lose too much water. Not only would healing take place less rapidly but the poisons they're putting in my system to kill any remaining cancer wouldn't be flushed out properly – plus, as my throat becomes more and more blistered from the radiation (they are irradiating BOTH sides of my neck as well as parts of my head and my chest – yippee) and my salivary glands shut down, fluid is going to become even more precious.

Although I was already taking double doses of an anti-nausea medicine as well as another that should have prevented headaches, I suffered from a migraine whose quality was unlike most I've ever experienced – easily an 8.5 out of 10 (excruciating – by the way, did you know we get the term 'excruciating' from the Latin 'excruciatus' which was developed to describe the intense pain brought about by crucifixion?).

This morning I went back for another treatment and I asked for stronger medicine to help control the vomiting etc. They were able to prescribe me some other meds but WOW the cost is amazing ($75 co-pay per prescription). You know, I'm beginning to fully understand why it is that people have to choose between their medicine and food. If we didn't have insurance it'd be even more expensive. Thank goodness prayer is free. ☺

I was also given a prescription for Pilocarpine (Salagen) which is considered the 'gold standard' for treating dry mouth (one has to wonder if it's been given this distinction because it costs almost the same as the precious metal). Unfortunately, Pilocarpine, while helping to increase the flow of saliva, can also cause nausea and vomiting (why can't I catch a break here, folks?).

Enough about me...

I'd again like to send out my love for all of you. It's pretty overwhelming that you've taken the time to include me in your prayers, to forward my needs to others, and to surround my family with love (this last one means the world to me). So many of you have asked how you can help. Frankly, I'm not even sure. Right now it's a day-by-day process and it'll probably get to be an hour-by-hour process. I say that to say this: I don't even really know what to ask for. Well, that's not exactly true. One of the things I do need, if you happen to run across them, are coupons for Boost or Ensure meal replacement drinks. Those would be GREAT since money is tight.

I also need to again ask your forgiveness if you've called or written me and I haven't been able to get back to you. My sleep habits are horribly out of whack (it's like my body is being fueled by a combination of Red Bull and Valium and I'm never sure which one is going to kick in when – so if I ever slump over the pulpit during a sermon, I probably haven't died, my body has just decided to nap – sure does make driving a car sound like a bad idea, doesn't it) so I never really know when I'm going to feel like talking or writing (I started this email yesterday).

Well, it's nearly 1 AM and I'm going to try to get some sleep. Another treatment is waiting for me bright and early tomorrow morning.

Love all of you dearly! Rev. Lonnie Honeycutt

11-15-07 From: Robert (Bob) T.

Subject: Your First Day of Treatment

Lonnie: How did your first day go? Bob T.

(My Reply to Bob) Bob, to be honest it's been brutal. I don't know if it's because of the amount of Cisplatin I received, the stress of trying to prepare for the length of the treatment and the long-term results, or the way my body has to be contorted to receive the radiation treatments. In any case, I've got a migraine that's worse than any I've had in about 8 weeks – they actually let-up for awhile once my jugular vein was removed (go figure).

Anyway, I'm definitely not looking forward to this but, emotionally, I'm doing pretty good. How was your day/week? Rev. Lonnie

(Bob's reply to me) Lonnie, I am sorry the treatments started off not good. Mine were not that way. Actually, it was almost nothing until about halfway through the radiation. Then the side effects began to show up. Eventually, the medicine they gave me, ethyol, just before the radiation treatments, did make me nauseous, but they gave me anti-nausea medicine for that. It worked pretty well. I did get sick to my stomach on a number of occasions.

How many treatments, both radiation and chemo are you scheduled for?

Since I am ahead of you, I can tell you once the treatment is over you will get better in small increments each succeeding day. That's how I am doing. I am nearly 2-1/2 months out from my last radiation/chemo treatment. I can tell it's getting better day by day, so hang onto that thought. I've also visited with another guy who is about eight (8) months ahead of me and he is doing fine. Hang in there. I am pulling for you. God bless. Bob T.

11-16-07 From: Kathie M.

Subject: Re: First Day of Cancer Treatment – Whew

I was sorry to hear you were so sick from the initial chemo treatment. Was that new (and expensive) medicine the doctor prescribed after the initial horror by any chance the Emend I told you about in an earlier email? If so, hang in there. My chemo nurse says there's orders of magnitude in difference between how sick you get without Emend versus how much better you are with it – but it does work best when taken BEFORE your Cisplatin dose (and Cisplatin can continue to make you sick for something like five days after the treatment), so you might not get the full benefit right away.

And do prepare yourself for sticker shock – that $75 for the anti-nausea medicine is going to begin to look cheap! I've already told the doctor I'm convinced I'm not going to die from ovarian cancer – I'm going to die of a heart attack brought on by opening all those Blue Cross/Blue Shield PPO Explanation of Benefits statements detailing the costs of treatment! For example, you will sooner or later no doubt be treated to Neulasta shots to keep your immune system functioning well (I'm not sure whether I get it because of the Gemzar, the Cisplatin, or the combination of the two, but I get a shot once every three weeks). It's sort of like getting a flu shot, only it takes maybe 15 seconds longer. Well, this little 30-second wonder bills at $6,500!! BC/BS pays the doctor roughly $2,400 (I pay $20) and the doctor writes off the rest. The nurse said the $2,400 is just about what the drug company charges the doctor. She also said that patients old enough to be on Medicare generally can't even get the shot at their doctor's office, because Medicare doesn't reimburse anywhere close to the $2,400 – so the doctors send the Medicare patients to their local hospital, because hospitals, with all their endowments and nonprofit foundations, can better afford to write off the difference between the cost of the medicine and the amount reimbursed. I have no idea what happens if the local hospitals aren't flush with endowments. Sort of a sad commentary on our medical system.

Here's hoping they manage to find something that will make you feel a bit better! Kathie

Week 15

11-19-07 From: Lonnie Honeycutt

Subject: Thank You – From the Bottom of My Heart – Christmas with the Honeycutts

As a Pastor, I'm often called upon to listen to the grief-stricken voices of those who are praying for sick loved ones or those who have been personally afflicted by disease and I am moved, through compassion, to hear below the surface – to hear their hearts. Each person has a unique story with commonalities woven throughout; a lost job, a wayward spouse, an estranged child, an illness, or some other devastating event. In each and every case, the common denominator is that the person with whom I speak wants, desperately, to connect to someone, almost anyone, who is willing to show him or her compassion. In other words, they want a relationship that can look beyond the limitations of locality, time, circumstances, and even personal mismanagement. They want to find someone who is willing to 'walk the walk' of love rather than someone who 'talks the talk' and then turns away.

I'm writing to you today because Arlen, a friend and a Brother-in-Christ, has introduced me to YOU – people I don't know, who don't know me or my family, but who have shown a willingness to demonstrate their kindness in a very practical manner. Though I cherish the thought of being able to give each and every one of you a hug and to personally say 'thank you,' such isn't possible in my present condition. It is my most sincere hope that this letter will help me to express the extreme gratitude I feel in my heart.

As you probably already know, I've recently been afflicted with Stage IVa cancer of the head and neck. I've had radical surgery which resulted in the removal of 9 malignant tumorous masses (neck, head, chest and the base of my tongue) as well as the extraction of a major nerve and my left jugular vein. Having healed sufficiently from this trauma, both my oncologists agreed that it was time to begin simultaneous and very aggressive chemotherapy and radiation treatments. These treatments are conducted at two different clinics (the chemotherapy is pumped into my veins – it takes about 4 hours for the entire procedure – and the radiation treatments are directed at both sides of my neck towards the center mass which lies deep inside my neck, head, and chest cavity). I will undergo treatments 5 days a week for a total of 40 treatments. Supposedly, most patients begin to experience negative effects after the first three weeks of treatment – I began to experience both raging nausea and vomiting as well as a sore throat and neck within 4 hours of my first treatment.

With Christmastime approaching, my wife and I were having a frank talk about what Christmas Day would look like. Perhaps it was because I was on pain-killers that I'd never considered the impact that co-pays, medical stays, and other cancer-related issues would take on our finances until that night. In any case, I was totally unprepared when my wife looked me squarely in my eyes and made the matter-of-fact statement: "*Lonnie, we have NOTHING for*

Christmas." While I tried to minimize the impact that her statement had on me, I didn't sleep for nearly two days. I kept running scenarios through my mind that might allow me to create a flow of income that would benefit my family and some of the people we know who are in dire straits. The realization that my body was simply not able to function like it had been able to two months ago – meaning that my strength (both physical and mental) and my emotions were on uncontrollable, virtual roller coaster rides, was like a slap in the face. It became apparent that I would need to 'talk with my children' about Christmas this year. Please don't get me wrong. In my family we really do value what Christmas means even without gifts but, for a four and an eight year old, the understanding that presents aren't going to be a part of the season is just a bit harder to grasp. To say the least, I was dreading this conversation.

With that being said, I'd like to say that your ability, both personally and as a corporate whole, to grasp some sense of the desperation my wife and I felt in having to deal with the ordeal of cancer and the treatment of the same, especially as the Christmas season approached, is commendable.

Allow an ailing man to tell you a brief story...

At the tender age of 8 years old (the same age as I find my own son today), around the time of Christmas, my family and I were living in the foothills of the Carolinas in a one-room shack (it was literally a shack that had been designed not to house a family but to serve as a repose for hunters). To say that we were poor would be an understatement of grand proportions. The floor on which we walked was made of warped 2" x 4"s so unevenly spaced that you could see the earth below them as you moved. My Mother, in an attempt to reduce the cold drafts as much as possible, stuffed newspaper in between the boards. A single wood stove stood alone in the center of the one-room shack and served as both heater and cooking stove. When it came time for baths, my sister and brother (two and four years younger than I am respectively) and I would build a small fire in the backyard, fill a #3 washtub with a couple of inches of water (as much as two waddling toddlers could manage to carry without spilling it), warm the water, and then carry it inside to a small porcelain tub. This procedure would be repeated four or five times until there was enough water to soak all of us. It became my 'job' as the eldest child, and as the resident pyromaniac, to chop wood, prepare fires, and, make coffee. I can't help but imagine that to most children the preparation of a cup of coffee would rank somewhere around tooth extraction and fingernail clipping on a 'fun scale.' As I grew older I came to realize that the reason I relished making coffee for my mom was because in doing so I could show her a modicum of love. You see, we didn't have a coffee pot in my youth. Instead, I would fill a small tin cup with water, scoop a small amount of Folger's instant coffee into it, stir it slightly, and patiently hold it over the flickering flame of a single candle, my fingers wrapped in a washcloth so as to not be burned, until the dark, bitter liquid bubbled. I'm quite certain that Mom never even got an adequately tasty cup of coffee from my hands but she never let on. To this day, making those cups of coffee ranks high on my favorite list of memories.

It's rare for me to share what I've just shared with you concerning my early childhood days because the memories are sometimes painful and difficult to relate. The reason I've chosen to do so is because I sincerely believe that the events that took place during this period of time helped to mold me into the man I am today. It's important for us to remember that the seemingly small, almost insignificant actions we take can have a major impact. Read on...

Even though our home didn't have a television or, from what I can remember, even a radio it was evident that Christmas was right around the corner. The children of our neighbors, who were ostensibly just as poor as we were, had done what kids do – they made ready for the special day of presents with what they had at hand. Colorful bottle caps from soft drinks and beer were pierced with a nail (there were no pop-tops or plastic tops then) and strung together with yarn, brightly designed paper snowflakes of assorted sizes were taped to windows and on windowsills there were propped, looking outward, a hodge-podge of Christmas elves, Santas, evergreen trees, and reindeer, most of whom looked either horribly skinny or bloated from too many Christmas cookies. The memory of these trinkets along with the expectant excitement of the children who lived on our side of town, has seared into my heart an almost palpable sense of what Christmas feels like – in two words: hope and wonder.

Though I didn't realize it fully at the time, the reality of what Christmas morning was really going to look like for my family was bearing down on my parents. My father, a full-time, long-haul trucker had been out of work, except for the occasional monthly run between two states, for nearly three months. My mother, having three young children to care for and no transportation had done what she could to earn money so that she could keep us fed, however leanly, for weeks. Still, while we had shelter over our heads, drafty but warmish beds in which to sleep, and two parents who loved us dearly, Dad and Mom knew that this would provide very little solace the morning after Santa was supposed to have arrived.

Unbeknownst to anyone (even my parents) a small group of people had other plans for our home and several of those in our neighborhood. Late on Christmas Eve, it must have been nearing 5 PM because the sun was going down and most of the stores in town were closed or closing, three grown-ups appeared at our door. Mom knew two of them as members of a local church from where we occasionally collected food stamps and they were invited in. As I remember it, within minutes my sister, Lillian, my brother, David, and I were all bundled up tightly and herded into a waiting station wagon. Even though I know it took much longer to arrive at the five and dime store (having driven to it as an adult), we seemed to only be in the backseat of the car for seconds. As youngsters, the time simply flew by.

Prior to departing, the grown-ups in whose temporary care we were had quickly gathered notes on our sizes of shoes, pants, underwear, coats, and other essentials from our parents. As my brother and sister were taken to and fro throughout the store in search for presents, I was asked by a young husband and wife what I'd like to get for Christmas? My question, *"Can I get anything?"* might have seemed a bit impertinent or even impolite to those who were there to serve me but, if so, they never let on. When they answered *"Yes,"* I immediately found what I'd been mentally drooling over. It was a small, acrylic, paint-by-numbers set for ages 12 and up. I remember the age grouping because the lady helping me mentioned it at least twice. The second time she asked me about my proficiency at oil painting she inquired, *"Sweetheart, are you sure you can do this, it says for boys ages twelve or more and you're only eight?"* It was then that I truly realized what she was asking and was able to give her a reasonable answer.

"No, Ma'am,' I can't do these pictures but my Momma can and she really likes doing them. This is what I want to get her for Christmas." She objected kindly, *"But, this is supposed to be for you..."* I nodded

my head and smiled as if what she and I were saying were one and the same, *"I know. This is what I want my present to be but I want to get it for my Mom. Painting makes her happy."*

In my mind, the issue was settled. If they wanted me to receive a present that would make me happy, then the paint-by-numbers set was it. Period. End of discussion. Maybe it was my determination or the fact that I had been continuously nodding my head up and down in a manner that declared, 'Yep, this is what we've been looking for all along' or maybe it was just that the man and woman with me understood that Christmas simply wouldn't be Christmas if I weren't able to get my mother a wonderful present. Whatever the case might have been, that night I was able to wrap-up a 25-cent paint-by-numbers set for my mom.

Honestly, I don't remember a single item that I personally received that Christmas although the small tree that bedazzled us on Christmas morning seemed packed to the hilt with gifts. While I don't remember the names of the man or woman, I do, however vaguely, remember their faces. More than anything though, I remember the way they helped me feel. I remember and I cherish the fact that they took the time to enter into a young boy's heart to see what was important to him and then to help him deliver a Christmas present that he will never forget. It's been 33 years since that happened and the memory has never faded.

I tell you this true story as a gift from my heart to yours. Your unselfish act of kindness to a family you have no relationship with, just like the people in my early years, is a gift whose magnitude you'll probably never truly know on this side of eternity. While I've never been able to express my gratitude to the folks who so kindly gave of themselves on that cold, sleeting night over three decades ago, I didn't want to miss the chance to do so this time. Thank you so very much – from the bottom of my heart I thank you.

I promise to tell my children YOUR story for as long as I am able so that it too becomes part of our Christmas story – a inspirational lore grounded in your faithful works that, over time, becomes more alive than mere tradition.

Sincerely, Rev. Lonnie Honeycutt (RevLon)

11-20-07 From: Melinda Y.

Subject: Your First Cancer Treatment...

I'm so sorry about your recent diagnosis. I'll pray for you and your family. You seem to be taking it in great stride. Of course, I always find it difficult to understand God's greater plan when these kinds of health issues arise within the body of true believers. I just keep coming back to remembering that God's ways are not our ways, and we don't have the ability to see the bigger picture. Many Blessings, Melinda

11-21-07 From: Eddie Honeycutt (Mom)

Subject: Just to Say Hello

Hi, I Just wanted to let you know the reason I haven't called you was that I know you are beginning to sound rusty when you talk. Your throat must be hurting so badly. So, I said to myself that I would just email you from time to time to let you know I love you. I really do love you and I'm so very sorry you have to go through this without me being there by your side.

I Hope Brance is okay from his bee sting the other day. Steve and I are doing o.k. I talked to David today and they are okay too. Gay took two more tests for her G.E.D. last week but she hasn't gotten the scores back yet. But, Gay said she felt like she did well on both the tests. I also talked to Helena this week and she is doing good as is Jay and his family. Mother!

11-21-07 From: Lonnie Honeycutt

Subject: Thanksgiving Thanks from Lonnie to DLF Members

Hi guys! Due to the fact that I haven't felt well and that I usually do the cooking, we had decided to pre-order Thanksgiving Dinner from Winn-Dixie – at least part of it.

When we went to pick it up today the lady behind the counter got all giggly and handed it to us with a note. The note said, *'Just a practical way of showing God's love.'* We don't know whom it was who picked up the tab but we recognize the motto. Thanks from the bottom of our hearts for your kindness. Lonnie (RevLon)

11-21-07 From: Lonnie Honeycutt

Subject: Thanksgiving Update from Lonnie (RevLon)

Hi Folks, this is one of my weekly updates but this one is going to be a bit different. It mostly has to do with a conversation I had with a fellow patient (Janet). A second email will be forthcoming as to a second conversation I was privileged to have with Greg, an elderly, very intelligent atheist.

First, about me...

Thanksgiving day has been rough. Vomiting, mouth sores, upset stomach, weak, and tired – all the things that make get-togethers difficult. Fortunately, the friends we were going to get together with understood why we couldn't. That's always nice – to have understanding friends in times of trial. I missed being with them terribly. We're also blessed because we sought out and found some people who needed food today who otherwise wouldn't have had any. Like Jesus said, the need is always going to be there.

I tried some of the artificial spit today and it's the definition of yuck!

My wife won't have read this before it goes out so I'd like to publicly thank Dawn for being such a wonderful caregiver and provider. This whole process has been difficult and it'll probably get worse. She's done such a super job with the kids, school, business, and, of course, me. Being a man and getting some of my worth out of what I can do to provide for my family means that the last several weeks have been extremely hard. Throughout this ordeal Dawn has sought to minimize those things pertaining to finances while accentuating that which is truly important – family and friendships. Personally, what this has meant to me is that she's helped me keep my ego somewhat intact – she's helped me understand and accept that while I'm not earning the money needed to keep a family of four 'above water,' that I am earning the respect of our kids by teaching them to graciously rely on God and friends and by continuing to serve in areas that I have the strength to do so. Dawn has been a beacon to me in this darker time and has allowed her feminine strength to protect my masculine self until such time as I'm physically able to provide like I want to.

To all of you – my friends and brothers and sisters, both in the natural and in Christ – THANK you. Thanksgiving is all about family to me and I am richly blessed to know how many family members I have who are thinking about me. Thanks for the rides to and from treatment, thanks for letting me borrow music and games and movies, thanks for the food and the laughs and thanks for letting me be part of your life even if it's just via emails. Y'all are TREMENDOUS.

Okay, I'm getting really very tired so I'm going to take a nap. The following is what I wrote during my stay at the clinic while getting Chemo. It's the first of two conversations I didn't expect to have that day. Please pardon any grammatical and spelling errors as I just don't feel up to editing right now. ☺

Love, Rev. Lonnie Honeycutt (RevLon)

Greg and Janet

Today I met Greg and Janet. The differences between the two couldn't have been more dramatic or similar. They were a study in contrasts and parallels.

Upon entering the Chemo Ward I found myself alone, with the exception of a few nurses who began flitting around me as if they were moths and I was a sugar-coated light in a dark alley. By the way, concerning the name of the ward, I really think they need to reconsider that designation because, to me, it smacks of people who are 'hooked ' on chemotherapy. Thus far, no one I've met has admitted to having midnight cravings for Chemo or any telltale signs of addiction such as itchy gums, crawling flesh, the jitters, or the occasionally irrational concern that someone, somewhere (mostly likely their miniature schnauzer who, they've noticed, monitors their every movement as if he were a pint-sized canine NARC), is monitoring their whereabouts in order to find out where their stash of chemotherapy drugs are. I don't know what the best new designation would be but someone needs to come up with something. Since they provide easy chairs (which are quite comfortable – although they smell a bit like antiseptic), warm blankets, and very comfy pillows, maybe they could call the room 'Chemo Camp' and then decorate it with balloons, streamers, bear rugs, and mounted deer heads? On the other hand, that might not be such a good idea. One popped balloon or one hallucinating patient who either has a flashback or thinks the decorative fixtures have suddenly come to life could ruin the day for everyone.

Anyway, back to reality…

I began talking to Janet, who was so full of fright that my eyes welled up with tears for her. This was her first day of Chemo and surgery is looming only a few weeks away, due to the positioning of the cancer in her body. While her staging of cancer isn't as great as mine (II vs. IVa), the two tumors on her lungs need to be shrunk considerably before they can operate. She's in major pain. The tumors, one each on the right and left main stem bronchus (the tubes that transition into your lungs from your trachea and allow you free-flowing oxygen), cause each breath to be constricted, thus reducing the overall circulation of blood-filled oxygen throughout her body. This restriction, in turn, has caused oxygen starvation throughout her system and is actually mimicking what might best be understood by most as organ-wide inflammation. For instance, the inflammatory response was so high in Janet that her M.D.'s initially believed that she had a combination of rheumatoid arthritis and rampant MODS (multiple organ dysfunction symptoms). In any case, she's in a LOT of pain. When she first arrived she could barely walk (wheelchair bound). It wasn't until they started an I.V. with high levels of both Benadryl (diphenhydramine) and Morphine that her pain subsided and she wanted to talk – and boy did she want to talk.

Her sister (Catherine) and her brother-in-law (Ben), both in from out of state, hovered over her like a mother hen hovers over a chick. It looked very sweet. After they went back to the waiting room Janet told me she wished they'd quit hovering and then admitted that she needed them to hover. The situation was infuriating to her. She wanted her independence, was used to being independent, and now knew that she couldn't be independent and have any quality of life. Frustrating. I empathize.

The next words out of Janet's lips were these, "*I never thought this would happen to me. I can't believe how awful it is. I used to watch these shows on Lifetime where people were diagnosed with cancer and now I hate those shows. I can't believe I've got* _cancer_."

While the words she spoke were interrupted by intermittent, tiny sobs and broken breaths one word and the emphasis she chose to put on that word came through loud and clear – *cancer*. Imagine as if that single word were hissed through the lips of a serpent. Janet feared that word – respected it – and her body language said so. Even as it passed through her lips she averted her head as if she might accidentally see the word sort of slither away from her. When she turned back towards me tears had filled her eyes. Anyone could see that she thought of cancer as a death knell too early in life.

Within seconds I had engaged her in conversation about the type of cancer that had invaded her body and what the protocol was for treating it. She had a fairly firm grip on what was to be expected and what the doctors were hoping would happen. She also seemed to have almost no hope in the words she repeated. It was like listening to my son recite for the umpteenth time our encouragement that if he gets a good education on the anatomy of bugs (or whatever) that his career opportunities might one day blossom so that he's no longer simply making 'chore money.' Janet, like Brance, at that point, was more than happy with chore money (just getting along in life) and didn't fully understand anything beyond that.

I moved two chairs closer to Janet because we were both too tired to speak loudly across the room to one another. She seemed to appreciate my consideration. It was then I became bold.

"Janet, may I have permission to say something to you about the cancer in your body?"

She hesitated but nodded her okay.

"Janet, don't be scared of cancer. I know that the word cancer is scary but it's just because most people hear or think about it in the most devastating terms. To me it's just another one of those 'things' that happen to a body for reasons we sometimes can't explain. The 'good' thing about cancer is that it isn't like the flu or a cold. You can't get it by just breathing germs from someone and it doesn't mutate as quickly as a virus. The bad thing is that people often don't find out they have cancer until it's all over their body – kind of like having the flu and waiting too long to go to the doctor to be treated for it. But, in your case, my case too, they know what type of cancer you have, they've told you they'll be able to operate, it's at a relatively low stage, and the worst part is what you're going through now – I know it is for me. What I'm telling you Janet is that you shouldn't respect cancer anymore than you respect a common cold. You've got to treat it differently but at least it can be treated. With a cold you just kind of have to wait it out and hope your body can overcome the effects. With your type of cancer, you're not going to die from it."

I went off on a few rabbit trails during my discourse but she didn't seem to mind. At the end of my 'talk' her body was more relaxed and, for the first time in about ten minutes, she smiled. I did take into consideration that it could have been the drugs kicking in, but I also decided that some of what I'd said had gotten through.

"What type of cancer do you have and how long have you been doing Chemo?" Janet asked me and nodded towards the three bags of solution hanging from my pole.

"It's my second week. I go 5 days a week for radiation therapy on my head, neck, and chest in the room across the hall and then I come in here and do chemo. I've got what's called oropharyngeal cancer and I've been staged at IVa."

Her tired head shot up from her pillow, shock etched across her face. *"Stage four A? Isn't that bad?"*

I laughed and grinned like a fool (which made the etching on her face deepen a little – I think that she considered sharing her IV line with me. *"Well, it's not as bad as being dead or being audited by the IRS but, yeah, it's not real good."*

"What's going to happen to you?"

"Janet, I'm going to get through this. Just like you. I've already had a major surgery (I showed her my neck, she grimaced at the scar and my description of what the surgeons removed) and may have to have another one before it's all over with. Whatever it takes, it's just going to take. I've had other problems and will probably have more before I go home to be with the Lord. For right now, I'm pretty calm about this because He's here at home with me."

Snort!

The 'snort' was the first sound of life I'd heard from Greg and, as with most snorts of the caliber he gave, it didn't bode well. It was kind of a harbinger of doom snort. I'll get to his/our story later.

"So, you're religious?" Janet asked.

"I'm a Christian. Some people call that religious, others call it a crutch, some call me a nut, but, yeah, I'm religious if by that you mean I've accepted Jesus as my personal Lord and Savior."

Agitated movement from Greg.

"How about you Janet?"

"Well, I don't got to church or anything but I believe in Jesus. I just don't know why He'd let me get cancer?"

"I don't know why I got cancer either but I don't think Jesus gave it to me directly – He might have, but I don't think so. I just think we live in a fallen body, a body that's been hurt by sin, by the way we live, and that cancer is sometimes a result of living in a world that evil is allowed into. Since you brought up Jesus, would you mind telling me who you think Jesus is? What's He like? What does Jesus think of you – of Janet?"

Talk about silence. Tick, tock, tick, tock, hmmmmm, tick, tock, tick, tock, hmmmmm, beep, beep, beep (the sounds of a wall clock, the hum of our dripping chemo, and alarms alerting the Chemo Nurses that a bag somewhere needed to be changed could be heard as if they were playing over your favorite iPod).

Finally...

"I don't know how to answer those questions. Not really. I mean, Jesus, the Jesus of the Bible, if I remember, was a really nice guy. He never got angry, He never called anyone names, He never hurt anyone, and He healed people. I guess. I mean, he died and rose on Sunday – that's why people go to church on Christmas and Easter. I don't really know what religion He was if that's what you mean?"

The look of disquiet on Janet's face was obvious. She was searching for answers she just didn't have.

Skirting the many obvious theological 'jump-in' points this lady had offered me, I asked Janet how old she was and when she said 52 I was honestly taken aback. She looked much, much older than her chronological age (I found out why later but that's for her to tell you if you ever meet).

"Janet, do you mind if I tell you a little about the Jesus that I know?" She indicated that it'd be okay and I quickly prayed that what I was going to say would minister to her. This was not a sermon I'd prepared.

"Janet, we read in the Bible that Jesus was not only a good man and a good teacher but that He Was and Is God. As you said, the reason we celebrate Christmas and Easter is because Jesus decided to come to Earth as a human, that's a fancy word called the Incarnation, and to live among the people He'd made – in other words humans – and then He rose from the dead, that's called resurrection. Did you know that He was a pastor whose ministry only lasted about three years and

that after those short few years He was killed?"

She nodded hesitantly.

"Did you also know that Jesus was almost 20 years younger than you when He willingly died a horrible death, a death more horrible than anything we could ever suffer from cancer or a car wreck, or even torture by the hands of other people? The reason it was so brutal and horrible is because Jesus wasn't dying for things He did – because He did absolutely nothing wrong, even the judge who sentenced Him to death admitted that Jesus was sinless and that He was pure and innocent. What made Jesus' punishment and death so horrible is because when He died, while He was suffering, He asked God the Father to allow Him to be punished for every single, solitary, bad thing that you and I and everyone who has ever lived or will ever live will ever do. When we do things that aren't pleasant to God, that's called sin and it makes God very unhappy – sometimes mad – but always sad. We're told that when Jesus died, He took to His grave ALL of the things that make God mad or sad at us and they were buried with Him. Janet, what happens to a pet, no matter how much you love it, if it dies and you bury it? Is it still around or is it gone?"

"It's gone. You can't get it back."

"Right. So, when the sins Jesus took with Him to His grave were buried, they were gone – forever. Period. No coming back."

"But, what about when He came back from the dead?" Her eyes were piercing now, as if she were inspecting me for any amount of falsehood, though she still wasn't certain where this was going. *"Didn't they come back with Him when He got back alive again?"*

"Janet, that's a good question. Here's what happened. When Jesus, who is God the Son, died, His Father decided that every sin for which Jesus had died for would be forever forgiven as long as the person who had or will commit them would accept His Son's payment for those sins. You see, sin is just like a debt. It's something we owe someone for. In this case, God initially made us perfect – starting with Adam and Eve. Since that time we've been really doing ourselves in by sinning in ways our original parents probably never even imagined. Each sin is like a red mark against our name and against God's name since He's the One who created us. So, the ONLY way to get those red marks removed was to have someone come up and pay our tab, so to speak. That person is Jesus. So, when Jesus died, it was like He said,

cover Me in as much red as you need but let Me take on their debt. I'll pay it all. Once it's paid, I'll return and give them the chance to become the person We wanted them to be in the first place, only they won't have the weight of debt hanging over their heads. Janet, do you know what redemption is? Do you know what it means when you redeem a coupon at the store?"

"It means you trade something in for something new?"

"Right! And, what happens to that coupon you redeemed on something new? Can you use it again, or is it all used up?"

"It's all used up?"

"Right again. But, what does the store do to that coupon you just used for the new thing?"

"Oh, they tear it up so it can't be used again. I used to work at Sears and sometimes people would try to reclaim a used coupon but we couldn't let them do that because it had already been used by the original owner."

"Janet, that's what Jesus did for you and for me. When He died and was put into that grave He took with Him all the coupons of debt, of sin that you and I have or ever will accumulate and carried them to His Father. Even though it didn't happen like this, I like to imagine that Jesus carefully placed each and every coupon out on a huge, big ol' desk, each coupon bearing the name of a person with all their sins on it. Then, God the Father, looks down on all of those coupons, all of those certificates of debt, maybe Lonnie Honeycutt's being the most stained with red check marks, and says to His Son, Jesus. "Jesus, who is going to pay for Lonnie's debt to us? It's a really big bill and there's no way he can ever pay for it himself." Then, Jesus smiles at His Dad and says something like, "If Lonnie will accept my payment for his debt and willingly turns his life over to Me so that he can truly be free and live the life I've always wanted him to live, I want to redeem Lonnie's coupon. But, it's up to Lonnie. It's still Lonnie's decision. I want to do the same for Janet. That coupon has everything on it that Janet has done or will ever do, that is offensive to Us. It's full of red. But, if she'll accept Me as the redeemer of her coupon, I'd like to pay the price that she'd otherwise have to pay."

Jesus Father looks at His son like a judge looks at a familiar but known criminal – wanting to show mercy but also knowing that justice has to be served and He asks, *"What type of payment do you offer for Lonnie and Janet and all the rest of humanity."*

Jesus steps back from His father and hold up Hands. A light shines on the young mans body and even though blood covers Him from head to toe, gashes hang with flesh from the torture He'd received just hours ago just before and while He was on the cross, and even though He's been so hideously beaten, beaten so that He doesn't really look human, Jesus smiles. *"I offer as payment the ONLY THING you and I can accept as payment. I offer a completely pure, sinless, debt-free life, given up for those who have sinned against Me, knowingly or not. I offer My life for theirs. I offer the life of the One who made them in the beginning, Who sustains them even now, Who loves them eternally, and Who never had to face mortal death but who did so because I knew they could never repay the debt they owed to Me themselves. Since it is to Me they owe the debt, I ask that You accept My payment for them so that those who will can live with Us forever and ever."*

The Father smiles, agrees, raps a heavy gavel, grabs His Son and, together with the Holy Spirit, they rejoice that all the coupons have been redeemed. With that Jesus scoops them all up, hands them to the Holy Spirit and says, *"Okay, here's the plan. Before the people are going to catch on to what just happened, I need to go back and visit with them a bit more. So, you take these redeemed coupons, keep that one for Lonnie handy, he's going to really be excited about it, let me get cleaned up, and in a couple of days I'm going to go back to the ones I just left. After they see me I'll tell them to spread the word that I have power not only over life but of death too. Once they start telling everyone about what's just happened, You get ready to start redeeming those coupons each and every time anyone says 'Yes, I'll accept Your payment for me' and truly wants Us to help them change their lives. Of course, You and I both know that some people will 'just say the words' but We'll know so, if they just talk the talk, the coupon doesn't get redeemed until they really mean what they say. If they don't really accept My payment for them, if they're just agreeing as a kind of 'get out of jail free card,' their coupon will be given back to them at the time of their death, unredeemed. Also, once a coupon is redeemed I want You to throw it into the Sea of Forgetfulness so that no one, especially the devil, has any access to it again. That'll really irritate him. Got it? Good."*

I gave Janet a couple of seconds to grasp what I'd said and then I continued, "*Janet, three days later, on Sunday morning, Jesus brought His own body back to life, came back from the dead and do you know what He used to show that He'd redeemed all of our debts? A redeemed body! I mean when He came out of His grave, the tomb He'd been laid in, His body was completely NEW. Even though it still bore the scars from His old body so that people would know who He was, everything else about it had been changed. Gravity, time, space, nothing had a hold on this newly redeemed body of His. Oh, He could still touch, taste, smell, hear, see, and hug people but His body was perfect – it was never, ever again going to die or hurt or even get old.*

Better yet, He went around and started telling people that the body they were seeing now, a body that used to be dead but was now alive, was one they could have, too. All they had to do was accept the payment He'd already made for them.

Of course, some people believed Him. Some didn't. Some do today. Some don't. But, here's the point, Janet: Jesus is NOT mad at Lonnie. He's NOT mad at Janet. Does this make any sense at all?"

Janet had closed her eyes and for long, long moments she was quiet – so long that I thought she might have drifted into a restful sleep. Finally, Janet opened her eyes and just stared at me. Honestly, it was kind of eerie. I could see the drugs had been working on her because she looked a bit loopy.

"*It makes sense. A little sense. But...*" There was another very long silence, punctuated by tears welling up in her eyes and when I heard her voice again it was a bit more raspy than before. "*I know that the Bible says that Jesus, since He's God, can forgive sins before we believe in Him when we accept Him as God and Savior but... what about the things I've done after I tell Him I want him to be my Savior?*"

It was my turn to choke up a little – not just because I felt sympathy for Janet but also because I could empathize with her. I know what it's like to personally know, without a doubt, that I've let my Lord and Savior down even after telling Him I'm sorry and trying to do what would be acceptable in His sight.

"*Janet, remember that we talked about the redemption of coupons?*" She nodded. "*You said that when you worked at Sears sometimes a person would come back in and try to use the same coupon again, right?" Another nod. "Were they allowed to?"*

"No, because they'd already cashed it in and it was either torn up or marked through."

"Well," I smiled. "You know what Jesus would tell us if we tried to use the same old coupon that He'd already redeemed? He'd say, 'Nope, can't do that. I've already used the one with Janet's name on it. Lonnie's too. They're mine now and nobody else can ever have 'em. Since there's only one coupon per person, you don't have any left. You might want it back but you can't have it back. All the debt that was on the ticket has been wiped out. I paid for it all and I'm not putting any of it back on your account. If I did that I'd have to die for you all over again and I'm NOT going to do that. So, sorry, you're out of luck. You're all mine. Besides, Janet, even if I wanted to get the coupon back I couldn't because I've already forgotten where it is – it was put at the bottom of the sea so it might as well be as far as the East is from the West as far as you're concerned.'"

"*Does the Bible really say that?*" She was staring at me again but this time there was less dopiness in her eyes and more desire for the truth.

"Yeah, it really does. I mean, it says it differently but it means the same thing." I gently took her hand. "Janet, you don't have to be scared of God. He really does love you. You know what you've done that isn't right and so does He. But, He's willing to cancel out every bit of your debt, to erase every bit of sin from your soul because He's already paid for it. The best thing is that if you'll allow Him to do that, He'll adopt you and you'll actually become His daughter – an honest-to-goodness, real-life princess. Whaddya think?"

"I'm really tired but could you tell my sister where to find that stuff in the Bible?"

"Sure."

"You really seem to believe what you're saying." She let my hand go and settled back into her neck pillow. *"You have a piece of Doritos on your moustache."*

With that Janet closed her eyes and we stopped talking. I almost laughed out loud at her parting comment. Sure enough, I'd been talking to her the whole time with a small piece of Doritos corn chip on my moustache. What a bonehead. Hahahaha.

As an epilogue to my conversation with Janet I'd like to say that I don't know if anything I said actually penetrated but some of it seemed to. For those who are professional theologians, I apologize for using what you may think are base examples of the redemptive plan of salvation. Also, if you're wondering how I could have gotten so much of what I said and what Janet said accurately dictated, my laptop has a recorder on it and I used it – yeah, I felt like one of those double-naught spies that Jethro Bodine of *Beverly Hillbillies* fame used to talk about, but it was worth it.

To all who are Christians I'd like to remind you of the exhortation we're given in Scripture: *"But in your hearts set apart Christ as Lord. Always be prepared to give an answer to everyone who asks you to give the reason for the hope that you have. But do this with gentleness and respect, keeping a clear conscience, so that those who speak maliciously against your good behavior in Christ may be ashamed of their slander. It is better, if it is God's will, to suffer for doing good than for doing evil. For Christ died for sins once for all, the righteous for the unrighteous, to bring you to God. He was put to death in the body but made alive by the Spirit, through whom also he went and preached to the spirits in prison who disobeyed long ago when God waited patiently in the days of Noah while the ark was being built. In it only a few people, eight in all, were saved through water, and this water symbolizes baptism that now saves you also – not the removal of dirt from the body but the pledge of a good conscience toward God. It saves you by the resurrection of Jesus Christ, who has gone into heaven and is at God's right hand – with angels, authorities and powers in submission to him."* 1 Peter 3:15-22

The first part of this verse says that we are to set Jesus apart in our hearts as Lord. This means that He either IS or ISN'T our Lord. If He IS that sets us up for following (whether we really feel like it or not – I definitely didn't 'feel' like chatting this much) His command to *"Always be prepared to give an answer to everyone who asks you to give the reason for the hope you have. But do this with gentleness and respect…"*

The construction of this command in the original language is remarkably similar to commands that we give our children in English when we tell them, *"Always be on your best behavior so that people know what kind of parents you have."* In other words, it's not a 'letter of the law' command. We aren't being told that we should wait until the moment that someone says specifically, *"What's the reason for the hope you have in Jesus?"* It's a general command to tell everyone we can about the hope that Jesus gives us. It's synonymous with the Great Commission in which we're told to tell the Word of God to everyone who will listen. Just like manners shouldn't be used *only* when people ask us to use them, our witness to others is a continuous action. Sometimes this means that we'll come under attack just for telling the truth or for acting in a manner that pleases Christ. The rest of this Scripture is a great summary for what Jesus has done for us and offers to everyone who will accept His will for their lives. In short, 1 Peter 3 tells us that 'Jesus died for all our sins ONE TIME – the Righteous (Jesus) was sacrificed for the unrighteous (Us) for the single-minded purpose of bringing us back to God.' We're also told that God is patient (before He destroyed the world with water He waited for nearly 1000 years for people to 'get the hint' – a pretty big hint – preaching, a huge boat being built out in the middle of nowhere, the threat of a downpour of rain (which had never been seen before) but that His patience can be exhausted – after the Ark was built, judgment came. Finally, we're told that we are saved by the resurrection of Jesus who holds ALL authority in His hands. All-in-all, if we were to only study this one passage, we'd get a pretty good glimpse into the condition we're all in before asking Christ to be our Savior, our condition after accepting Jesus as Savior and some of what we have to look forward to because of our decision – life with Jesus FOREVER!

So, I encourage you… the next time you have the opportunity, step out on a limb and do as Jesus commands us to do, tell people about Him. Don't worry if you have the right words. Don't worry whether or not you're going to 'mess it up.' Just do what you know you're supposed to do and trust that He'll take care of the rest. I promise, He can!

As I close this email, allow me to put myself 'out there.' If I've brought up issues that you take issue with or that you have questions about, please write me and let me know. This may especially be the case if you aren't a Christian or if you've got 'religious background' but just aren't sure what the Bible says. If this is you, fire away – don't worry if I know you or not. I may not be able to respond quickly, but I promise I'll respond. I don't know who is going to end up reading this so, whether you're a family member, a friend, someone

I've never met or anyone inbetween, let me hear from you if have any questions.

Folks, have a happy, happy Thanksgiving! I will tell you about the conversation I had with Greg in an upcoming email.

11-22-07 From: Barbara B. and Libby B.

Subject: Dear Friends of Lonnie...

This email is going out to a select few people. You have been chosen because we know Lonnie considers you close friends. Deeper Life Fellowship Eastern Shore is asking your help for Lonnie. We are not asking you to take one penny from your tithe. But if any of you can give a little extra to Lonnie to keep them going financially right now, not as a Church, but as a family, it would be greatly appreciated.

Some of you may want to give a one-time offering, others a little bit a month. However God leads you. If you will make out your checks to DLF designated to Lonnie and Dawn it will be on your giving record for tax purposes. Please pray and see what God would have you to do. Christmas is coming for the Honeycutt family also.

Above all continue to pray for Lonnie's healing and for him as he is going through some terrible times right now with the treatments. Thanks to each of you for your consideration. Your response will be held in strict confidence.

11-23-07 From: Lonnie Honeycutt

Subject: Re: Dear Friends of Lonnie...

Ladies... THANK YOU. I know I say that a LOT nowadays without much energy to be able to do anything more to express my gratitude but please know that, in my heart, the use of the term hasn't diminished what it means to me – true thanks to those who care enough to care thoroughly.

It thrills my heart that you and Melvin are so thoughtful as to want to put my family and me, once again, before the eyes of others. My heart aches with joy that Barbara would act as a go-between on this matter. But, alas, I simply don't feel it's appropriate as it stands. Please allow me a moment to explain.

While my family and I are definitely in a financial crunch and Christmas is right around the corner, when I received the diagnosis of cancer and was told about the therapy I'd have to undergo, Dawn and I knew it was going to be tough.

Libby, you and Melvin have already asked that a special offering of gifts be made to the Wyatts, as the Pastor and family of DLF Mobile, for Christmas. I think that it is wonderful that you seek the best for Mark and his family. While I'm still called upon by members of DLF Mobile for counsel and prayer and advice, I accept such calls as a friend, a Brother in Christ, and as a man charged with the mantel of Pastor – not as their associate Pastor. To suggest that I receive 'something extra' whilst Pam and Neal aren't included, simply doesn't seem fair to me. It may be that Mark has already asked for extra offerings for them seeing as how these two fine people have 'stepped up to the plate' and been full-time with the youth for nearly half the life of DLF Mobile. I don't know so I can't comment on that. What I most desire is a joyous attitude in all things. As such, while I so appreciate the thoughts and the thoughtfulness behind the email I've read and while I acknowledge a real need, please do not send it to those I know as it stands.

Obviously, we also don't want to take anything away from Mark and what his family might receive from DLF. Further, I know that, in the past, Mark has stated that he doesn't often feel compelled to send out requests such as the one proposed because it puts 'too much power' in the asking since it comes from the Pastor directly. I guess I feel, in this case, that if Mark believes an open letter to DLF members is appropriate, it should come from him. I say this because of the aforementioned reasons but also because there's always a possibility someone would 'talk' about a specific 'friends of Lonnie' list and someone else might get offended. I'd rather have it all in the open or not at all. Honestly, our friends really are helping us as much as they can right now – take the four of you for example (Libby, Barbara, Melvin, & Regis). What I really don't want is for the same friends who care so much about us to feel obligated, in any way, just because they've received a special letter asking for help. A 'general, open letter,' if it's deemed appropriate would allow freedom and, regardless, we aren't going to think any worse of anyone anyway. ☺

Please do let Dawn and I know if there are any smaller children who need anything this year that we might be able to help with. Danielle and Brance have both outgrown clothes and shoes (many of which either are or practically are new) and both have toys that they no longer play with. We would consider it an honor to give to those who otherwise might have too little.

Barbara and Libby, as I close I want to make certain that you both know how much your special thoughts of us mean. Please do not take anything that I've said in this email to be a slight towards your heart(s). I love you both dearly. You are truly Sisters-in-Christ and I am more than honored to know you and can't wait to know you more. His and yours, RevLon.

11-24-07 From: Lonnie Honeycutt

Subject: To Robert T. – How did you do it?

Hi Bob! Lonnie again. Gotta question... How in the world did you get through this? I'm on my second week of radiation and it's about to do me in: sore mouth, sore tongue, lack of taste, less spit (a LOT less), and I feel miserable. Brother, I can't imagine what the next 6 weeks hold in store. Even with a feeding tube inserted, which I don't want, it's hard to imagine things being much better. Any words of encouragement?

(Bob's reply to me) Lonnie: I am sorry, but no words of encouragement, except it will all be over someday. What you are asking about is exactly what got to me. I heard all that they said would happen to me. I knew it by heart. The problem was, I had never experienced anything like it so it did not sink in. I thought it was unnecessary to have the feeding tube. But, about halfway through for me, I abandoned eating and even swallowing. It was strictly the tube for me. I did not know what dry mouth meant until about the end of the treatment. My mouth would foam up with mucous. I went through countless rolls of paper towels as I literally wiped my mouth out. I finished my last treatment the Friday before Labor Day. I still do not have any saliva that I can distinguish. However, I am eating and I am not using the feeding tube anymore. This coming week I am going to talk to the Doctor about removing it, along with the port-o-cath in my chest. Food does not taste like it once did, but I think that's because the saliva is not there. I can taste things better finally, but the taste is not close to the old taste. I wish I could tell you something good about the side effects of the treatments, but it is something you will just have to endure. Remember, it is saving your life.

Basically, you will just have to find your own way through this treatment ordeal. I slept a lot. The odd thing is now, I cannot sleep without something to make me sleep. That happened just after the surgery. I think I am beginning to get to where I can sleep. That was my worst week. I couldn't eat anything, I couldn't taste anything, my throat hurt and felt twisted and distorted, and I couldn't sleep. That was about a month and a half ago. When December 8th rolls around, the surgery will be two months ago. When December 31st rolls around, the treatments (for me) will have been done for four months. I am healing slowly for whatever reason from both the surgery and the treatments. It is just that way for me. I guess I can say I heal a very, very small bit each day. I am a long way from being able to eat normally. HOWEVER, I do have the acquaintance who is eight months ahead of me and he tells me he is back to normal. So, there's hope. Hang in there. I am praying and pulling for you. A lot of people were pulling for me and I have made it this far.

I hope I answered your question. Not quite what you wanted to hear I am sure. But you will beat it all and be the better for it. Bob

11-24-07 From: Mike Woods

Subject: How are you?

How are you doin? Mike.

(My reply to Mike) Whew! Mike, it's really, really rough. To be quite transparent – I'm dealing with heavy depression right now (along with some physically irritating stuff – from constipation due to the medicines to severely dry mouth and sore tissues). Plus, I'm Tired (with a capital 'T' as you see – Hey! I'm a poet but don't know it but my feet show it because they're Longfellows – haha, okay that's an old joke!)

Hope to see you at church tomorrow but don't count on it. Love, Lonnie

Week 16

From: Lonnie Honeycutt

Subject: Wednesday to Friday

Hi everyone!

Wednesday

Well, the last week has been a hodge-podge of ups and downs. I've felt good for several hours straight, felt horrible for even longer, thought seriously about whether my doctors are just guessing or if they really know how much treatment I need (you know – 'it'll probably just take a teaspoon but let's go ahead and give him a cup'), and the pain is inching, sometimes leaping up the scale. The weirdest thing as of late is that while I can only distinguish a couple of different tastes as 'good' (such as cherry Kool-Aid and, well, that's almost it – not that I think about it all that much), my nose is smelling things that I didn't even know existed in my house. In all probability, with what's going on with my olfactory senses, some of what I smell probably doesn't exist. But, most of the smells I smell, smell smelly in a yucky sort of way. Let me regale you...

I used to enjoy the nice fragrant mist that comes off a freshly opened can of cola – now all I smell is the caramel and the phosphoric acid – yum. The other day my daughter took off her socks and playfully threw them at my head. Quite honestly, I'd gotten used to the fact that sometimes a four year old girl who follows her eight year old brother around like a misguided groupie doesn't always smell that nice. But these socks... whew! They smelled like our 18-year old cat had worn them while break dancing in a garbage bin and working up a sweat. I actually gagged. Just tonight I was cleaning up (well, I call it 'cleaning up,' Dawn calls it 'moving the molt') a couple of cans of Ensure. The tops were removed and I caught the gentle wafting aroma of something that's supposed to be Milk Chocolate Milkshakes. The fact that this flavor of Ensure is the #1 seller for Ross Labs leads me to believe that it's supposed to smell okay and taste even better. Well, not tonight. These things were only about 30 minutes old (in other words, they hadn't soured) and I can tell you with much assuredness, chocolate milkshakes were not what I smelled. Instead, something I can only imagine as the residue from the recessed bowels of an heretofore non-sterilized 10,000 gallon mixing unit had been sucked up and placed in the two bottles of Ensure I received. Imagine moldy cheese. Imagine someone trying to disguise the taste of the same cheese with dark chocolate. Now imagine that instead of pure dark chocolate they used congealed chocolate flavored buttermilk and swirled it all together. Okay, you've got the picture of what climbed into my nose and held on for dear life.

Since your taste buds are connected to your nose buds (I mean olfactory nerves) and vice-versa, you might imagine that foods taste equally as bad. Not really. Most everything (Cherry Kool-Aid for example), just tastes bland. Really bland. Bland to the Nth degree. So bland that if they were to make a movie about it there would be only one actor and the camera would focus squarely, but through dimly-lit shrouds, on Hayden Christensen (the actor who played Anakin Skywalker of 'Star Wars' fame) for two solid hours. Keep in mind that during his entire performance, the actor would be doing his best to remain 'in the character' of Anakin BEFORE the force started getting to him and giving him a range of emotions. For those of us who need an older comparison – think of Mr. Spock (Star Trek) in deep meditation while on a fist full of Valium. That's the kind of bland I'm talking about when I place food in my mouth. I tried a couple of spoonfuls of Blue Bell Tin Roof ice cream tonight. Normally this is my absolutely favorite treat. I'm talking I'd choose it over a tenderloin (and for those of you who know how much I like tenderloin, 'nuff said). The first bite was... underwhelming. It was cold and wet. That's about as far as I can really describe the taste of the first bite. The second bite was cold, wet, and grainy. Yeah, grainy. Isn't that weird? It was like someone had taken ashtray sand, coated it with something brown and tasteless, threw in a few lumps, and froze it all. That's what I tried to eat. I got through three bites before pouring it down the sink. Steak tastes like fiber board. Minced chicken in chicken soup tastes like I'm eating small pieces of string.

So, you might wonder how I'm getting through eating? Mostly I hold my breath and swallow. Yep, that's about it. I try not to eat much of anything that requires chewing because my mouth and gums have started to crack and shred fairly easily. Yum, huh?

Friday

It's taken me three days to get this email done if that tells you anything about how my days have been going. Yesterday and last night were the worst so far. My mouth is so dry that I try not to even breathe through it. I'm going to the docs this morning for IV fluids and nausea meds because I've been vomiting for the last 15 hours or so. When I swish water around in my mouth it tastes like sodium and when my throat contracts to swallow I vomit. I've only been able to eat one half of a pear in almost a day. It's strange to be so hungry yet not have an appetite. I don't want to sound like a complainer but I don't know how I'm going to get through the next several weeks emotionally. I thought the chemo was going to be the worst part of things but it's the radiation I fear now because of what I'm starting to experience daily.

I've had a lot of people email me who want to know what's going on so I'm going to cut this short. I'm on painkillers 24/7 now – via transdermal patches and oral meds. But, to tell you the truth, I can't tell any difference in the levels of pain whether I'm on the meds or not.

Thanks for all your prayers! Keep praying because I need it. Lonnie

11-30-07 From: Cindy C.

Subject: Re: Wednesday to Friday

I'm crying and praying and praying and crying. That sounds worse than horrible. The yucky odor syndrome may be a B12 deficiency.

Know that you are loved. Cindy

11-30-07 From: Lonnie Honeycutt

Subject: To Mom

Hi Mom! Thought I'd write you a short note just to say I love you dearly.

Things on my end have been the pits but it was GREAT to hear about Gay's grades.

Mom, I can't remember a time in my life when I've felt this terrible. Emotionally it is so devastating. I'm surrounded by people in the chemo ward who are just having chemo and even though their treatment is further along than mine, I'm having so many problems. Sorry to complain but I know you'll keep me in your prayers. Miss you a lot. Love, Lonnie

Week 17

12-02-07 From: Eddie Honeycutt (Mom)

Subject: Re: From Lonnie to Mom

Hi, I got your email and am just now getting back to you. I just want to let you know that it's o.k. to complain all you want to, I don't care. I placed you in the Lord's hands when you were born and He has kept you in His care, so Baby don't give up no matter what for you are loved not only by me but by the Lord. So you just complain all you want – He and I WILL understand. Know you are loved. Love, Mom

12-02-07 From: David H.

Subject: How You Is?

Hey Lonnie, Just wanted to see how you be. I tried to call a few times. LOVE YA MY LITTLE BUDDY!!!!!!!! Dave

(My reply to David) Dave, I just got back from the hospital about 15 minutes ago. I feel a lot better than I did a few days ago but that's not saying much. I've still got 2/3rd of the treatments to go (about 6 weeks) and it's almost a foregone conclusion that a feeding tube is in my future. Who knows, though? Right?

Anyway, I appreciate you calling and emailing. I can't talk right now because the acid I was vomiting scalded my vocal chords (yum).

Hopefully, once all of this is over with and get my taste buds back you can treat me to some of your world class steaks and pork chops (I had a dream about them last night – no joke). Love you David! Lonnie

12-07-07 From: Lonnie Honeycutt

Subject: Update from Lonnie and the 81-Year Old Atheist

What an interesting season this has turned out to be.

With my good and bad days becoming almost indistinguishable – they're all kind of like bland, grayish days (I think I have more of an idea of what Jesus was talking about when He said, in the Book of Revelation chapter 3, verse 16, that He'd rather have us hot or cold but not lukewarm. The word for 'lukewarm' used in this passage is the Greek word 'chliaros.' It means, simply, tepid. In other words, it's not hot enough to be any good and it's not cold enough to be any good. When my children taste something that's tepid they have a sound for it, 'yechhh.' So, for the most part my days have been 'yechhhy.'

Of course there have been very bright spots in the yechhhiness and I welcome and await those bright spots. Most often the bright spots surface when someone calls just to say, "*I'm thinking of you*" or "*Is there anything you need*" or some such greeting or query. Even though both parties instinctively know that there's very little that can be done to make my day intrinsically better, it really is the thought that counts. Plus, I know that if I were to ask the person calling to check on something for me they would make a genuine effort to help me in whatever capacity they could. That's an abundance of solace. Then there are the get-well cards, the financial support, the food, the musical aides (from Lance – a very good friend of mine) and the rides to and from my treatments (these have been especially helpful since even my radiation treatments have been zapping me more than usual – no pun intended). With so much in our lives seeming to be going topsy-turvy (my illness, Dawn needing to find a new job, my own business drying-up albeit temporarily, hopefully), and probably a half-dozen other things no one needs to know about, your prayers mean SO MUCH TO ME. Know also that I'm taking the time to pray for others as I get the requests. It's an honor and a privilege.

Okay, onto happenings in my life thus far... A neat one first!

Normally, around Christmas I like to go to the Mall by myself, grab a cold drink and just watch all the hustle and bustle. Well, since I can't go to the Mall right now because I have to watch my white blood cell count and with so many potential 'sick' people at the mall – not those with poor taste in shoes, but those who are actually ill – it's not a place I can afford to chance. Also, I can't have cold drinks since they burn my tongue. With all this in mind, I chose to visit Big Lots the other day.

Big Lots isn't exactly a mall but it is 'mallish' (with the exception that there is a conspicuous absence of eateries on the inside) in that lots and lots of people travel through it at a fairly hectic pace. The isles are small and you have to brace yourself to get around the turns and bends of the same so tensions can run quite high – especially since breakables are almost always in the easy reach of any toddler.

I found a place to stand and I waited. As I waited and watched I casually sipped from a bottle of Spring Water that tasted, to me, as if it were emptied into the container after having dripped directly off a stalactite from the Salt Lake itself. Sure enough, just like at the mall, it soon became pretty frustrating seeing families going by in hurried and harried fashions (some quite a bit more harried than others depending on the number of children they had in tow and how many conversations they were trying to carry on at once). My spirit, sensing that 'it was about time,' prompted me into action and I found myself walking casually through the crowd, observing situations as if I were casing the joint or sizing up my competition. Soon, I realized that there was no competition and the joint was HUGE. I made ready and, when the moment was right, once I saw a disaster about to happen – an argument, a spilled drink, a mother with too many grumpy, tired, screaming kids on her hip and one too few nerves – I went into action.

Armed with a couple of plastic, a few assorted wrapped pieces of candy (suckers), and a big smile, I calmly walked over, thanked the woman for shopping at Big Lots (as if I worked there – you know as many times as I've done this, regardless of how I've been dressed, no one has ever questioned me), and asked if I could do anything to help. As usual she said 'no' at first because I'm a stranger. Then, she noticed that my shirt had a Church logo emblazoned on it with the words *The Church Has Left The Building*.' She calmed noticeably. I took a moment to distract her children – they were already a bit distracted just from having a stranger enter the fray – and I asked them if it would be okay with their Mom if I gave them a sucker? They nodded – a shaky, uncertain, twisting nod (the kind I give when my wife wakes me up in the middle of the night asking if I'd mind going into the bathroom to root around the back of the toilet for the sole purpose of killing a wood spider she's certain is bent on either world domination or attacking her derrière when she least expects it). It isn't the best start, but it's a start.

I glance back at the adult stranger I've now known for all of maybe ten seconds and smile at her, trying to exude a reassurance that I'm not secretly carrying out a 12-step plan designed to lull her into a deep sense of relaxation so that I can abscond with her heretofore disquieted heathens – heaven forbid, I'd rather take on the rabid, derrière-munching arachnid who has made his stand behind the porcelain god in our lavatory and is planning an after-midnight assault.

I could see that she was mentally having to fight through years of protective maternal instinct, hacked away I suppose by all the hype of the now ambiguous holiday sales preseason/season presentations for a number of holidays or holy days (depending on whether you're religious or not) including the three biggies of December (Christmas, Hanukah and Kwanzaa). As an aside, I've noticed that while you can mention either Hanukah or Kwanzaa without much eyebrow raising, mention a clerk should have a 'Merry Christmas' and the clerk to whom you've wished this upon silently tenses (as if he/she suspects that a hidden supervisor is secretly monitoring their reaction and response, ever-ready to call in squads of ACLU goons at the slightest inference of preference of Jesus over African culture or dreidel spinning). Maybe we should rename the season 'Consumermas' or something similar since that's what it's becoming (bold, in-your-face consumerism).

In any case, Christmas or the holiday that's kinda-sorta-like-Christmas but not really (only the colors, songs, and sales prices), and other holiday sales as well as the ever-present 'help' in the form of employees whom you have never seen in between these seasonal sales (unless you're trying to buy a paper from the side of the road or you happen to frequent midnight jam sessions at the heavy metal-laden SKREACH room near downtown – whose destination changes quite often because of noise ordinance issues), has weakened her defenses and the mother smiles back. I can see that she too knows, inwardly, that even a tiny respite would be welcome.

After another full minute of cajoling, commenting on how pretty *this* ice-creamed stained shirt is, or how pretty *that* pair of semi-scuffed princess shoes are (or at least were), or how tough a little boy standing in front of me wearing a G.I. Joe costume *is* (even though he's holding onto his dear mother's leg as if it were his last bastion of safety for miles around), I finally get one child, just one, mind you, to open up their hands and take a sucker. I get each one to ask their mother's permission and then I unwrap the circles of flavored sugar, discard the wrappers into a plastic bag, say *"Thank You and Merry Christmas"* to the kids and then I stand to face the Mom. I smile at her and she smiles back. For a moment there is a bit of tranquility because, for one thing, I've given out all the same type of suckers so there's very little bickering ('I wanted orange', 'No, I wanted grape'). I reach into the other plastic bag, and take out a small token of my appreciation for her. It's a simple 33-cent dove candy bar with our church card placed neatly just inside the wrapper. Here's all I say as I depart:

"Ma'am, have a wonderful, Merry Christmas. Thanks for being a Mom to these kids. I hope you have a great day."

After that, I was gone. I was like the masked Lone Ranger, riding off into the sunset, my white cowboy hat glowing and my boot spurs jingling a good old song of the prairie – the only differences being that I wasn't masked, I don't have hair, I'm not a ranger, I don't have a horse, I wear very quiet sneakers and a baseball cap and the only 'prairie song' I know by heart is *Old Dan Tucker.* So, while I was wearing Levi's jeans, which, as we all know, only real cowboys wear unless they get a seven-figure income deal to wear some other kind, I probably substituted the song of the prairie with whatever contemporary Christian song I happened to be muttering under my breath at the time.

Anyway, the effect is pretty much the same. I've done my thing. I've been a hero for all of 3 minutes, made her world a bit nicer, introduced her to the love of Christ, even if it's on a very small scale, and a stranger (me) who didn't know her five minutes ago just left a way for her to learn more about Jesus Christ and the reason for the season if she'd like to. Maybe she already knows, maybe she doesn't – either way, if she calls, I'll be there. If she doesn't call me but wants to know about Him, I'm certain Jesus will put someone in her path. You can do the same thing, anytime. Consider it 'outreach on a microcosmic scale.' Amen!

I Wanna New Drug

Remember Huey Lewis & the News' song *I Wanna New Drug*? Well, that reminds me of me Tuesday. Only, while the rocker was wanting a new drug to get over a girl (or something), I wanted one that'd keep me from having a bucket by my bed. So, the new lyrics to my song goes something like this...

"I wanna new drug, one that won't make me sick... one that won't make my eyes bug out or make my head feel three-feet thick. I wanna new drug... one that won't hurt my head, one that won't make my mouth so dry or keep me in my bed. One that won't make me nervous, wondering when I'll spew, one that makes feel like I don't have the flu."

After last week's episode of vomiting from the moment I got out of a small convenience store all the way to my truck (about 50 yards –

yeah, I wonder what people were thinking too) and for a day or two after that, I decided it was time to do some hard-nosed investigation.

I was on Cispatinum (Cisplatin), now I'm on Erbitux. Let me give you a little of the skinny on Erbitux. First and foremost, it's not platinum-based. Should cost less, right? Wrong. It's about 4 times as much. It's been tested although not studied in double-blind tests against Cisplatin so it's still a shot in the dark. For those of you with a technical bent, it's a complex of recombinant, human/mouse chimeric monoclonal antibodies that binds specifically to the extracellular domain of the human epidermal growth factor receptor.

I think if you can say that 4 times really fast in pig-latin all cancer is automatically cured but since I've only made it through 3 times, don't take my word on it. In plain English what Erbitux is supposed to do is to keep in-check fast growing cells (like Cisplatin) but without the harsh side effects of the stomach upset and vomiting of Cisplatin. I'm all for that. If I were a bit more suspicious I'd say the formula sounds like something that turns you into, at the very least, a 4-foot mouse. Having watched loads of Star Trek and other *completely science-based* television shows and movies (Battlestar Galactica, Logan's Run, Pod People, the Attack of the Killer Tomatoes, Resident Evil, Frankenstein, Plan IX, X, XII ad infinitum From Outer Space – and played the game Halo), I've come to learn that when the terms 'recombinant' is combined with any other term that knits a human with some other species together it usually ends up in a national disaster. All I can say is, FEMA better get prepared because there may be a new breed of Honeycutt showing up any day now.

Honestly, Erbitux really should help with how badly I've been feeling if I don't experience any of the bronchospasms, stridor or hoarseness (I've been told to expect this one since hoarseness is already part of my life). Also, I'm having to be monitored for high and low blood pressure, anaphylactic shock (throat closing up and that sort of thing) and sudden onset of cardiac arrest. No kidding, I was told that if the last two happen I probably won't even be aware of it – good, good, now I can rest easy. ☺

Due to the nature of Erbitux, I have to be infused with it (infusion sounds like something ladies are supposed to do to keep their roots healthy or a type of herbal tea) and then the nurses sit around and look at me for an hour. Well, at least for the hour I've got a captive audience and if anyone starts to leave I can always start 'ticking' the side of my face or hold my breath until I turn a slightly alarming, though not anywhere near an emergency zone, shade of red and they'll sit right back down. Hmmm, wonder if I could try this at church during my sermon when I see someone falling asleep??

Losing Everything (Well, at least it feels like it)

Three days ago I had to shave my goatee. It had started coming out in clumps and I didn't feel that Elmer's glue was really an option. So, I shaved it off and the first thing Brance, my son, asks my wife is: *"Why does Dad look so weird?"* and *"Is he always going to look that way?"* Ah, the innocent acceptance of a dad's firstborn. Kind of warms the cockles of an old man's heart.

The hair on the top of my head is keeping it's own for now but I've been told to get ready so I went ahead and shaved again today. The hair on my chest and arms now look like something akin to a patchwork quilt because of all the IV's and the tape that holds onto follicles like hips hold onto fat. On the upside, I can now carry on a non-interrupted conversation while 18-gauge needles puncture my skin. I've even helped one nurse 'thread the vein' once – I just thought of myself as a surfer dude riding the venous waves of Lani on the Southern Hemisphere of Guyo's canal (if you know your anatomy you'll get that one, otherwise don't even bother reading that last sentence). The only difference between being in Hawaii and in the Chemo Ward was that I was in a recliner, I could only smell and taste sodium chloride instead of fishy saltwater, and I was sans swimsuit (something I'm pretty certain the nurses appreciated).

Speaking of conversing, my voice keeps coming and going, as does my energy – kind of like a manic-depressive Energizer Bunny. By the way, it's been a day or so since I started this email and the new drug does seem to be better. I still often feel queasy but I've only vomited twice. Yay!

My taste buds seem to have gone the way of the dinosaur although my tongue isn't giving up the fight just yet. If it had vocal cords it'd be screaming most of the day in pain. Actually, come to think of it, if my tongue had vocal chords it'd probably be in some foreign laboratory all by itself. That wouldn't really solve anything but it'd probably get me a lot more national media attention.

Pleading With My Salivary Glands: "*O mighty glands, my teeth, my gums, my uvula doth beseech thee, leave us not alone and dry but quench us so that bread and honey tastes as such and of gel-like mucous there's not so much. To you, I ask, spit don't split!*"

Yep, as I said in my first few emails, my saliva is drying up. I awake during the night probably some 15 times because I'm choking due to a dry throat. I reach over, uncap a bottle of water and take a swig of liquid salt – not actually salt but it tastes like it. In fact, everything liquid tastes a bit like salt (some more than others). It's getting really, really annoying – but supposedly I've only got around 8 weeks to go before I get new taste buds. Yipee!

Finally, some of the skin around my neck and face is losing integrity. I'm beginning to experience advanced signs of what is technically termed 'photo-aging.' This means that the radiation I'm being bombarded with is not only cooking the inside of my body; the effects are showing up on the outside via capillary fragility, loss of collagen, etc. So, by the time this is through I may be calling on some of you ladies to help me decide which cosmetic facial cream is the best.

My jaw line is almost always painful and it's extending into my gums. At least my gums aren't receding – yet.

Folks, I'm losing so much so fast that when this is all over I may ask your help in putting together a Scavenger Hunt for all things pertaining to Lonnie.

What I'd Like For Christmas...

I've been asked this more than a few times and I can honestly say that I've got little to want for. I've got people praying for me, people who care for me, and I've got a God who loves me.

Here's one thing that I could ask for as a 'temporary' gift. Since it's becoming more and more apparent that I'm going to be homebound more than I want to be... if you have any Xbox 360 games that you're done playing with and you'd be willing to let me borrow, I'd really appreciate that. Just make certain you put your name with the game so I know who to get it back to. I don't have the money to go and rent many (buying them is out of the question) so borrowing them to play is the next best thing. I will warn you though, I'm not a fast player. I use the Xbox 360 as a way to distract myself from pain so sometimes I just 'explore' rather than 'play.'

Greg – The 81-Year-Old Atheist

You were last introduced to Greg on 11-21-07, he was the older gentleman who kept grunting as I talked to Janet (the new Chemo patient). Sorry it's taken me so long to include this story but, to be completely honest, I'd forgotten to do so until today. In any case, after Janet had fallen asleep I began a conversation with Greg and found that he was a very interesting fellow who had led an interesting life.

One of the most interesting things I found out was that Greg had been one of the first African American men placed aboard a fighting ship in the Navy. It was a destroyer but I couldn't make out the name when I listened to the recording of our conversation. He may have said it was the Manley but that probably isn't correct. Anyway, he and I talked about this part of his life quite a bit and I found that he'd not only been in both WWI & WWII but also in the Korean War as a consultant of some type (he mumbled a bit and I didn't catch it). To bring you up to speed on his military history, he'd 'applied' with the Navy at the age of 16 because he was tired of working on a cotton farm. He didn't have a high school education, he was black, and he was underage. To hear him tell the story, none of that really mattered. The recruiting station he'd signed-up under was 'progressive' and wanted blacks in the military (he kept using the term 'blacks' so I'll use it liberally here). He didn't have a birth certificate to speak of but, then again, neither did the nineteen other young black teens who went with him to the station. Once accepted they were put to work below decks as cooks, janitors, and the like. Their quarters were a distance from the 'white boys' and sometimes he just slept near his station so as to not get into trouble. Even though the Navy wasn't very accommodating to his needs as a minority, Greg figured that he'd be able to 'see the world' better from a ship than from a field in Alabama. And, apparently, he has.

This is how our conversation began once Janet fell asleep.

"So, you're one of them pastor guys, huh? Never found much use for priests myself. Did you hear about the preacher the other day what was caught with them young boys. He had all this money out on the bed and these fancy watches and told 'em, 'y'all take whatever you want because you know what I want!'"

He waited for a response while I stared blankly at him. I couldn't believe what an upfront attack he was beginning.

"Well, it's pretty apparent that he's a poor excuse for a minister, isn't it?" I told him. "I hope the cops got him and locked him away – not only for being a pervert but for impersonating a man of God."

"So," he continued unabated. "You get your jollies from coming in here an telling fairy tales to people like her? Don't you think it's a little unfair to take advantage of her since she's so sick and all? She's likely to believe anything just to have some hope."

"Greg, I figure we're on a level playing field here. I'm just as sick as she is. In fact, I'm much sicker. Now, between you and me, I don't know which one is worse off. You're old and getting feeble and I'm in a younger but just as feeble body, speaking immunity-wise. Besides, I don't consider them fairy tales. You did notice that I didn't once mention Peter Pan, Santa Clause, or Allah."

"You think Allah's a fairy tale?"

"Sure, don't you?"

"It's just, I thought all you religious fanatics said that Allah was just another name for 'Gooodddd.'" He let the last word roll out of his mouth as if he were a preacher with passion.

"Well, it is the name of 'a' god, just a false one. Allah isn't anything other than an idol – just like the gods worshipped by people who construct likenesses of their deities on totem poles."

"So, you think that lady needs a crutch, do you? Don't think she's strong enough to face up to her disease all by herself?"

I smiled. "That's an interesting question coming from someone who is wearing glasses and two hearing aids and who is also being treated for cancer. What's wrong? Do you think you need that many crutches? Aren't you strong enough to face up to weak eyes and ears and a body that's infected?"

Greg sat up straighter. "Hey, these aren't crutches. I need these because there's something really wrong with my body. If I didn't have this stuff I wouldn't get through the danged day [he didn't say 'danged' but since I don't know who is going to eventually read this I'll soften the language whenever possible]."

"So, crutches, things that help you make it through the day, are okay, as long as there's something really wrong with you?"

"Yes." He snorted and blew his nose. "But the garbage you're feeding her isn't anything but poison. Talking about some fool who *died for sins and who is supposedly god almighty and who brings peace to all the people of the world. All we've got to go on is what other people have said is true. That's just hogwash and you're a moron if you believe it!*" His accusations dripped with sarcasm.

"*Hmmm,*" I sat back in my recliner and looked long and hard at Greg, praying that I'd know how to respond to what was an obviously hard heart.

"*What's the matter? Did I hurt your sensibilities?*" He mocked and wiped something out of his nose.

"*Mine?*" I smiled. "*No, not at all. I mean seriously, you just called the God I love and adore, the God who has changed my life forever, the God over Heaven and Earth, over Life and Death, the One who is above all a 'fool' and you've told me that believing in Him is hogwash. Believe me, calling me a moron doesn't bother me one iota. I've been called a lot worse by people who know me a lot better than you.*"

We sat there in silence for a few minutes until I nodded to capture his attention away from the New Price is Right starring Drew Carey.

"*Greg, can I ask you a question or two?*"

"*Shoot.*"

"*What's your real beef with God? Why won't you even consider the possibility that He's real?*"

Without a seconds hesitation he said, "*Sickness for one. Evil for another. If God's supposed to be all-loving then why would he allow either to exist.*"

"*But, how do you know He's supposed to be all-loving?*"

"*The Bible says so, doesn't it?*"

"*Ah, so can I assume, for the sake of argument, that we can limit our discussion to the God described in the Bible rather than the one in the Quran or the Book of Mormon?*"

"*If that's the one you know best, sure, but they're all the same.*"

"*Well,*" I shook my head, "*They're not all the same but I just wanted to wrap my mind around some kind of foundation. So, what about sickness bothers you?*"

"*It just shouldn't happen. I haven't done anything in my life to deserve this. This makes you feel lousy. And, look at you, you're supposed to be some kind of 'man of god' and he won't even cure you."*

"Who says He won't? He just may not have done it yet."

*"That's just childish thinking. It's like someone saying, I'm really first even though I came in last because it's my attitude that determines my altitude. Something stupid like that. The fact is the person who comes in first is first and the person who comes in last is last. I'm sick, you're sick, everyone in here is sick of something –
we're born dying. It's just not fair and it's not something a loving god would do if he had the power to control the health of those he created."*

"That's a mouthful. Greg, do you have any kids?"

"Sure. A passel of them. Some I haven't even met. Reckon I got about half dozen children that I know of, three who live around here."

"When your children were growing up, maturing, and they asked you to do something you had a reason for not doing would you go ahead and do it?"

"No."

"Even if they couldn't understand what your reasons were for not doing it?" My point was made and I saw it register on his face. He'd been backed into a corner, but he was agile.

"Well, yeah. But, we're talking about you being sick – with cancer. Why wouldn't God cure you – especially someone like you – of that?"

"Greg, first of all you don't know who 'I' am." I made a grandiose flourish with my arms – the I.V. tubes bounced to and fro as if they were the tentacles of some emaciated, stainless steel octopus. *"I could be like the preacher you hear about on the news who molests children or the truck driver who secretly hides bodies in the back of convenience stores, or the little, unassuming white guy who also happens to be the Grand Wizard of the KKK. But, thankfully, who 'I' am or who 'you' are doesn't really matter in this case. You're looking at sickness as if it's something terrible in and of itself rather than just being what it is. Besides, it's not like I'm going to die."*

"Heck, you might, you never know. Being a Christian doesn't give you immunity to death. Cancer could kill your butt just like mine." Greg gestured with a meaty finger as if to mark '1' on some unseen chalkboard in the air.

"That's where you're wrong, Greg. As a Christian, I am immune to death. Absolutely immune. I'll never die. Oh, this body I'm in might die but even it'll be redeemed, made alive and better one of these days. So, I don't have to fear death. Your butt, as an atheist, has one cheek in the fire and one in the frying pan so to speak. What's you're escape plan?"

Greg just looked at me. His face screwed-up in a fashion that I couldn't really read. It could have been that he either thought that I'd just crossed over the line and was about to lambaste me with a tirade on being nice to your elders or he was contemplating running from the Chemo Ward just in case I was a cancer-riddled uni-bomber. Or it could have been gas pains. Who knows. Whatever it was, the silence between us lasted a long, long time. Finally, I was prompted by the Holy Spirit to continue.

"Greg, you said you were stationed on a battleship. Did you ever see wartime action?"

"You mean did we ever kick the living poop out of people. Yeah."

"Greg, what's a depth charge like? What does it feel like when one of those go off?"

"Oh, man, it's something else." His eyes lit up and you could see him remembering the events he was about to unfold as if they had happened just yesterday. *"You drop one of those babies and when it blows I don't care where you are in your ship, it feels like it's going to rip something apart. I used to almost poop myself every time one of those things went off and they went off a lot sometimes."*

"So, you used to drop them yourself?"

"Me? Heck no. I was mostly a cook during those days. I never actually saw any of 'em being dropped. I'd just hear the command and feel the shock."

"So, how do you know it was a depth charge they were dropping?"

"Oh, the guys above deck were in charge of that. The C.O. would give the 'go,' those boys'd swing into action and pretty soon – BOOM! Hot darn, that must have scared the stew out of anybody in a sub." Greg was swinging his arms to and fro, being a little too loud, and coming precariously close to knocking over his own I.V. pump. It was fun to watch but I was glad I was over on the other side of the room.

"I've never been in the military." I continued. *"What's the C.O.?"*

"That differed depending on the shift."

"I mean, in general."

"Oh, it's the Commanding Officer. He's the one who gives the orders to fire the guns and drop the charges. You either listen to him or you're in the brig. I learned that the hard way one day and it cost me a week."

"Were there any African Americans dropping the charges?"

"Blacks? No. Not when I was there. We was just cooks and janitors and cannon fodder. Unless things got really bad me and my boys kept our butts down, tight and out of sight. Once I went up on deck when we were in the thick of things and I puked all the way back down into my hole. It was like hell had come to Earth and satan himself was throwing body parts at me. But, I got to see the world."

"Did you ever drop one yourself?"

"Me? No, boy, I'm black."

"I mean after blacks were accepted into the rank and file of the Navy."

"No, I never got that close to them."

"Then," I inquired. *"How did you know they were actually dropping depth charges and not just hand grenades?"*

Greg looked at me with a look that posed the silent question, 'does your Mama know how stupid you are?'

"Well, for one, they ain't no grenade in the world what could make an entire ship rattle like one of them charges. And, when we went back up on deck to help clean up or to disembark I was shown the depth charges and where they were packed and kept."

"Oh, so you actually saw a depth charge that had exploded?"

"No," Greg rolled his eyes at me. *"Those would be the ones at the bottom of the ocean."*

"Greg, what would it take for you to believe in Jesus as God?" The question caught him unprepared but he recovered nicely and seemed to appreciate the new question.

"That's easy. I'd believe if he would come down and speak to me face-to-face. If he'd show himself to me then I'd believe. Otherwise it's only so much hearsay and you can't count on hearsay."

"Ok, let me get this straight." I started using my fingers to count points. *"You never actually saw a depth charge go overboard and explode. You never saw a depth charge that had exploded so that it could be checked against one that hadn't. You were told where the depth charges were kept. You were told what depth charges were supposed to do. You were told what depth charges were supposed to do to subs. And you assumed that when your ship rocked it was because of one of these supposed depth charges. Further, you took the word of a superior officer and of the rank and file military men that what you knew about depth charges was correct. Did I miss anything?"*

Greg hesitated. He could tell that something had just happened. *"Um, no. I don't think so. That's about right."*

"Greg, you might just be only 81-year-old idiot I know." That comment stopped every conversation in the room. Finally, he said, *"I've never had a Christian talk to me like that."*

"Well, maybe it's about time." I shook my head in astonishment. *"Do you realize how hard it is for a pastor to talk to people who are hypocrites?"*

"What? I ain't no hypocrite."

"Sure you are. It sounds like you have a double standard for Christ and just about everything else."

"What do you mean?" Greg was obviously angry and the blood pressure machine he was hooked up to showed a rise.

"Well, you tell me that all we have to go on when it comes to my faith in Jesus Christ is hearsay – what others say is true – and that we can't trust that type of hogwash. Then you tell me about an experience in the Navy and you admit that you've come to a conclusion based on the exact same 'hogwash' you don't want me accepting, namely, the testimony of other people about something you don't know anything about firsthand. That sounds pretty hypocritical."

Greg finally 'got' where I was going. *"That's not fair. What you're doing is trying to convince me that I should accept the same evidence for a supernatural being as I should for something natural!"*

"No, no. That's not what I said, that's what YOU said. You said that you'd believe if He came and talked to you and showed Himself to you. That's what I would call wanting the same evidence. But, I don't

necessarily disagree with you, that's called plain evidence. Still, you didn't wait until you had 'plain evidence' before deciding that depth charges were real."

"That's because I KNOW depth charges are real. I've felt them. I've heard them. I've..."

"...Assumed that what you felt and heard and were told about were depth charges. That's all you've done."

"Well," he pointed a work worn finger at me. *"What kind of evidence do you have about God?"*

"I've seen Him work."

"Bull."

"Nope, not on bulls, on people. He does probably work on bulls but, as for what I've seen, He's worked on people. In the past 2 years I've seen two people completely cured of Hepatitis C, without going through any treatment protocol, mind you, and one man completely cured of Parkinson's disease. Plus, I know all three of these people personally. That's pretty strong testimony."

"It's no different than mine with the depth charges," he argued.

"Yes, it is. In at least one way."

"What?" His arms were folded.

"The guy who let you into the Navy at sixteen years old and assigned you to a battleship... did you know him very well?"

"No, he was just the guy at the recruiting station."

"How about your C.O.? Did he really care about you or were you just another number, a token to get a feather in his cap as long as none of the blacks under his care got hurt or killed?"

Greg hesitated. *"No. Those guys didn't care about me or my boys. All they cared about was numbers. That's all we was to them, just numbers."*

I gotta tell you folks, my heart went out to Greg at that moment. He'd just verbalized something that he probably hadn't really wanted to think on in a long, long time. It showed on his face. I continued, much softer now.

"Greg, even though you knew those men didn't really care about you or your friends, you still had to trust them with your life. Even with your death. You literally put your hands in the hands of men who saw

you as a number instead of 'Greg, a man of importance.' You followed their orders to go into harm's way even when you didn't understand why they wanted you to go there and you believed, at some level, that their 'word' was their bond. All that's commendable and I'd like to thank you, from the bottom of my heart, for everything you've done for me and my family and the country you and I share. I saw the Purple Heart on your license plate so I know you were injured at some point. You don't have to tell me how. But, I know you've made sacrifices that I haven't had to make.

"Greg, the reason I take the time to talk to people like her (I nodded to the sleeping patient on my left) and to you is because I know that your life is precious. Personally, you and I don't know each other from Adam except for when we come in here. But, God does know you. He wants you to know Him. He's not only granted your wish of coming down and talking to people like you and me face-to-face, He's also taken care to have what He said to us written down and preserved. I know you'd like for Him to meet with you one-on-one and maybe He will. Maybe He won't. Maybe He's like your former Commanding Officer who expected you to carry out his orders even if he wasn't around to give them to you personally. I believe that Jesus is the type of Commanding Officer who speaks to us in such a way that we can't help but understand His clear words of instruction. Further, I believe they come from the Bible. So, if you'd want to look into this 'hogwash' to see what's got someone like me, someone forty years younger than you are, so bent out of shape and on fire, I'd be more than happy to get you a Bible and even suggest where you might want to start reading from it if you'd like."

For long, long, long, long minutes all you could hear was the sound of the machines in the room and the lady gently snoring. I had no idea what kind of impact I'd had on him and I had no idea if I'd offended him. Finally...

"I don't know about the Bible thing." He took off his hat and scratched a graying head. *"Would you mind if I chewed on this and asked you some more questions later? Then maybe I'll get a Bible."*

"That'll be fine." I said.

Folks, that conversation took place a couple of weeks ago. Since that time I've seen Greg EVERY TIME I've gone to radiation (before, he was never there) and EVERY TIME I've gone to Chemo.

Death, Heaven and Back   215

Coincidence? Maybe, but I don't think so. He's still pretty obstinate but he does know that I honestly care. It took me twice to get him to hug me (I'm a hugger) but now he expects it. Pretty neat, eh? I'll let you know if this goes anywhere else. Perhaps I'm just the seed-flinger in this case and YOU will be the one with the water? Hopefully, someone down the road will be involved in the gathering. In any case, Praise God!

Saying Goodbye to Margaret Ann

For those of you who have pets, you'll know how hard this last issue hit Dawn and me. Our family pet of nearly 19 years, Margaret Ann, died earlier this week. I can't even write this without crying. Dawn got her when she fit in little more than one hand and she grew to be a constant companion to my dear, loving wife. She had the perfect little nose and was always so quiet. It was like she knew she had her place in the family and there was no way anyone was going to usurp her. I'd call that confidence. She survived countless hyper dogs, two children who never understood how little she really was, and she ruled the roost over our 85-pound watchdog. To this day, I remember the first time I met her. I walked into the trailer in which Dawn was living and Margaret bounced up to me, flopped on her back and let me rub her tummy. I'll never forget that. Animal behavior specialists would say that's a sign of my dominance. I disagree. I think it was part of God's confirmation that I could be trusted by Dawn. I miss Margaret Ann so much. That's it for now! Love you all! RevLon

Week 18

12-15-07 From: Lonnie Honeycutt

Subject: Acne, the Taste of Salt and Pain

Hi everyone! I thought I'd try to get out a brief update before my body goes back into the twilight zone – I'm telling you, some of the meds they've got me on make me have some very strange dreams.

As you probably know, they changed the Chemo drug I was getting to Erbitux. I was forewarned that it'd probably give me some acne but I thought *"What the heck? It's better than vomiting, right?"*

Well, the vomiting has become less of a problem (only once or twice a day now), but the acne – sheesh. I didn't have acne this bad when I was a teenager with hormones racing around my body as if they were tiny NASCAR drivers.

My face, head, chest, and shoulders look as if I've been attacked by a swarm of militant mosquitoes bent on the destruction of anyone with A+ blood (when you see the pics you'll know what I mean – and the pics don't do justice to how bad the rash is at all). Not only does the rash itch, it's actually painful. They've upped my dose of pain meds to 3x what they used to be and I'm still having a bit of trouble coping. In all seriousness, I may have to see a dermatologist once this is all said and done.

Everything I put in my mouth that's liquid tastes just like salt – still. Good news: I can smell almost everything now and it's the 'correct' smell. Sometimes it's torture though because while food smells good again, I still can't eat any. 98% of what I'm on is liquid right now. By the way, if you think drinking one type of drink would get redundant and boring after awhile, imagine only tasting salt when you drink anything for several weeks – it redefines boring.

As the salivary glands in my mouth have begun to decrease in function, the other mucous membranes in my mouth, nose and eyes are following their lead. I'm going through a LOT of Visine and have pretty much stopped wearing contacts – I don't have a pair of glasses or I'd wear those (glasses are one of those luxuries that'll have to wait). My lips are splitting for no reason and it seems that I have new blisters popping up on my tongue and around the inside of my mouth almost every single day (the most impressive one is about the size of a dime – ouch!).

It seems that I'm slowly but surely losing what little voice I had left but I can't tell if that's just from the inflammation caused by throwing-up or if it's a side-effect from the radiation treatments (probably a combo of the two).

A bit of good news is that I get from next Monday until the 26th of December 'off' (except for the jars full of medicines I have to keep taking). So, with any luck, I'll have some energy for my kids on Christmas day.

Let's see... Anything else?

Well, on a very bright note, we were able to help out a LOT more people with Angel Food this month. Dawn and several other folks are across the Bay loading-up cars as I type this (I was going to go but I was sick at my stomach a bunch last evening).

Oh, a note on Greg (my friend who claims he's an atheist)... The last time I saw him he actually introduced me to a couple of people he knew from cancer treatment. This is what he said: *"This is Lonnie. He's a pastor but he don't talk to you like most of them do."*

I can think of perhaps two or three dozen other ways I'd rather be introduced to someone but something must have clicked because there were several conversations started that day. I'll take anything that'll start a conversation.

Finally...

THANKS for all the stuff you've been sending us in the way of food and paper goods, etc. Seriously, I now have a whole new perspective on what it means to have stuff available when you need it instead of having to worry about when you're going to be able to get it because you have to schedule stops at the store around being sick. And now that I can't drive any longer (remember the upped dosage of pain killers?), it's even more appreciated.

That's it for now. I really do need to get some more sleep.

Love all of you! Rev. Lonnie Honeycutt

Week 19

12-16-07 From: Robert (Bob) T.

Subject: How are you making it?

Lonnie: How are you doing? I haven't heard from you in several weeks. I sure hope you are making it through this hard time. I know it is rough. Let me know how you are doing. Bob T.

(My reply to Bob) Hi Robert, I thought I'd included you on this one. Sorry about that. I sent this out yesterday I believe.

Today the rash is worse than ever. I saw my medical oncologist today for about 15 minutes. He said that he was going to order a reduction in the amount of Erbitux I'm getting because it's working 'too good.' He's also going to see if there's anything stronger they can give me to stop some of the pain from the sores in my mouth and on my tongue – that may be the worst part of this whole thing.

To be quite honest, I'm getting tired of it all. Not knowing how well the treatment is actually going while having to live through the problems of the treatment is getting to me. I can't really be around anyone so I'm homebound for the most part. Not being able to get to my own church is really bothering me. To be quite honest, I'm having a hard time not saying 'to heck with all this' and just seeing what happens. But, my personality is such that I need to know that I've done all that I can to lick this disease so that I can look into the face of my children and tell them that I did everything possible.

Hope you're having a good night. Lonnie

12-18-07 From: Lonnie Honeycutt

Subject: Feeding Tube to Be Put In Tomorrow

Well, folks, tomorrow is the day I've been expecting but dreading. Ever since the treatments for cancer began I've been getting smaller and smaller due to my inability to eat or drink much. So, it's been decided that I MUST have a feeding tube placed into my stomach. This should allow me to get the proper nutrition I need to make it through the rest of my treatments and beyond. Let's hope so.

Supposedly, the procedure is a simple one. All the doctors should have to do is feed a tube down into my stomach, shine a light towards the outside and puncture my stomach flesh with the feeding tube. That's really all there is to it.

Okay, I'm going to sign-off now and go lay down again – it seems like all I do nowadays is lay around. Sigh…! Lonnie Honeycutt (RevLon)

12-18-07 From: Libby B.

Subject: Lonnie Is In the Hospital NOW

Dear Friends, they have taken Lonnie back to the hospital. Dawn called to tell me and as we prayed we had a meltdown together.

Lonnie has not been able to eat in several days. He can barely whisper. He and Dawn both are SO depressed. Lonnie will have a stomach tube put in his stomach. Also an I.V.

Now, Deeper Life Family, is the time to pray fervently and relentlessly, to fight aggressively, to shout loudly! Dawn requested no visitors. If you know you are an exception, call Dawn. You know who you are.

When Gideon said to the Lord, "*I don't have what it takes,*" the Lord replied "*I will be with you and you will strike down all the Midianites (your enemies)*" Judges 6:16.

We must join God in fight for our Gideon (Lonnie) NOW! Thanks so much!! Love, Libby

12-19-07 From: Libby B.

Subject: Latest Update on Lonnie at 5 p.m.

Dear DLFers, I have been with Dawn and Lonnie for most of the day. Lonnie was supposed to have the feeding tube put in today but because of having his spleen removed when he was 1 day old they could not get through the scar tissue. He has more scars now from their trying to get this feeding tube put in. They will try again tomorrow in a regular surgical room, using stronger medication and go in another way. Also today they put a port in so they don't have to give him so many shots.

Lonnie's had a hard day today. BUT GOD.......! I believe He felt the prayers of God's children as we all were praying. Please pray against demonic attack as Lonnie has had some horrible nightmares under morphine. If you don't understand why they are both depressed, just go spend one day in that hospital room, and watch what Lonnie is going through. BUT WE BELIEVE HE IS GOING THROUGH and coming out better on the other side. Now that I am home God seems much larger than the mountain I looked at today.

Lonnie thanks everyone for praying.

The money is dwindling down and it looks like they are dealing with whether or not Blue Cross will allow Dawn and Lonnie to stay on Cobra, since she is losing their insurance coverage. Finances are certainly secondary, but it is a burden to both of them. Dawn is so pulled because she needs to work but Lonnie needs her more.

Let us all listen and hear God for what He tells each of us to do.

The Children's Christmas has been taken care of. I think all that Lonnie will have for food is Ensure or Boost. I will let you know more later. So glad God works through His people! We are never alone.

Love and Blessings, Libby

12-20-07 From: Dawn Honeycutt

Subject: Re: Latest Update on Lonnie at 5 p.m.

Hey Libby. Thank you for being there today and for all the support. The latest is that they have scratched Lonnie from the surgery schedule tomorrow because they are too booked. They said that they would try to fit him in on Friday, but no guarantees. They are also talking about sending him home tomorrow until they can get the surgery scheduled. Now, I'm not seeing how they can do that when he can't even swallow water!!! Even though he is getting fluids right now he is getting weaker and if they send him home without the feeding tube, he will dehydrate quickly again. Please pray for a breakthrough at the hospital and that all the doctors can coordinate this better.

Tell everyone that we said 'Thank You' for their support. I really do know that God is bigger than all this, it is just so hard to see someone you love suffering.

Also, Lonnie requested prayer for the surgery for the feeding tube. He is still VERY SCARED of having a repeat of what happened yesterday. I'm not certain how to word this request, could you please phrase it properly? Lonnie was still pretty out of it today, still imagining things. Thank you, Libby. I will let you know how the surgery goes tomorrow.

Love to all, Dawn

12-21-07 From: Dawn Honeycutt

Subject: Hallucinations

Hi everyone. Just a quick update on Lonnie. He has been in the hospital since Tuesday. He went in for fluids and a feeding tube. They had trouble putting the feeding tube in on Wednesday, he had too much scar tissue for the needle to penetrate. Since the attempt, Lonnie has been suffering from hallucinations that have not been improving.

I just got done speaking with Lonnie's nurse. Lonnie is still imagining things this morning. She spoke with the doctor and they are fairly certain it is not from the medication. It could be a lot of things – progression of the cancer, a stroke, etc. We are praying that it is just because he hasn't had any nutrients in quite a few days. Please pray that mentally he clears up quickly with no lasting damage.

They are still planning on doing the feeding tube today, though I don't have a time yet. I will try to contact you again when I have more information. Thank you for all the prayer support. Love, Dawn

12-21-07 From: Libby B.

Subject: Spinal Block

Lonnie had to have a spinal block in order for them to cut open his belly. He will not be able to use the feeding tube until the Spinal block has lost its effect. Lonnie's surgery is much worse than they thought at first.

Dawn is very concerned about the pain he will have from the surgery. Lonnie will be there until Sunday. Libby

12-21-07 From: Libby B.

Subject: Urgent Prayer Request – COMA

Dawn just called and said they cannot wake Lonnie up. The nurses are saying this should not have happened. They are not sure why. This could cause cardiac arrest. Option 1. To give him a shot of Narcan which would stop the all pain meds in his body and he would be in excruciating pain. Option 2. To get him on a respirator as quickly as possible. PLEASE PRAY DAWN CAN WAKE LONNIE UP!!! Libby

12-21-07 From: Mark Wyatt

Subject: Urgent Prayer Request – Pain Crisis

Hi, Libby, we just got home and I didn't want to call and wake you (it's almost 1 a.m.). When we (Mary Ann, me, Neal and Pam and all our kids) got to the hospital, there was quite an army there. The kids went into a waiting room while the rest of us went to Lonnie's room. Alicia came out and said that they had given Lonnie the shot that effectively wiped out all of his pain medication, so he was having a pain crisis and wouldn't let go of Dawn's hands and didn't want anyone else in the room.

We all stayed in the hallway and prayed until Dawn came out about 20 minutes later. She said that the crisis had been averted and that they were giving Lonnie some anti-nausea meds in an effort to help him relax. We also got to pray for Dawn before we left. Her brother is here now and her sister-in-law is with the kids at home. Mark

Week 20

12-26-07 From: Dawn Honeycutt

Subject: Update on Lonnie – Dec. 26th from Dawn

I hope you and your family had a really nice Christmas.
We had a wonderful day. Lonnie slept most of it, but was able to be
present while the children opened their gifts. And what a blessing we
received! There were several people who really wanted to make
certain our children were taken care of this year (and some folks who
never left their names). Well, the children had the best Christmas. I
was able to tell them about how much God loves us, and that when He
blesses, it is not just what we need, but poured out and overflowing
with blessing. It was an awesome time.

Of course, just having Lonnie home was a blessing. The tube
feeding is going okay at a very low dose, but we have not been able to
increase the amount. We need to get him up higher because right now
he is still only absorbing about 500 calories in 24 hours. Please ask for
prayers that his body will start accepting more nourishment. He
started back for radiation today and we are waiting to find out when
chemo restarts.

Love to all and thank you again for your many provisions, prayers
and calls. I am sincerely overwhelmed by the love of Christ. Dawn

12-29-07 From: Charles Lewis

Subject: Pastor Lewis: New Life Baptist, Converse, TX.

Brother Lonnie, we have been praying for you and the family during
this most difficult time in your life. Brother Mark [my brother-in-law
– Lonnie] has kept us posted about your health and we realize it has
been a real struggle. I appreciate your faithfulness to the Lord.

We at New Life wanted to be a blessing to you folks so we are
sending a check for a $1000 to be used at your discretion. We are
continuing to pray that God will shower his blessings on you and your
ministry. I believe in God's healing power and am trusting Him for
His divine will to be accomplished. God bless each of you as you
serve Him.

In His Service, Pastor Charles E. Lewis

Week 21

1-01-08 From: Lonnie Honeycutt

Subject: Re: Pastor Lewis: New Life Baptist, Converse

Brother Charles, please forgive my tardiness in getting this 'Thank You' card to you. The last several days have been EXTREMELY DIFFICULT on me physically and, quite frankly, I simply haven't been up to doing anything except lying down (there's gotta be a country and western song in there somewhere – *"All I felt UP TO was a-Lying Down"*).

In any case, your email letter could NOT have arrived at a better time. The amount of non-covered items when you're being treated for head and neck cancer is staggering. I remember opening your email and simply folding my arms and weeping. Please let your congregation, my brothers and sisters in Christ, know that my heart is filled with joy that I can point to another group of us who tries to live out John 13:34-35:

"A new command I give you: Love one another. As I have loved you, so you must love one another. By this all men will know that you are my disciples, if you love one another."

and James 2:26:

"For just as the body without the spirit is dead, so also faith without works is dead."

Charles, so many in the body of Christ attempt to talk the talk instead of walking the walk. You, as their shepherd should be righteously proud at the manner in which your flock is conducting itself.

Thank you again for your help, your service, your love of Christ, and the love you've all shown my family.

Yours in Christ, Pastor Lonnie Honeycutt

1-02-08 From: Libby B.

Subject: What Lonnie Needs

What Lonnie needs now is:

1. For his body to accept the food coming from the feeding tube and for his digestive system to work. He needs more calories. When he sees the doctor tomorrow pray that he will have wisdom

on how Lonnie can get more nutrition and calories.

2. Pray for strength and endurance for the next 3 weeks. I am praying that the doctors will see all this and that God will work so he won't have to go through this but will begin to regain strength.

3. Pray for rest and sleep.

Until Lonnie is able to thank you for himself, I can only say *"that words cannot express how grateful he and Dawn are for every big and little thing done for them (with tears)."*

Lonnie is usually not up to visitors now, but if God puts it on your heart to visit, just call Dawn first and she will be honest as to whether or not he can handle it. Lonnie had some relatively good time for Melvin and I to go visit him this afternoon and so I took that message of thanks just as I received it from him.

The Kids are just thrilled with their Christmas and we got to see most of Danielle's gifts. The kids look wonderful and are doing great. I just had to tell Dawn how proud of her I am. She went into this not knowing all it meant and wondering if she was adequate. Thank God, through Jesus Christ, she is more than adequate. Dawn is a hero among us women now. Dawn and Lonnie both give all the glory to Jesus Christ for how God has helped them through this battle. So let's keep holding their arms up so that they will not just prevail, but CONQUER!

Exodus 17:9-15

"The Lord, my banner, the God who fights for us." Libby

1-05-08 From: Lonnie Honeycutt

Subject: A Reader's Digest Time at Chemo

This is the first email I've sent out in awhile and I guess the first thing I should do is apologize. A very good friend of mine called me and said, *"At least send one that states – 'It's been a hard week but I'm still alive. I'll write more when I get the chance.'")* I'll try to heed his advice since so much really can happen over just a few days.

It's hard to know where to start so let's start at the most obvious – there are a LOT of needs out there so I'd like to suggest something that should also be very obvious... let's all take at least 10 or 15 or more minutes and spend it in prayer with our Father for the salvation and healing of others. If nothing else, we'll all be 'connected' with someone we should want to spend time with anyway (God).

Even though I'm going through what I'm going through (and it's rough), there are a LOT of people who need us to intercede for them. This week let's try to be the prayer warriors we always wish we could be.

Thanks!

I've been saying a lot of thank yous this Christmas season and I'm not about to stop now. The generosity (physically, emotionally, and spiritually) you've shown my family went beyond my comprehension a month or two ago. When all of this began I knew there'd be a toll to pay for surviving it. I even thought I had an idea as to how much that toll would be. Now that I'm within 30 treatments of ending this round of the war, I realize that I didn't have a clue as to how much the toll would be.

When this began I tried to assess things through cool, logical insight (how much money would be needed to survive, how much this would affect my income, mortgages, things like that). Basically I was keeping my concerns and my emotions on a surface level. But, when it comes right down to it, the hardest part has not been the finances (although those have been daunting enough), it has been the emotional and physical strain coupled with periods of spiritual weakness.

When my children got up on Christmas morning and were able to open gifts given to them from people they didn't know – many of these gifts weren't signed by anyone – my heart leapt for joy and my eyes reciprocated with tears of appreciation.

Days and days prior to Christmas morning Dawn and I had spent a decent amount of time telling Brance and Danielle about the generosity of those we know and don't know. Your gifts to them gave us the perfect opportunity to demonstrate what Jesus said was the greatest commandment "*Love the Lord your God with all your heart, soul, and mind, and strength and love your neighbor as yourself.*" (Matthew 22:34-40).

While it may be some time before we know how this season of teaching has gotten through to Danielle, Brance seems to have 'gotten it.' As he was going through his toys he started making a separate pile to one side. After awhile I ask why. His reply was simple: "*I don't want to accidentally open and play with those because some other little boy or girl might have a lot of fun with them. How do we find kids that haven't gotten a lot of presents?"*

While the charity in his heart made me want to cry, his challenge to me to find needy children shocked me back to the reality that we're here to serve – all while 'gearing him up' for fundamental evangelism, I'd failed to do fundamental pre-preparation. Oops – that was a 'call on the Lord moment.'

It also brought back to mind a saying that's very rampant in the Christian community – *"Don't worry, the Lord will take care of it."* I couldn't agree more that we shouldn't worry about the things over which we have no control (or even if we do have some control over it). So, I think that first part of this admonition ('Don't worry') is proper regardless of our situation. But, all too often, I think some people use the second part of the declaration as a way to shirk off personal responsibility. Here's the reason why: Even though we're told that the Lord will take care of it, how does HE usually take care of things? I think there are only two obvious answers:

1) Through miraculous acts (healings, plagues, parting of seas, etc.) and

2) Through the action of the men/women who serve him.

If I've missed any other way, please let me know – seriously.

In considering this admonition I noted that even as it concerned our condition of sin, God sent a man (Jesus – God in the flesh), to take care of the problem.

When Jesus returns, we're told that we'll be asked about faith that resides. We'll be asked if once we found someone who needed to eat, 'did you feed them?' or who needed to be kept warm, 'did you clothe them?' etc. All of these actions involve relationships and they involve God moving through man. So, when we pray for God to help 'so and so' let's make certain that God isn't asking us to help 'so and so' since, if we're His children, His storehouse is open to all of us.

A Reader's Digest Time at Chemo

Hahahaaha – okay, I guess it must be getting towards the first of April.

While I was getting a chemo treatment both Sandra and her brother Andrew made a trip to see me.

With my eyes closed they were certain that I was asleep and that they had the drop on me.

Sandra simply took a small folded blanket and spread it across my torso. Andrew had another idea altogether. Kathi, his mom, had hand-knitted me a 'neck pillow.' Through my somewhat closed eyes I watched as he looked for the best location to put it. Sandra kept whispering, *"No, you'll scare him."* to which Andrew replied. *"That's the point – he'll love it."*

Andrew had made up his mind and it was apparent what he was going to do. The neck pillow's arms were very long (she must have had either Andrew or Daniel in her mind when making it because I could have wrapped them around my head and neck almost twice.

Anyway, he moved very slowly so that he might carefully place the pillow both behind my neck and around my eyes.

Just as he got close enough for me to touch him I acted. [On second thought, this could have been dangerous because I was still hooked to an I.V. bag. But, as it turns out, it didn't matter.]

Jumping forward in a kind of sitting/lunging position I pointed my index finger at his belly with the intention of 'goosing' him. Simultaneously, I yelled, very loudly, *"Ah-HA! Gotcha!"*

I opened my eyes fully so that I could take in the spectacle of Andrew jumping back.

There I was in my chemo chair (you know the old lime green reclining one – I think I've mentioned it before) with my finger pointed towards the abs of the young man. Trouble is: He wasn't there. Neither were Sandra or the comfy neck pillow.

But, it's not like I didn't get the intended effect of a jump and some frayed nerves. No, that part went by fine. Everyone, and I mean everyone, raised up, stood up, or ran to where I was to see what was wrong. The lady directly across from me spilled her cup of cold tea and threw one of the cookies she'd been eating so that it seemed to be some sort of antiballistic missile in search of a lime green curtain.

What could I do? Realizing that I'd been soundly asleep and had dreamed the whole episode, I pointed to the I.V. bag, mumbled 'drugs' and covered my head with my hat. I was so embarrassed that even Sandra and Andrew had sense enough not to even join me in my next dream. It's weird how the mind works, isn't it?

In Closing:

People are still wondering what we need? To be honest, I don't know right now. My short-term memory is pretty bad so praying for it to get better would be great. Dawn and I still need some time away from the kids after all of this is done. They are 'upping' the dose of radiation on my neck for the next 3 weeks so it's going to really get painful now – just an hour or so ago I rubbed my neck and that action alone caused the skin to start bleeding.

Tell you what, if you really want to help right now, just continue to pray that I'll be healed, that I'll find more people to witness to, and that I'll know what it is we really need. Love all of you! I'll write more later. Lonnie

Week 22

1-08-08 From: Dawn Honeycutt

Subject: Boost Started on Lonnie

Hello all, I just wanted to send out a quick update as Lonnie's last one didn't talk about a lot of the medical stuff.

Lonnie had a couple of really good days (Friday and Saturday) and was able to visit with a couple of friends. I'm afraid since then things have not been as good. Last Friday they started a 'boost' for the remainder of treatment. The boost is actually an increased dose of radiation each treatment. After the first treatment, Lonnie's neck was burned and continued to redden over the weekend. Monday he had another treatment and now his neck looks like a combination of raw hamburger and cooked hamburger. It has also started to crack open and bleed. Lonnie went to treatment today but was not able to get radiation because he was vomiting too severely. They did send him home with a whole arsenal of things to topically treat the open sores on his neck. They said that by the end of this week his jawbone would be painful too.

They tell us that these last two weeks will be as bad or worse than the first six weeks all rolled into one. Yesterday they told us that his last radiation date would be Jan 17th but today they said that was wrong and it is more like the 21st. Since he missed today, who knows what that will do to the end date.

Please pray for pain relief, protection from infection, control of the nausea and (preferably) that we can get an appointment with Bill Johnson and that the Lord heals him completely through prayer.

Thank you all for your support and prayers. Love you, Dawn

1-12-08 From: Lonnie Honeycutt

Subject: Right on track except for a few missteps…

January 7 – Monday

Talk about not knowing what tomorrow is going to bring...

The day before yesterday was pretty good as my days go... no nausea, no vomiting, fairly high energy levels as the day wore on (early morning hours were a bit tougher but that's okay). That evening I noticed that I had an 'abrasion' spot' on the left side of my jaw (it looked as though someone had scrubbed it with a brillo pad). I 'doctored' it as best I could following the scant information I'd been given from my oncologist's office and went to sleep.

Yesterday morning I woke up feeling lousy with a capital 'L.' My face hurt, my back hurt, my jaw hurt, I just plain ol' hurt. It probably didn't help that I wasn't looking forward to getting my treatments. As I may have mentioned they redesigned the mask they'd been using to hold my head in place and this new piece of gear has no slack in it whatsoever. This mean's it is TIGHT. With the small amount of saliva I've been producing coupled with the amount of artificial spit I've been using AND adding to that the fact that my range of view from inside the mask has been cut from around 60% to 25%, you can understand why I'm having a bit of a problem.

January 10 – Thursday

I went to see both my radiation and chemo oncologists today. Boy are they a team. One says, *"Well, we're right on track except for the few missteps we've taken* (he means 'me' but uses the 'majestic plural' of language so that I might feel his empathy – yeah right)." The second doctor takes a look at my face and says, *"Good Lord, what'd they do... miss turning off a switch or something?"* His reaction is more in line with my own. The reason for concern from either has to do with my face. I've included a couple of pictures so you'll be able to see what's causing such an uproar. If you are SQEAMISH do NOT look at these pictures (while they aren't of me in a Bart Simpson thong, they're almost as disturbing).

As you can see from the pictures of my neck, I'm exhibiting classic 2nd and 3rd degree radiation burns. The kicker to this type of burn is that it's 'to the bone.' Yeah, ouch! There isn't a moment I'm awake that I'm not aware of the pain in and around my face. I got to talk to one gentleman today and he said, "*Yeah, sleep has become something of an escape for me because when I'm asleep I don't know that I hurt.*" Boy, can I empathize.

Throw on top of all that the Chemo they're giving me is creating more and more acne and the fun just never stops!!!!

A few of you have asked me what my feeding tube looks like. Well, for those of you who want to know, here are some pictures. Gotta tell ya' a feeding tube presents challenges that I never thought I'd have to personally consider. First and foremost is that I've got the option of either letting it flop around willy-nilly or taping it to the hair on my stomach. Neither are great options – the tape hurts while a flopping tube opens up the possibility of actually snagging it and pulling it out prematurely. I usually just wear a nightshirt and hope for the best.

Bill Johnson Prayer Time

Dawn drove me to the Municipal Civic Center tonight and a couple of the prayer warriors from Bill Johnson's team (Brent and Kyle) came over to pray for and with me. They were nice young fellows whose faith seemed to be strong and whose care for others definitely showed through their actions – it was getting colder and it was starting to rain yet, there they were, praying for others. About 12 hours later found me at a luncheon with Bill Johnson. Actually, I wasn't going to the luncheon, I was 'invited' to be the 'man on the mat' by some dear friends of mine who wanted Bill to pray for me in person. That was accomplished as Bill walked through the door. Though God, for whatever reason, hasn't healed me of the cancer or, at the very least, the residual effects of the cancer I'm experiencing, Bill took a few minutes of his time (as did around 20 other men) to pray that the Father's will would be done in my life as His will is done in Heaven. I am so happy to have received this prayer – not just because I want to be healed of cancer (and BOY do I want to be healed) but because some people whom I didn't expect to be there (such as Mike Woods, one of my associate Pastors), were.

Guys and gals, please understand that when I say I covet your phone calls and your letters, I REALLY DO COVET THEM in the most positive manner. I feel as though I'm a man trapped within a familiar prison but a prison nonetheless. Knowing that there's a church, a congregation, meeting together on the Eastern Shore because the Lord caused me to plant it is pretty difficult to take when I haven't been there for a single service in almost 3 months – whew! Praise God He is who He is and that He has people in place. Thank all of you for being my friends and family.

Something I Need

I'm always being asked what I need, if anything. Okay, I've found something that I need.

Since my skin is so burned, wearing shirts is incredibly difficult, I'm having to cut the pull-over shirts I have at the collar so that they don't rub against my wounds and make them bleed – actually the bleeding isn't as bad as the pain. So, if you have any old pullover shirts (large or extra large) that you wouldn't mind me destroying for the sake of comfort or any tank tops, I could really use those.

Please continue to pray for my emotional stability because I'm beginning to wear down. Love all of you! Lonnie

1-12-08 From: Cindy C.

Subject: Re: Right on track except for a few missteps…

OH Dude! I'm not very squeamish but those pix make me wince. What do you dress them with? Don't they make something that can anesthetize that skin?

I love you guys and I'm praying for you but it makes me cry. Cindy

Week 23

1-15-08 From: Lonnie Honeycutt

Subject: Treatments Delayed

Hi everyone!

I went to the physician this morning and was told that due to the damage done to my skin that it would be at least 1 week but more than likely 2 - 3 weeks before I can resume treatments.

I'd also like to say PRAISE AND THANKS TO GOD and to you for all of your faithful prayers because today has been a relatively pain-free day. Believe me, when one of those days comes along you notice. So THANKS!!!!!!!! In Christ, Rev. Lonnie Honeycutt

1-17-08 From: Frances W.

Subject: Prayer Update – SFUMC

Hi Brother Honeycutt, I am typing the prayer updates for the Spanish Fort United Methodist Church for the next two weeks and I would appreciate you sending us an update on your condition. I pray you are better. In Christ, Frances W.

(My reply to Frances) Hi Frances, Thanks for contacting me.

At this point in my cancer treatment I'm on hiatus due to massive burns I received from the radiation I was being given. My neck actually started to bleed and they had to give me a break to allow it to heal. I also had to have a feeding tube put in place.

Once enough healing has taken place I'll undergo the last 2 weeks of intensive, very localized treatment of radiation and broad-spectrum chemo. I've been told that these last 2 weeks will hurt just as much or more than the previous 6 combined (can't say I'm looking forward to that).

Personally, this is very, very hard. Emotionally, physically, and financially this is extremely rough. My wife just recently lost her job due to a merger of companies and the pain (along with the pain meds) have worked to make me extremely depressed. Not having the energy to play with my young children (4 and 8 years old) or to help my wife with basic, essential housework doesn't help my overall attitude.

Thankfully, I've had the time to really delve into our Lord's Scriptures and to pray for those who need spiritual undergirding.

If you need more specifics, just let me know.

Thank you and thanks to everyone who pray for folks like me on a daily basis. In Christ, Rev. Lonnie Honeycutt (RevLon)

Week 24

1-23-08 From: Lonnie Honeycutt

Subject: Intense Treatments & Claustrophobia

Hi Everyone! I wanted to let you know that I'm doing great on T-Shirts now. Thanks for your donations – they helped more than you can know.

I've also started on what should (hope, hope) be the last of the series of radiation treatments. I hope to know by tomorrow (Wednesday) how many I have to go exactly.

Please pray that I'll get through this last series okay. Today I had a major bout of claustrophobia (something I usually don't suffer from) – to the point that I was sweating profusely, I became very jittery, and I started vomiting. I took an anti-anxiety pill and was finally able to get through this first one after around 45 minutes.

Also, these treatments are intense. I came home and was in bed from around 11 AM - 6 PM. Love all of you! Lonnie

Week 25

1-28-08 From: Libby B.

Subject: How is this week going?

Last report I got was last Wednesday. What did the Doctors say last Wednesday? Are y'all ready for some more food or anything? We are ready and waiting to serve you and honored to do so. Love you, Libby.

(Dawn's reply to Libby) Libby, I am sorry I haven't gotten with you today. Life has been on hold awaiting the radiation people to get their machine working again. I got the call finally and have to take Lonnie to the hospital at 4:30pm. Is that too late to get with you? If so, I can get with you in the morning. Please let me know what works best.

Lonnie is going through treatments again. At this point they are saying February 1 will be the last day. Otherwise, things have been kind of going along as they have been. We are just looking forward to the victory at the end of all this. Love you and will wait to hear from you. Dawn

1-29-08 From: Lonnie Honeycutt

Subject: A Conversation with Delores, the End is Near, and an Update on Greg!

Today was pretty interesting. First, it was the first time I've been back for both chemo and radiation on the same day. Second, there were a number of new people here I hadn't met (which led to some good conversations). Third, due to a couple of the conversations, I started processing through some of the things I've not been up to thinking about until now.

One of the conversations I had was with Delores. Delores was diagnosed about the same time I was last year (in July rather than September) with stage IV breast cancer. Like the cancer I currently have, it metastasized into other parts of her body. Unlike me, she's not been given a decent chance of cure. In fact, her chances of survival are only around 30%.

While we waited on our radiation treatments, Delores confided in me that she wasn't certain what was going to happen if she died. Not knowing if she was talking about herself and eternity or about what was going to happen to her family, I asked. While she was genuinely concerned about what her family would do without her, as am I should this cancer be the cause of an untimely death (she and I are similar in age – she's 48 and I'm 42), Delores was very concerned about eternity.

When I asked her what she believed would happen to her soul/spirit when she died, whenever that might be, Delores admitted that she'd never really considered it before. I asked her why it was that she was now considering it and what she said confirmed my suspicions. I thought that it might be because she was now facing her own mortality and she told me, *"It's because I might die at any time now and I just wonder what it'll be like. I mean, is it just like sleeping forever or do we come back as something else like an insect or an animal or maybe another person or what?"*

I smiled and chuckled a bit at her assumptions and she was prompted to ask me, *"What?"* That led us into a much deeper, albeit short, conversation about Heaven and Hell. As I recall I asked her something like, *"Did you know that there is a way to know exactly what happens after you die?"* and she said, *"No way, really?"*

Once I had her 'locked in' to the conversation, I mentioned the Bible. At this point I almost lost her because she obviously had some preconceived notion that the Bible was full of fairy tales. In fact, she told me as much. She asked me, in a tone that affirmed her skepticism of what I consider to be the Word of God, *"You don't believe in the Bible, do you?"* I answered her, *"As a matter of fact, I do. Not only do I believe in it, I also believe that it's the only Holy Book ever written that can be confirmed by history and by personal testimony, among other ways."*

"*Why would you believe in such an old book?*" was her next question. "*Well,*" I began my answer, "*Wouldn't you agree that the age of a book doesn't really matter as long as the information in it is correct and can be counted on to be accurate?*" She agreed so I continued, "*Well, that's why I believe in what the Bible has to say… because it is correct and accurate. You know, when you asked about coming back as an insect or another person, that's reincarnation, right? Do you know of anyone who has ever supposedly 'come back' as another person who is credible?*" She admitted, after we spoke for a few minutes, that no one who ever claimed to have been reincarnated, was credible in their testimony. "*What about annihilation? Does that make a lot of sense to you? I mean, do you truly believe that once we die that that's it. That nothing else ever happens to you – forever?*" Delores confessed that such a view of the 'afterlife' didn't make much sense to her. "*So,*" I concluded, "*Wouldn't it make a lot of sense to seek out information from someone who actually knew and knows what the afterlife is really going to be like? In other words, if you could get info from a person who has firsthand knowledge of the afterlife, wouldn't you like to?*" She said "*Yes*" and that one word allowed me to witness to her of Jesus Christ and what He had to say about the realities of both a literal Heaven and a literal Hell.

Honestly, I don't know if she'll accept Jesus as her personal Savior or not but I certainly hope she will. And, I know for certain that I'll continue to witness to her anytime I get the chance.

The 'End' Is Near for Me

As many of you know, if everything goes as planned, February 1, 2008 will be the last of my treatments. After that, they'll give my body somewhere between 8 and 12 weeks to heal. Once this time has elapsed, they'll send me through a PET Scan and allow us to see what's happening.

I've been talking to a couple of oncology counselors and the one thing they keep trying to get me to understand is this: 'I won't be able to just jump right back into what I was doing before.'

That's not exactly great news to me because there are so many things I feel need my immediate attention; church – concerning the reservation of a building to worship in and because there are so many things that need to get done; steady, on-going advertisement that tells others what we're all about; and a number of other things. Praise God that we've grown a little since I've been gone and high praise that the people who are in attendance are those who like to get involved.

In any case, suffice it to say that I'm going to try to 'beat the odds' and jump back in with both feet. The way I feel today, though, makes me wonder if that's going to be possible. Still, I know that with God 'the end' is often only the beginning of something new and exciting.

Greg – Revisited, Reformed, and Renewed

For those of you who have been keeping up with the 'going's on' of my life via these emails, you'll remember that a month or two ago I wrote about Greg – an older, African American gentleman who had definite reservations about the Bible and didn't mind voicing the same to me and others. As I think I told you, He and I have been able to have some quite spirited (pun intended) conversations about God, Jesus, and the afterlife. Once I had gotten through his rough exterior (it wasn't all that hard to do – just a few hugs and he melted), I found out that he's also one of the nicest guys I've had the pleasure of getting to know. Anyway, I had the opportunity to speak to him again a couple of hours ago and I've got some wonderful news. Greg, the once belligerent, almost always sarcastic man with a biting wit, who used to be an atheist (note the phrase 'used to be') is now our Brother (if you're a Christian, that is)! Yep, he told me to my face that after he'd considered all that I had told him and had confirmed much of what I'd said through other Christians, including his own brother and another minister at a church in Bay Minette, that he'd accepted Jesus as his Lord and Savior. YAY!!!

I don't know about you but I personally think that's pretty neat! Greg is now attending Sunday School on a regular basis and says that a lot of the questions that he's had up until now are being answered. He also told me that he's now telling everyone he can about Jesus and the fact that the Bible is true and the fact that people don't have to die and the fact that God is real! He used the word 'fact' quite a bit so I used it to illustrate my/his point. Again, YAY!!!

Well, guys and gals, that's all I feel up to writing about right now. I'm devastatingly tired so I'm heading to bed (in my easy chair).

Thanks for all of your prayers and well-wishes! Lonnie (RevLon)

Week 26

2-06-08   From: Dawn Honeycutt

Subject: Date Set for Lonnie's Last Treatment

The doctor just told us that Friday will be Lonnie's last radiation treatment!!! I can't tell you how excited we are. He is taking his last chemo as I write this note.

The doctors tell us that recovery from the treatment will last 2 - 3 months. The therapist warned us not to rush things or we will be doing one step forward, two steps back. In a few weeks, he should start to slowly improve. We are so looking forward to all the Lord has for us as we move forward from this experience.

Thank you to every one of you who have come alongside us during this time. Please continue to pray for healing from the treatments and that there will be no lasting or recurring side effects. With His love, Dawn

2-09-08   From: Lonnie Honeycutt

Subject: Last Cancer Treatment – Yay!

First, my apologies for not writing sooner. The last couple of weeks have been a roller coaster for me mentally, physically, emotionally, financially, and otherwise. About the only thing that's stayed stable is my spiritual walk with Christ – that's been nice.

The amount of pain medication I've been taking has really taken a toll on my body (as of this morning I've lost 40+ lbs. that I didn't need to lose). I'm praying that my throat and my tongue heal fast enough for me to begin eating at least semi-normally soon. Crushed ice has become my friend because the inside of my mouth is so blistered – I won't even begin to explain that. Yesterday saw my voice take a dive for the worst – I almost couldn't talk. Today isn't much better.

On the positive side, Friday was my last treatment for this cancer. Am I cured? I believe so. It'll be another 13 weeks before we know what the PET SCAN says. Also, I'd like to thank all of you who have given to us – the paper towels, canned fruit, t-shirts, Boost, Ensure and other nutritional supplements, prepared meals, money, and everything else has been such a blessing.

When Dawn and I sat down and went over the numbers the other night, I realized that I'd not been able to work for literally months. Since our church (DLFE) isn't big enough to afford a salary for me, I know the Lord is going to have to provide another avenue for income. So, please keep us in prayer financially. Something's gotta give (in the positive sense) either church-wise or in the way of business in the next couple of months or... well, we'll talk about that when the time comes. Suffice it to say that I'm very anxious to get back to doing some normal stuff – preaching, teaching, making a living.

Conflicting Emotions

Knowing that today is my last radiation treatment makes me giddy with happiness but it's a giddiness tempered by a kind of dread – the kind of dread you don't experience (or at least I didn't) until you've been through something like this. The fantasy I have is that after my last treatment I'll go back to doing everything I used to do immediately. Oh, maybe my body will take the weekend off but, more or less, everything will be the same. The reality is nothing like the fantasy. First, there's the weight loss – 48 pounds is nothing to shrug your shoulders at. It takes a conscious effort to bend down, pick something up, and stand upright again without passing out. As for the intake of calories, right now it's so terribly hard to swallow that even gulping down water is a chore. My salivary glands have all but shut down and, well, it's just tough. So, please pray that my throat and taste buds heal quickly because I need to gain at least 10 pounds back pretty quickly – just for the sake of energy and repair. Also, if I'm able to regain my speaking voice and energy I'll be able to present those things God has quickened in my heart beginning next Sunday (thanks to Mike Woods, Richard H., and Drew R. for stepping up in that area and to everyone who supported them).

What Has This Taught Me?

This ordeal has definitely taught me a few things. First, regardless of how alone you feel, there are others who will surround you and help you and just be a comfort – if you let them know that this is what you need. Relying on God really is harder than it seems it should be, but once we realize that our own 'bootstraps' are infinitely incapable of keeping us out of the muck and the mire of life, seeing Him for Who He is really does become easier.

Another lesson I've learned is that reaching out to others who are hurting has a healing effect on your own heart. There are many stories I haven't related simply because I haven't had the strength to do so. These stories are of a young woman (around 15 or 16) whose father was going through cancer treatments and who was so frightened she found it difficult to put into words the questions she wanted answered. A lady whose heart was stone-like and whose attitude hurt those she spoke to. An older gentleman who 'gave out hugs.'

One of these days maybe I'll get around to telling you these stories and more.

Finally, lest I run out of time again to get this email out, I've learned that having people who don't really 'know' what you're going through but try to enter into it anyway and who do their best to uphold you even though it inconveniences them, is another of those blessings that simply can't be described. Thanks to all of you who were like these – the ones who called, who prayed, who battled with me against a foe that can scarcely be described – all without expecting or even wanting a 'thanks.' Yours in the Love of Christ! RevLon

Week 27

2-12-08 From: Lonnie Honeycutt

Subject: Recovery From the Cancer Treatments…

Who knew that recovering from a treatment would be so difficult? I certainly didn't. Of course, having spoken to a dozen or so professionals at this point and having been told essentially the same thing from all of them, I knew that the next few months would be far from a 'walk in the park.' Still, I didn't expect what I've already been experiencing.

Last week I underwent the last of the radiation and chemo treatments for the cancer that had invaded my body. It was a milestone in putting this saga behind me and getting on with the rest of my life.

Today Was Different.

Monday, for the past several months, has been reserved for visiting one of two (or both) clinics and allowing my body to be bombarded with a variety of poisons or high intensity radiation. As you can imagine, I haven't looked forward to Mondays for quite some time. It made going to bed on Sunday night much less exciting. While most people don't really look forward to Monday morning, I began to almost dread it. The dread was tempered by the fact that I usually got to visit with some great individuals, all of whom were undergoing similar treatments for the same type of illness. Still, there were fewer 'sweet dream' Sundays than before. So, as I've already said, today was different.

Interestingly, but not altogether unexpectedly, I kind of missed not going to the clinic(s) this morning. Of course I didn't miss getting poked and prodded (many of the veins in my arms have collapsed and the others that remain have become so scarred that it's often difficult for the nurses to get a needle in without causing me a considerable amount of discomfort) but I did miss seeing some of the friends I'd made. I really care about these people and how they're doing and I believe they care about me (one of the gentlemen I've gotten to know rather well gave me a crate of homegrown green onions last week – it was a sweet, though pungent gesture of friendship). Fortunately, I have their phone numbers and email addresses but, all the same, today felt 'odd.'

This Monday also found me feeling rather terrible, physically. I woke around 3 AM nauseous and the rest of my rest was fitful – so fitful that by the time I gave in to getting up and getting on with my day that I needed to see a chiropractor or massage therapist. Plus, to make things even more delightful, my throat, tongue, gums, and uvula were all so sore or swollen from my last set of treatments that even swallowing water is impossible because of the pain. It's tough when you know that taking a long draw of cool water would make you feel much better but you physically aren't able to do so because of the high risk of aspiration. I've been reduced to taking short, miniscule sips of water, sloshing it around in my mouth and spitting it out. Adding any type of flavor to the water at this point makes even the smallest of sips very painful since most of the flavors that my taste buds can detect are acidic in nature. Thankfully, I know that as long as I can keep from vomiting, this issue should resolve itself in about two weeks. Knowing this helps me tremendously because it gives me a time frame within which I can work.

Weight Loss and Weight Gain

Another issue I've had to begin to seriously consider is weight gain. As those of you who have actually seen me probably remember, I've lost almost 50 pounds, 30 of which I really need to put back on, 20 as quickly as possible. But, as you can imagine, since drinking something as smooth as water is all but out of the question, eating is impossible. Even if I were to be able to disregard the very real potential of aspiration (breathing food into your lungs instead of swallowing it), not even foods whose texture is as smooth as yogurt is comfortable enough to eat. Honestly, I'm very concerned about not being able to consume enough calories. Currently, the only calories I'm getting is coming from either the Boost or Ensure that I'm pouring into my PEG tube (feeding tube). So, please pray that my mucous membranes heal quickly.

Walking Gets Exciting!

While talking to my neighbors this afternoon I bent down to pick up a small branch (they were in the midst of cutting down three enormous trees so it was the least I could do). As I rose everything started going black. I'd had this happen enough in the past to know that I was about to lose consciousness. Thankfully, I also knew enough to simply stand still and be silent.

While I know that getting exercise is important, doing so has become increasingly difficult. I remember that I used to be in fairly decent shape – doing 100 push-ups at a time was something I 'prided' myself on being able to do. Today, if I tried to do a single push-up I'd probably faint. So, instead of major calisthenics I've chosen to simply do my best at walking up and down the street on which I live. Honestly, it's a chore. I'm so absolutely tired of being tired all the time. I can't wait until I get back to some type of normalcy in my life.

Oh, well, just knowing that I'm still alive and relatively well, especially when compared to some of the other people I've met in the past few months, does my heart good. I thank God for the provision He's made for my family and me during this trial. He is good all the time! Amen! Take care!

Love all of you! Lonnie (RevLon)

2-13-08 From: Lonnie Honeycutt

Subject: I Still Need Your Prayers

Hi everyone! I'd really appreciate your continued prayers. It's been about 7 days since my last treatment and my body is still going through major turmoil. I need prayers that I'll be able to sleep through the night, that vomiting will be a thing of the past, that my throat, mouth, and tongue will stop being so sore that drinking water hurts (eating is out of the question), and that I'll just feel better in general. Feeling this badly for this long is causing me to really become depressed and that's not something I want to be.

All of this has got to be taking more of a toll on Dawn than she's admitting so I'd appreciate prayers for her as well. Thanks to everyone for everything. Lonnie

2-15-08   From: Eddie Honeycutt

Subject: Thanks for Standing With Lonnie

I am Lonnie's Mother (Eddie Honeycutt) and I wish to thank all of you who have not only kept Lonnie in your prayers but have helped him and his family in so many ways.

I know that everyone (including our own family) feels that we should be there to help them (Lonnie and his family). I can only say that if I was able, I would be there in a heart beat, but, as it is, I can only be there in my heart. Lonnie and I have been though a lot together in his life and this is the first time that I haven't been right there with him.

I have a very caring and loving son as I am sure you all have found out. He's one of those kids who grew up doing 'without' and never complained. Instead, he's always looked to find out how he could help others who need just as much or more than he or his family did. Even with physical abnormalities he was born with, even though the doctors said he would live but a few days after birth or would have bad injuries as his body grew, Lonnie just kept on going and I'm very proud of him for that.

Knowing that he's got a home church of people who love him helps a mother, this mother, sleep better at night. I've watched my little, shy, Lonnie boy grow up with his eyes centered on what those who are in the world need. Even when he went to work and people would unfairly promote someone else above him or simply not pay him what his work deserved, he rarely complained. Oh, he might throw his hands up in despair or complain once or twice but that would be the end of it. He told me that what the Lord required of anyone, including him, was that we Love God and do our best towards others. How he went from being a tyrannical terror as youngster to the man he is today is beyond normal explanation. I'm convinced that he does what he does because he loves Jesus and he has such a trusting heart. Please pray that his heart will also be protected throughout all this mess.

I wish to also say that my daughter-in-law is something else too. She has had so much put on her and has held her head up through it all and still is. She has stood by my son when so many wouldn't have. Dawn has my love and my thanks. Words cannot say what I feel for her and all of you. Let me say again thank you all for standing by my son and keeping him in your prayers as well as for the help you have given him and his family.

Every one of you (whomever you are) I love you for all you have done that I haven't been able to.

Please keep Lonnie in your hearts and in your prayers. I know my son is strong but he still needs all the love and prayers he can get.

Thank you and as I tell Lonnie "*you know you are loved*" not only by us but by Christ our Lord. Lonnie's Mother, Eddie Honeycutt

2-16-08 From: Melvin B.

Subject: Emergency Prayer for Lonnie

When Dawn went in to wake up Lonnie this morning he was not breathing. Dawn called 911. He's being taken to a hospital emergency room. Pastor Mark is on the way to be with him and Dawn. Pray! Pray! Pray! Alicia B. and Pastor Mark called... That's all we know now. We will keep you posted when we get more information... Melvin

2-16-08 From: Melvin B.

Subject: Update on Emergency Prayer for Lonnie

As of around noon Lonnie was transferred from the Emergency Room at the hospital to ICU Room 1011. He is on a ventilator. He has had some seizures while there and he has not awakened since Dawn found him unresponsive in bed this morning. The doctors say it can go either way. We know God is able to raise him up. Dawn is having a very rough time emotionally with this. Please pray for both Lonnie and Dawn. Family and friends are in the ICU 2 Waiting Room, just outside the doors into ICU 2. From Melvin (Libby is still there).

2-16-08 From: Libby B.

Subject: Update on Lonnie

Good News! Lonnie began to be responsive this afternoon. We were all encouraged when the nurse came out and told us he was responding. Please Keep Praying. On Earth as it is in HEAVEN King Jesus!!! Libby

Week 28

2-18-08 From: Libby B.

Subject: Great News About Lonnie

As of 10:00 this morning they turned the Respirator off and Lonnie is breathing on his own. They have left the tube in, (just in case.) Because of the tube still being in, he can not speak but used sign language to say to Dawn, "*I love you*." Hallelujah!!!!!! YEAH GOD!!!! Libby

2-18-08 From: Libby B.

Subject: Another Prayer Request for Lonnie

The Nurses noticed that it was wearing Lonnie out to breathe on his own. They ran some tests and found Pneumonia on both sides of his lungs. So they turned the Ventilator back on to help him rest and heal. They are giving him antibiotics through his I.V. His spirits are still good and he is still very responsive! We just can't give up or stop praying for Lonnie! God is good all the time! Libby

2-20-08 From: Mark Strick (Brother-in-Law)

Subject: Miracle Turnaround for Lonnie

Well, to say his turnaround is a miracle is probably true. On Saturday night his blood pressure bottomed out and his pupils were fixed and dilated. Today he was moved from ICU to a private room and he is doing fairly well. He is weak but he does know who people are. He doesn't remember the past week and the troubles he had leading up to his situation by Saturday but he is able to talk very weakly and he can smile and cry. It is a blessing to see him where he is compared to what I saw Sunday when I got here. Please continue to pray for him because he needs to do a lot of recuperating. He probably can't walk or won't for several weeks so he still needs prayer. Thanks for the prayers you have already offered up. Mark

[Note: From this point forward all emails noting a CB in the subject line were first placed on the Caringbridge site that my wife setup.]

2-22-08 From: Dawn Honeycutt

Subject: CB: Lonnie Is Doing Better

Hi, this is Dawn. Lonnie is doing well, a little better each day. This is the quote I want everyone to hear. There was a nursing student assigned to Lonnie during all this. He got very wrapped up in this case and asked a lot of questions of his instructors and doctors. What he came and told us was this:

"My instructors and doctors have never seen someone who was so bad off come back so quickly, so well, and with such a good prognosis. Sometimes there are things in medical science that defy medical reason, and this is one of them. It is a miracle."

Lonnie still has some battles ahead. He is having short-term memory issues, trouble remembering things from yesterday even, also occurrences in the past few months. He recognizes most people, though may get names wrong. His breathing is still an issue. But, all things considered, he's doing wonderfully – especially considering that he wasn't supposed to even be awake for three weeks and that I was told that when (and if) he woke up that he'd be in a vegetative state and that he wouldn't be the same Lonnie I (and we) love. He is being evaluated by a neurologist today (probably) and is having a 'swallowing' test done to see how bad his throat is. Please also pray that during his 'fuzzy minded' moments, he doesn't do anything dangerous. Last night he tried to remove his central line (which is in the main femoral artery) and he also tried to get out of bed and fell.

Please know we love you and appreciate all the prayers and calls. I started this page to try to keep all who have called from around the world updated. I will update it as often as possible. Isn't God good!!!!!!! When the prognosis was so grim, God really showed up. Can't wait to tell you all the miracles worked this last week. Dawn

2-23-08   From: Dawn Honeycutt

Subject: CB: A Little Humor – At Lonnie's Expense

Just got home from the hospital to take a quick shower, feed the animals and head back. It has been a really emotional day today.

First, we need to start with a little humor. The introduction may not sound humorous, but hopefully the story will give you a giggle.

Lonnie has been having 'confused' episodes where he is not himself. Normally they freak me out, but with my wonderful brother Mark present, the one last night had me laughing hysterically while also crying for Lonnie. It started simply. Mark and I were talking and Lonnie was sleeping. Suddenly Lonnie sits up and says, *"Good-bye."* We both asked, *"What?"*

Lonnie repeated himself and said, *"Good-bye!"* Mark asked him where he was going and Lonnie said, *"I'm leaving,"* and started getting up out of his bed.

After Mark (with his one good arm – he recently had surgery on one of his arms) placed Lonnie back in bed, he asked Lonnie, *"Do you know where you are?"*

Lonnie response was simply, *"Space."*

Mark asked a clarifying question, *"Hyperspace or outer space?"*

Lonnie assured us that they were the same thing but that if he had to clarify, he would say outer space. Mark asked him if he should contact Scotty to beam us up. Lonnie thought that this was a good idea. After making transporter sounds we told Lonnie we were onboard and asked what our destination was. He responded, *"Home."*

Mark proceeded to give orders to set coordinates for our house and to engage warp engines. We 'cruised' fine for a while until the warp engines failed (made even more 'real' by Mark's making grinding and lurching noises), to which Lonnie responded, *"That's not good."* He was especially concerned after hearing that it would take 10 years to reach home on impulse power.

In order to dissuade Lonnie from attempting to 'transport' out of the Starship Enterprise (his bed), I asked him if he would like a tribble (a soft, furry, warm-blooded animal sold as a pet by interstellar trader Cyrano Jones on the old series Star Trek). Lonnie's face brightened at my suggestion of giving him a tribble and he replied *"Yes."* At this point I handed him a small, white stuffed goose our son (Brance) had given him to 'keep Dad company' while he was in the hospital. Lonnie laid back in his bed holding the goose in his hands for a bit as if he were petting a tribble. Suddenly, he tossed it aside and demanded, *"That's not a tribble, I want a tribble!"*

After my brother and I got through laughing and crying, we decided it was time to get serious. Mark asked if Lonnie knew him and Lonnie was able to correctly identify him as his brother-in-law Mark. Then Mark asked if he knew me and he again responded correctly *"Yes, that is Queen Dawn."* Mark quickly asked Lonnie, *"Queen Dawn? What is she queen of?"* Lonnie's reply was as matter-of-fact as anything I've ever heard him say, *"Queen of everything."*

Boy was I relieved to know that he is still clearheaded and knows everyone! ☺ Hahaha.

Seriously, no one knows what brings on these episodes but no one is concerned at this time. In fact, they aren't concerned about much right now. The urinary catheter is being removed as I type this, while our dear friend David B. sits with Lonnie. (We can always count on David for those 'special' hospital moments. Bless you, David.) Right now the only medication Lonnie is receiving is potassium and antibiotics.

Today we spent a lot of time with Lonnie asking questions about things he doesn't remember. He has shed a lot of tears today, even though I have reassured him that many of the memories from recent months are a blessing to have removed. I have also reassured him that these may come back in time. But you know Lonnie, he was crying for anyone or any event he might have forgotten. He invests so much in other people's lives that missing that time is very sad for him. Still, we were able to rejoice over what the Lord has done for him.

Oh yes, it appears that Lonnie's mouth and throat have been healed too. He is able to eat ANYTHING he wants – in fact, his first meal was pizza and chocolate-covered pretzels. His taste buds are still out to lunch (so to speak) but we have faith that God will restore those along with the memories he needs to continue forward in his calling.

Well, I'd better get a shower and return to the hospital. Thank you from Lonnie and me for all those who prayed for us and stood (and still stand) with us through this. We are truly blessed with such a wonderful extended family.

And just a special note to Lonnie's family who came this week… I love you and appreciate you more than you will ever know. Mom, thanks for standing with me through this. Jay and Valerie, thanks so much for coming here. I know Lonnie was helped by your presence. Our love to all, Dawn.

Week 29

2-24-08   From: Dawn Honeycutt

  Subject: CB: Worship Service, Memory Loss and Wanting to Come Home

Today DLF-East brought church to us in the hospital. Wow, what a wonderful time of worship and fellowship. Lonnie loved seeing each of you and was in tears afterwards because of all the love shown to us. Then came visits from friends. Please don't be afraid to visit. Lonnie thrives on company.

They took Lonnie's central line out today because they did a scan and thought there might be a clot forming. They believe it is either a clot or bacterial growth. We should know soon. I'm believing that it is neither one and that all concerns over clots will be considered vanquished.

Each day I get a better picture of the memory loss that Lonnie is experiencing. It covers the last few years plus things that happened as recently as yesterday. I have found myself repeating things today that were discussed yesterday. The thing is, he remembers pretty much everyone, but doesn't have memory of things or events in connection with people. He is very disturbed over this. I don't remember if I said this in the last note, but he knows that he and I have a close connection, that we're husband and wife and that he loves me dearly but he doesn't remember our life together during the last few years. It is a bit disconcerting. But, I am told that in time all those memories may come back.

For now Lonnie and I are looking at the now and what we have now. What we have is an awesome, loving God, friends who are truly the extension of God's heart (and as I've learned, you (our friends) really do love me as well as Lonnie, we have great children and we have this time – this moment that we are living in).

It has been such a faith-building time, even amidst the tears, fears and anger. God is good all the time. Sonya H. had a wonderful quote from a car commercial, though I can't remember exactly how it all goes. The important part is: *"Now is a gift, because it is called the present."*

Lonnie desperately wants to come home tomorrow. Please pray that the doctors do what is right and necessary and that Lonnie can accept this with no trouble. We all want him well, but when he comes home, I want it to be for a long while.

Well, back to the hospital. Starting tomorrow I will get my children back from Alicia. Thank you to Alicia, Melicia and Barbara for looking after our babies this week. It is so wonderful knowing that they were cared for by such wonderful, loving friends. Love, Dawn

2-25-08 From: Dawn Honeycutt

Subject: CB: Whirlwind Improvement!

Wow, today Lonnie has continued to show whirlwind improvement. Lonnie was removed from the oxygen, has had his PICC line removed, was removed from tube feedings, and was given a good report on his chest x-ray.

They may even remove his feeding tube tomorrow. The pulmonary doctor says that he is going to get the other doctors moving and get Lonnie home tomorrow!!

Man, when I think about things a week ago, I can't help but be amazed. Lonnie spoke with others today, including Mark and Mary Ann. He is starting to grasp the big picture and just how major this event has been. Some of the things he expressed amazement at have been talked about before, but I hope with repetition he will be able to grab hold of the amazing work our Lord has done.

Thank you to everyone who has brought food, prayers and love to us through this trial as well as over the last few months. I am tired yet exhilarated at God's greatness and blessing. Lonnie's love is still for God's people and so I am certain he will be contacting many of you this week to catch up. Thank you to everyone who allowed me to be real during this time. I don't know how I would have gotten through this without all God's people coming alongside and helping me feel and heal. Love you all. Keep singing God's praises!!! Dawn

2-26-08 From: Dawn Honeycutt

Subject: CB: Lonnie Is Home!

Lonnie is home!!! We left the hospital at 5:00 p.m. Everyone is so amazed at how well he has done. The nurses who saw him come in to ICU were in awe to see him walking the halls today. Some things have triggered Lonnie's memory but there are still so many things that are fuzzy. We are believing that God will open those memories as needed and in His time and wisdom. Please pray for Lonnie that he doesn't get too depressed that the doctors didn't want to remove his feeding tube at the present time because they want to make certain he's going to continue to eat well enough not to need it. I personally don't think that's going to be a problem as Lonnie is highly motivated to get the tube removed and regardless of the fact that he still can't taste most foods, he's eating very, very well.

We are working on getting settled in and will spend a lot of time working on bringing our lives back together as a family. Thank you again for all the love and support. Love, Dawn

2-27-08 From: Dawn Honeycutt

Subject: CB: Prayers for Lonnie's Memory

While we are rejoicing at all God has done, we are also now getting down to the reality of living. There is A LOT that Lonnie still doesn't remember. You know where Lonnie used to be the one carrying conversations, he just kind of sits now, not knowing what to say. It is really tough on him, not knowing what he doesn't know.

We keep trusting in God that the memories will return when they need to and not before then. This is a time to rediscover and redefine life, priorities and callings. Please pray for us during this transitional period. Also pray that we will hear the Lord's direction in ministry and life.

Love you very much and thank you so much for the love and support. I know I keep saying that, but I don't know how I would have gotten through this without my wonderful 'family.' Dawn

2-27-08 From: Lonnie Honeycutt

Subject: My First Day Home from the Hospital

Guys and Gals, yesterday was brutally difficult for me physically – insofar as I had a hard time getting around! Coming home from the hospital, while it was wonderful to get out of there, gave me a new perspective on feeling weak. Even though I was only a passenger in our vehicle, I found it difficult to sit-up straight in the seat. In fact, my wife kept looking at me with concern in her eyes because I was so slumped over. I remember pulling down the sun visor and lifting the lid on its mirror to see what I looked like and, to be honest, I scared myself. My face was and is gaunt. I've lost an incredible amount of weight and it occurs to me now that it might not have been the best idea for me to leave the hospital so soon. Still, what's done is done and now that I'm home, I definitely don't want to go back.

Eating, Drinking, and Being Merry

Do you recall that I told you prior to my going into the hospital this last time I was having difficulty eating and drinking? In fact, as I related to you at that time, I was only able to 'eat' or 'drink' through my feeding tube? Well, not any longer! Praise God! Three days after I woke up from being 'out of it' I was taken to have a barium swallow test to see how much food and water I was aspirating. If you've never had a barium swallow test, I highly recommend that you try to avoid them at all costs! Let me attempt an explanation of what such a test is like…

First, you're given a liquid to drink. Now, this isn't just any liquid… No, it's a very thick, heavy, white liquid that looks and tastes similar to chalk (yes, I've actually tasted chalk – as a child). If you're able to get that down (i.e., if you're able to swallow it without gagging), the docs and the techs move on to other substances that you're supposed to ingest. Thankfully, I only had to eat two things; a cookie and a piece of a nuclear green banana (both of which were smeared with a barium paste). Not having any salivary glands to speak of (these were burned-out by the radiation I underwent), swallowing both of these 'foods' was very difficult. In fact, by the time I got to the banana my mouth was so dry that I had to chew and chew and chew until, at last, I forced myself to swallow. It took me three swallows to get the banana down.

Finally, the test was over and one of the techs who was watching the fluoroscope (the machine that allows one to see the barium and barium-coated foods going from your mouth and into your body), asked me *"Mr. Honeycutt, why are you here?"* I replied, with a smile,

"I don't know. I'm here because I'm trying to be a good patient and someone wheeled me down here."

He asked this question because, as everyone could see (including me – they had kindly positioned the screen of the fluoroscope so that I could watch the procedure), I had zero aspiration of anything.

To make a fairly long story much shorter, I was given the go ahead to eat whatever I wanted to eat and drink. Unfortunately, the test was done in the middle of the afternoon and supper wasn't going to be served for a few hours. Fortunately, as God would have it, Felicia H., one of the nicest ladies you'll ever meet, called me almost as soon as I arrived back into my room. She asked me how I was doing and I said, *"Great"* – which was a slight exaggeration but only slight – and then she asked me if I needed anything. I told her that I could use something to eat. Felicia inquired as to what I would like to eat and I told her that it really didn't matter because my taste buds weren't working anyway. Still, I told her, I was very, very hungry and I'd appreciate it if she'd bring me something to eat when she came to visit. Lo and behold, about thirty minutes later, she walks into my room carrying a Dominos Pizza and a bag of candy-coated, chocolate pretzels.

Hahahahahahahahahahahahahahaha!

People, I have got to tell you that this story delights me. Why? It's because this is the first meal I've had, after not being able to eat or drink anything for the last month or so due to inflamed and bleeding lips, gums, throat, and tongue. That's right, I went from not being able to eat or drink anything (including water) to having pizza and pretzels as my first meal. Talk about a miracle! God had restored the tissues in my mouth and my throat to such an extent that the doctor who came in to look down my throat (not having known what I'd already eaten) told me, in an incredulous tone, *"Mr. Honeycutt, this is the first time I've ever seen anyone go from having such severe damage in their throat to what I'd call baby soft skin tissue."*

What a praise report!!

So, while I'm still not able to taste anything, although water no longer tastes salty to me (it has more of a malted flavor to it – that's something I'm convinced that God has done for me because I used to hate the taste of water and now I find that I'm craving it), I can eat and drink anything I want. This is very important to me because I desperately want to have the feeding tube removed from my stomach as soon as possible and I know that they won't do it unless I can prove that I'm willing and able to eat. So, bring on the food and I'll eat and drink and be merry about it all the while – who needs taste buds anyway?

Short-Term Memory Loss

If I had to choose the one thing that I don't like experiencing, it's short-term memory loss. I've been told that this is something to be expected for someone as bad off as I was but it's still disconcerting. You know, I'm still not certain why I even wound up in the hospital this time but, apparently it was because I had been overdosed on drugs about 12 days ago. Whatever the reason, the short-term memory loss I'm experiencing is bad. And, it doesn't seem to have any rhyme or reason behind it. I still remember my name, my birthday, and most of the important things in my life, such as my wife, but I don't remember other things such as how long Dawn and I have been married (I remember marrying her but I don't remember when we got married) or my daughter, Danielle. I do remember Brance, but I didn't when I first woke up. But, Danielle is like a stranger to me. You know, it's very interesting, I have a bunch of parental feelings towards this little blonde-haired girl who calls me Daddy but I have zero recollection of her. I don't remember my wife being pregnant with her, I don't remember feeding her or changing her diapers, I don't remember her birth. Everything is a blank when it comes to her. I'm definitely praying to the Lord that He'll allow my memories to return as far as it concerns Danielle because if I'm going to be her Daddy I need to have more of an anchor to her then I have now.

It's very depressing not knowing what I don't know. In fact, that's a subject that's a bit sore to me at the moment – not because of anything anyone has said but simply because I can't recall so many things. I do remember that when I was still in the hospital, Dawn asked me what I didn't remember and I said, incredulously, *"I don't know what I don't know, why don't you ask me some questions and let's find out."* That's when I figured out that I didn't know my own daughter.

Now that I'm home I find that I feel like a stranger in a strange place. Nothing seems familiar to me. I've been told, by Dawn, that I used to love to cook. Well, that may have changed because when I went into the kitchen today I didn't even know where the cups and plates were kept. I had to open every door to familiarize myself with things again. One thing I'm amazed at is the amount of food we have in both our refrigerator and our pantry – I mean we have a LOT of food. I assume it's because my wife has a pretty decent job (although, to be quite honest, I don't know what it is she does or did) and because of all of your kindness in bringing prepared meals to us.

Speaking of 'memories,' I'd like all of your prayers concerning a specific set of memories that I think I have. While I won't go into details now, suffice it to say that I have some very, very vivid memories that don't correspond to what I know as reality at the moment. Like I said, I won't go into the details at the moment but I would like you to pray for me that God reveals the whereabouts and whenabouts of these memories to me as soon as possible. They are pretty astounding!!

That's all for now folks! Take care, keep praying, and keep sending me prayer requests – I really like taking things before our Heavenly Father. Lonnie (RevLon)

2-28-08   From: Lonnie Honeycutt

Subject: Worship Service in the Hospital – A Funny Story…

This is a story I haven't told to anyone except my wife at this point. I thought it was pretty funny.

A few days before I left the hospital, I was called by Mike Woods. He inquired as to how I was doing and then quickly got to the heart of what was on his mind. Mike wanted to know if I'd like for him and his wife, Patti, to bring a guitar and some friends to my room and celebrate with me on Sunday morning. I said, "*That'd be great!*" So, the plans were made and, sure enough, on February 24, 2008 (Sunday), Mike and Patti and several people (most of whom I didn't know at the time – actually I DID know them I just didn't remember knowing them), piled into my hospital room and we soon began worshipping together.

Thankfully, I remembered (somehow) most of the songs that Mike played and was able to sing along. Then, at the end of our praise and worship time, Mike asked if there were any prayer requests and a couple of them came up. He began to lead us in prayer for those others had requested we pray for and then he started to pray for his pastor. As he prayed, I came to realize that whomever their pastor was, he was a very ill man. So, as any decent Christian should, I entered into prayer with them. I knew that even if I didn't know who the pastor was that God did. Knowing some of what I had been through and hearing how bad off the man was we were praying for, I really entered into the prayer time strongly. I 'prayed hard' that God would manifest His presence in the life of the believer we were praying for and that God would heal him. Soon enough prayer time was over and everyone slowly filed out.

About 30 minutes later I realized, with the help of my wife, that their pastor, the one I had been praying so hard for, was ME!

Hahaha!

What a hoot! No one can tell me that God doesn't have a sense of humor. ☺ Love everyone! Lonnie (RevLon)

2-28-08 From: Dawn Honeycutt

Subject: CB: Neurology Appointment...

I spoke with Lonnie's doctor today and he has referred us to a neurologist to try to find out more about this memory loss. Lonnie's regular doctor thinks that the memories should come back eventually. He can't predict how long but possibly 6 months or more. Right now he said that I need to put Lonnie on a very regular schedule to help him settle in and move on. That should be interesting as those who know us well know how 'regularly scheduled' challenged we are. ☺

Anyway, even though Lonnie wasn't feeling very energetic today, I took him out to the gym to watch the children take class. He is actually in the living room right now playing guitar. It is nice to hear. Especially since a day or so ago he couldn't remember how to make but one or two chords. Dawn

3-01-08 From: Dawn Honeycutt

Subject: CB: A Much Better Day

Today has been a much better day. It has been an emotional day as we mark 2 weeks ago that Lonnie died. Lonnie's emotions have been close to the surface with much joy and rejoicing. Lonnie is still very weak but is looking forward to getting stronger so he can begin helping God's people again. We both feel like we owe the Lord so much for all He has done in our lives.

Lonnie's memory is still not good, but in some ways it is getting a little easier for him to deal with. Right now he is enjoying getting to know his children and making connections with friends. We sat today and looked at all the cards and notes that we have received over the last few months and need to again say a tremendous 'thank you' for all the support and prayer directed toward us. It is such a wonderful feeling to be so loved. We would like to know if you have any needs that we can be praying for. Lonnie is enjoying putting pieces together, so please feel free to call and talk. It seems to really help. Dawn

Week 30

3-04-08 From: Dawn G.

Subject: Important Info for Cancer Burns

Hi Lonnie, I Pray you are feeling better! I belong to a company with my nephew. He runs the business and I pay for the advertising.

Well, he asked me to please get on the call tonight and so I am listening to the call as I write this to you... The reason I am writing is because they have a product that has tremendous benefits and testimonies from cancer patients especially in reference to cancer burns which you are suffering from. Lonnie, I am sooooo impressed with the benefits of the product and also how it takes away pain! I believe this may help you with your chemo treatments. I wish you could hear this... They have info on a CD... Have you heard anything about it??? I believe the product can help you. Blessings, Dawn

(My reply to Dawn) Hi Dawn, I appreciate you thinking of me but, quite honestly, since I died two weeks ago I haven't had a single issue with a chemo or radiation burn. In fact, not only is the outside of my neck healed completely, even the insides have healed to the point where I don't have to worry about what I eat – I can eat anything. Now, if the product you're speaking of is benefiting those who have undergone cancer of the neck treatments as it concerns their ability to taste foods – I'll be all over looking into it. Thanks! Lonnie

3-4-08   From: Dawn Honeycutt

Subject: CB: Check-up for Lonnie

Well, we went to the doctor for a check up yesterday. The oncologist is running blood work because Lonnie's platelets are very high (3x's higher than normal). Common causes of this are systemic infection or bone marrow dysfunction. It could also be because he doesn't have a spleen, but since all platelet tests before this have been normal the doctor doesn't think this is the cause. This is just one more chance for prayer and victory!

Friday Lonnie goes to the surgeon who put the feeding tube in, hopefully to have it removed. He is eating well and hasn't used the tube since coming home. We are also getting home health care in to do some physical therapy. Lonnie has lost so much muscle (all over his body but especially in this left neck and shoulder) and is very weak. This will allow him to get stronger and head off possible problems trying to rehab himself. After this we have the neurologist on the 10th.

The doctors have set the new PET scan for March 25th with an appointment on April 1st to see the results. Please join us in praying that the PET scan is clear and the cancer is completely gone.

Overall things are going well. There are many times when Lonnie is overwhelmed by what the Lord has done for him and all that he has been through. Right now there aren't memories from the cancer treatment – something for which we are very happy. Dawn

Week 31

3-10-08   From: Dawn Honeycutt

Subject: CB: An Eventful Few Days

It has been an eventful few days. Friday Lonnie had his feeding tube removed. That was a very exciting event.

Lonnie continues to get stronger and is beginning to get some taste buds back. Iced Tea was the first item that tasted normal and has been consumed by the gallons now. Lonnie is slowly returning to normal activities and has even cooked dinner once! Anyone who knows me and my cooking knows what a blessing that was for us!!!

Saturday we went to the Flea Market and walked around. I followed behind often just marveling at how amazing it was to have Lonnie with us and doing so well at that. He is doing better than he should be doing after just the cancer treatment (never mind the whole dying thing). There is still memory loss though that is something that Lonnie seems to be getting more comfortable with. Emotions are still really tender and many tears were shed when we visited Deeper Life Fellowship in Mobile on Sunday. It was so wonderful seeing so many people who have prayed and supported us during the last 5 months.

A doctor over in Malbis has donated time in a hyperbaric chamber. This oxygen saturation should really help him recover faster and could also help his memory return. We had a wonderful friend (Teresa H.) come by to give us massages and visit with us on Monday. It is so cool being able to catch up with so many and to begin enjoying our family and friends. Love you all and I think that Lonnie will soon be writing again. Dawn

3-14-08 From: Lonnie Honeycutt

Subject: CB: Another 'God Thing'

Hey everyone! This is Lonnie. First of all, THANKS SO MUCH for all of your prayers and both physical and financial support – they've all been needed and are truly appreciated.

Second, stay tuned for a full-fledged update on what I've already gone through, am going through currently, and what I expect to happen in the near future. Hopefully, I'll be writing such a synopsis by the end of this weekend – with the help of my wife and some of our very close friends whose memories are certainly sharper than my own at this point.

Platelet Count Sky High

As you may remember, around a week ago I had some blood work done (I think that I've probably lost at least 10 pounds of the 48 that's gone from my frame just because my body is having to utilize so many calories just to keep my blood volume up – haha). The blood work showed my blood platelet count to be almost 1000 (3 times more than it should have been). More blood was immediately drawn so that a conclusion could be made as to what was causing the count to be so high – we were told it was more than likely an infection of some type but I also knew it could have been a secondary cancer.

Well, I just got off the phone with my primary oncologist and it's all

GOOD news – no infection and no secondary cancer. When I go back for my Pet Scan on the 25th of this month (11 days from today), they'll do more blood work just to confirm that nothing is wrong. But, for now, I am definitely rejoicing because with a blood platelet count that high there was definitely something going wrong in my body. So, I think that what happened is another 'God thing.' Maybe I'm wrong but I don't think so.

Anyway, I sincerely appreciate everyone who has taken the time to hold me and my family up to the Lord our God in prayer. Thank you so much! Love, Lonnie

Week 34

3-30-08 From: Lonnie Honeycutt

Subject: CB: Easter, My Death, and Playing Fish Pathologist

Hi Again Everyone! I'm sorry it's taken me so long to issue another update. As you'll see from the way I start this, I meant to have it posted a while ago. But, as they say, 'life started happening' and I just haven't gotten around to it until now. With that being said, I'll begin...

I hope that you had a wonderful Easter (we certainly did). You know, this morning as we sang 'Arise' in church, I couldn't help but be in awe that I've been allowed to become one of those who have arisen from death. While definitely not as spectacular or as meaningful as when Christ raised Himself from the grave, my death and subsequent healing from the same has certainly meant quite a lot for my family and friends and myself.

For those of you who don't know the story, I died on February 16th, 2008. Here's what happened in brief: After my wife found me black, blue, and gray in my son's bed (I had fallen asleep with him the night before as we watched Smash Lab or Myth Busters), she couldn't find a pulse and I wasn't breathing. While she performed CPR on me, my son called an ambulance. My neighbors, Bob and Jenny P. and Cindy and Larry J., all came over as soon as they saw and heard the ambulance making their way to our house. I was so bad off that one of the EMT's on the scene asked Bob (whom I think they thought was my father), if I had a DNR (Do Not Resuscitate) form signed. Dawn told them that I didn't so that meant that they had to try to save me. Another EMT was asked by Cindy point blank *"Is he going to make it?"* She was told, *"No, I don't think so."*

Due to the fact that I had suffered from 2nd and 3rd degree burns on the outside and inside of my throat and mouth (both of which were blistered and bleeding), the EMT's called my primary physician to get the OK to 'tube' me. They were afraid that by inserting a tube for air that they'd damage my airway and possibly collapse it. My physician gave them the 'go ahead' since I had not signed a DNR.

Once at the hospital I began having seizures in the ICU. My wife was told that this was 'normal' for someone whose brain had been deprived of oxygen. She was also told that my flailing didn't mean that I was responsive but that my body was basically in death throes due to cerebral hypoxia. The medical staff also found that my respiration was extremely shallow (once every 33 seconds and less) and, eventually, they were unable to find either a pulse or blood pressure AND my pupils were fixed and dilated (indicating terminal anoxia – brain death). At this point my physician was asked what should be done for me and he replied (paraphrased), "*What do you want me to tell you? He's brain dead. You need to tell his wife.*"

My wife was told, in no uncertain words, that I was brain dead and she was given a DNR form to sign. Thankfully, she never had to fill the form out because, according to the medical staff, a couple of minutes later I was 'fighting the doctors and the tube in my throat.' While this was definitely a good sign, Dawn was again cautioned against expecting any great turnaround. Especially since I quickly went back into a coma. She was told that if I woke up, it'd be in 2 - 3 weeks and that if I did wake up I wouldn't be the same Lonnie she knew – I'd be more like a vegetable.

Well, as the Good Lord (praise His Holy, Holy Name) would have it, the doctors were wrong all the way around. First and foremost, He answered the prayers of the many, many people who were praying for me to come back from being dead. Secondly, He really did heal me. Not only was I completely awake and cognizant in the next 4-5 days, I was out of the hospital in 10 days total. If you'll remember, I mentioned the state of my throat and mouth a few lines ago. Well, once I came out of my coma, those were completely healed. I'm talking, COMPLETELY. Not only was I able to speak normally again but I was able to eat any and everything that people put in front of me (and people put a LOT of stuff in front of me – from pizza to candy-covered pretzels). A swallow barium test proved to everyone that I had been given, for all intents and purposes, a new throat and new tissue in my mouth and throat.

My CT/PET Scan

For those who are wondering, I had my most recent CT/PET scan on the 25th and I'll know what it said (if there is any cancer left in my body or not) on the April 1st (this coming Tuesday).

Survivor's Lap

On April 4th, I've been invited to join Pam P., another cancer survivor, on a Survivor's Lap walk (a 1-mile trek) to benefit the American Cancer Society (ACS) and to help make people aware of cancer in general and their treatment options. I'm definitely looking forward to that because of all the people that will be involved. I've got to tell you that I believe Pam is one of the strongest people I've ever met when it comes to going through diversity. She truly gives people (including me) hope and comfort just through her presence. I really appreciate Pam a lot!

What I'm Still Suffering From and Need Prayer About

As nice as it is not to be dead, I'm still suffering from a few things physically and mentally. Mentally, I'm still having some short-term memory loss issues. For instance, I can't remember a thing about Christmas day, nor do I remember almost anything during the course of the past 6 months. It's all a blur or a complete blank.

Also, as it concerns my mental state, I'm having quite a bit of difficulty communicating to people verbally on even a basic level. What I mean is that I sometimes forget how to use certain words or I simply can't immediately come up with the appropriate word to use in the midst of a basic conversation. For instance, the other day I was speaking to a young woman and had the need to use the word 'exception.' While that should have been fairly simple, it wasn't. I couldn't, for the life of me, remember the word 'exception.' So, I chose to use the word 'objection' instead and, as such, had to re-diagram the entire sentence I was going to say so that the term 'objection' could be used appropriately and would mean the same as 'exception.' While I'm glad that my brain was able to make the mental leap and gymnastics needed to replace one word for the other, it's uncomfortable to find oneself in such a position. So, please pray that I regain the mental and verbal lucidity that I once had when speaking to people. Not being able to effectively communicate with others will definitely hamper my ability to interact with them concerning their health and the health profiles that I rely upon to generate the income needed to feed my family.

Speaking of 'generating income,' that's another area that I need prayer for. Currently, I'm beginning to slowly interact with my former clients (most of whom are probably reading this email and have an idea of what I've been going through). Unfortunately, in my view, the process is too slow. But, due to my physical limitations, I don't have much of a choice but to take it slowly. In fact, I've been told that if I try to do too much too quickly that I'll take a giant step backwards. I definitely don't want that to happen. On the other hand, I'm more than aware of our need (my need) to make money. Not only is it my job to be a 'bread winner,' it's something that I feel I must do in order to please my Lord and to be a good witness to my family. But, the fact of the matter is that I still get very, very tired, extremely quickly. As you can imagine, this limits my ability to work. So, please pray that I'll not only get more energy and have more stamina but that I'll also be able to withstand the internal pressure to work regardless of the physical and mental price I might pay. Honestly, folks, this is one of those times that I realize how much the male ego sometimes gets in the way – while I don't want to admit that I need to take it easy, I am also very aware of my need to take it easy lest I hurt myself. It's a tough thing to have to deal with mentally.

Finally, as it concerns what you might want to hold up in prayer for me, my left shoulder is still giving me fits. It's extremely difficult for me to lift my arm above my head (simply lifting it even with my jaw-line is difficult). The pain is fairly intense even a few months out from having the surgery that removed the muscle and nerve. Thankfully, I have a couple of very good friends who are massage therapists (Teresa and Richard H.) and who volunteer their time and energy to making that area feel much better every few weeks. But, I'd prefer that new muscle be grown in that area so that I no longer have to deal with the pain. If that's not going to happen then simply pray that I'm able to handle the pain without complaining about it.

Playing a Fish Pathologist

This morning (the 30th) I woke up at around 5:30 a.m. (one of the many times during the night (about 7 or so) that I wake up due to the fact that my throat is so dry that I have to get a drink of water – which

I keep by my bedside). I rose from bed, went into Brance's room, and asked him if he wanted to go fishing. To be quite honest with you, I didn't really feel like going fishing but I also knew that he liked going fishing with me prior to my death. He immediately said "*Yes*" and, within minutes, we were on our way to the Cedar Point Pier.

Once at the pier I baited 4 poles with some shrimp that I'd had frozen for about 6 months and got them in the water. Brance then wanted to go and buy some live minnows – he only wanted 1 so that he could see if it would catch anything before we purchased more. Of course, the bait shop doesn't sell just one minnow at a time so we had

to get a half dozen at $2 – thankfully I'd brought $5 with me. When we got back to our poles he wanted to bait his pole with a minnow so I told him to grab one out of the water. He looked at me as if I'd gone insane. When I asked, "*What?*" he told me, "*No, minnows bite.*"

After I finished laughing hysterically, I asked him where he got the idea that minnows bit people. He said that a friend had assured him that this was true. After trying to assure him otherwise, based on the fact that minnows don't have teeth large enough to hurt even a baby, I finally had to reach into the water and grab a minnow myself. Once the tiny fish was outside the water, Brance saw what I meant about their small mouths and teeth and was immediately calmed.

I baited his hook, tossed it back into the water, and then watched as my son began to attempt to catch the still bucketed minnows with his bare hands. After he'd finally succeeded in catching a minnow, he calmly began releasing them back into the Gulf of Mexico. One by one he caught and released the minnows so that they wouldn't die.

If you know Brance at all you know that his actions were preceded, proceeded, and accompanied by a steady stream of dialogue. He talked to each one of the minnows as they were being caught and released and he spoke to me about the virtues of releasing the bait I'd just spent most of my pocket money on back into the wild. As luck would have it, a gentleman on the dock who had been about 100 yards away from us when we arrived and staked out our spot on the pier, had slowly been trolling with his line towards us. Just as he got within earshot of Brance's endless chatter, my son said, "*Dad, I wish I could keep one of these as a pet.*"

The man stopped trolling for a second and just looked at Brance – I assume to see what my son was talking about. As Brance brought forth another minnow, the man chuckled and I burst out in laughter. The gentleman smiled at me and said, as he pointed to his daughter some several feet away from us, *"I know, I've got one too."*

Soon after the minnows were gone Brance was ready to try another spot since we hadn't even gotten a nibble on any of our poles. I agreed to move and we released the one lone minnow that was still alive but hooked into the Gulf. As we moved towards another spot on the pier, one that took us directly past the bait shop, Brance began asking me to buy him a frozen mullet (a type of fish commonly used as bait – for you non-fishers out there). I said, *"No,"* but, of course, that didn't stop him from asking again and again and again – the way only children can do and get away with. Oh, he didn't just ask again and again if he could have a mullet. Instead, he began to tell me all of the great things about mullets.

"Dad, you know the fish really like mullet."

"Dad, mullet is much, much better than shrimp because we usually catch stuff with the mullet."

"Dad, I'd really like to cut-up the mullet for you."

"Dad, I have a lot of fun with mullets and so do you."

"Dad, if you get me a mullet I'll have a lot of fun even if we don't catch anything."

By the time we'd walked about 50 yards, he'd worn me down and I spent the $1.52 needed to get a mullet. Over the course of the next 30 minutes he was as happy as could be.

True to his word, he liked cutting up and dissecting the mullet. Since he'd just gotten through going over body parts in his science class, as he cut into the frozen fish, he wanted to know everything there is to know about the insides of a mullet. Surprisingly, at least to me, he was able to identify the heart, the liver, and, of course, the intestines of the fish. Then he began asking me to help him identify the pancreas, the stomach, and other assorted odds and ends of fish innards. Had anyone else come to our end of the pier for the next 30 minutes they'd have sworn that we were having a science class (which, in a way, I guess we were).

In any case, I ended up 'fishing' with so many different fish organs that I'm quite sure some of the fish in the gulf were throwing up at the site of what was on the end of my hooks. Once Brance had cleaned out the mullet we packed everything up and headed home. No fish were caught but, according to Brance, this was one of the *"best fishing days we've had"*" So, YAY for science! That's it for now folks. Have a great day! Lonnie (RevLon)

4-01-08 From: Lonnie Honeycutt

Subject: CB: Cancer Free

Hi and Praise God! Dawn and I just went to the doctors this morning and we were told that I am now officially CANCER FREE! Yay!!!!!

I'll write more later. I just wanted to let everyone know the good (make that GREAT) news! Love all of you! Lonnie (RevLon)

Week 37

4-23-08 From: Lonnie Honeycutt

Subject: CB: Changing Times and a Changed Me…

Changing Times

Since I've come back from stepping over to the side of eternity, I'm different. I've changed. At least that's what Dawn tells me and, to tell you the truth, I kind of feel that I have as well. Dawn assures me that it's not all bad – the way I've changed. In fact, just last night she remarked that she liked the way that I now enjoy rice and beans mixed together (something I used to hold in disdain, although I don't remember having such a dislike).

One way I do know that I've changed, is that I'm less of a conversationalist now. I remember that I used to be able to talk a blue streak with people on just about any subject (be it a subject of interest or one fraught with absurdities). Today, I find myself being very laconic (concise) with people in my speech. As such, she (Dawn) suggested that when I updated the Caringbridge site (which I'm doing now), that I apologize to any and everyone who may have spoken to me lately and explain that I'm not trying to be rude. So, with that being said, I apologize.

If you've been keeping up with me on the Caringbridge, you'll have read that I wrote about my inability to put together some sentences properly – at least when speaking. This, I'm certain, has been an accompanying factor in my shortness of speech with people (I simply don't feel comfortable speaking to others due to my inadequacy in coming up with a stock of words to describe whatever it is I'm attempting to depict).

Two Sunday nights ago, at our Church Meeting, I began teaching on the book of James. If you're familiar with the epistle, you know that it's a fairly straightforward study. Unfortunately, while I was very prepared mentally, I had such trouble putting together the sentences I knew were on the proverbial 'tip of my tongue' that I believe it was the worst lesson I've ever taught. I was completely mortified by my ineptitude. In fact, it was so bad that I'm not certain that I'm any longer cut out to be a pastor (at least not in the teaching department).

I'd appreciate prayer for this because talking to people is how I make a living. Speaking of making a living, things are slow-going on that end but, hopefully they'll pick up now that I'm 'back in business.' I recently began sending out postcards to my clients and on the front of the cards is the announcement: *"After Surviving Cancer and Death... Lonnie Is Back!"* I figure, if nothing else, that this card would at least get people to call and talk to me about dying.

Our Ministry

Whew! What a rough road it's been concerning ministry. Though I clearly remember ministering to many people over the years, I barely remember being a pastor at Deeper Life Fellowship on the Eastern Shore. As such, I'm uncertain as to the long-term survivability of the church itself – although the group we're meeting with on Sunday nights is certainly a committed group of Christians.

As always, I'm willing to do whatever it is that God would have me do. I'm just not certain what that is at the moment. You know, on a personal note (as if all of this isn't a 'personal note'), it's a bit disconcerting that I've gotten so much insight into so many different aspects of my life in the past couple of months, but none (or, actually, very little) concerning the life of our church.

One insight that I have gotten into our church concerns outreach. Currently, I'm in the process of gearing up for an outreach project during which we will offer a soft drink and a hotdog for a nickel (that's just five cents). The premise behind this outreach is two-fold: First, people will come over to us because a soft drink and hotdog for five cents is one heck of a deal, and second, when they've gotten their food and drink and start to pay us, we'll GIVE THEM a nickel instead of taking one. This is a paradigm shift for most people, in that they are used to paying for food rather than getting paid to eat food, and, because of this, it gives us a chance to talk to them about why we're doing this – because it's something we believe Jesus would do if He were still walking on the Earth (that is feeding people).

These types of outreaches aren't cheap, but they are effective and that's what counts.

Dawn and I are also looking into opening up a Soup Kitchen on the Eastern Shore and in Mobile as well as a non-profit restaurant that would directly benefit the Soup Kitchen. There is a definite need for such a Kitchen because of the number of working needy. If we are able to get enough volunteers we want to run the Soup Kitchen like a regular restaurant in that we want to seat people, take their orders, and serve them. To us, outreach is all about treating people with respect. If this is accomplished, then a relationship may come about. It's like a bumper sticker I recently read that stated: The path to Heaven is shown by footprints not signposts – in other words, just as St. James said, it is our works rather than our words that show people what is in our hearts.

By the way, I'll be meeting with the owner of a non-profit restaurant that operates in Mobile, AL. next week to see what is required to get such an operation underway. If you'd like to pray for either of these operations, I'd appreciate it.

I'd like to say THANK YOU to everyone who has supported us and our ministry for the past several months. I can't tell you how much this support has meant to us and to the others we've been able to impact.

Telling My Story at Two Churches

In a couple of weeks we'll be going on a vacation (something I've not had in a long, long while – just like many of you I'd suspect). In any case, we'll be traveling to Texas to visit my family and part of Dawn's. During that visit, I've already been asked to tell my story (of my death, resurrection, and what I saw on 'the other side') at two churches. I'm really looking forward to the chance to tell others about my experience(s). So, please pray that I'm able to do this with more grace and style than I've been able to muster lately when speaking in public.

I'm also going to be speaking at the American Cancer Society in Citronelle, Alabama on May 13th.

Well, that's all for now. I hope I didn't bore you. As you can tell, I've not grown short of things to say via email. Rev. Lonnie (RevLon)

Week 43

6-1-08 From: Lonnie Honeycutt

Subject: CB: My Trip to Heaven

Wow! I can't believe it's already June. Sorry about the very long delay in updating the site but we were out of town for a couple of weeks (we went to see our families in Texas).

Okay, as promised, I'm going to be writing to you today about my experience in Heaven. But, for just a moment, allow me to bring you up to speed on what's been going on with me on this side of eternity.

Memory Loss

While I've definitely regained many of the memories I'd previously lost, I'm still concerned about my ability to function 'normally.' I can't remember simple things like all of my times tables (I can get up to my sixes well enough but, after that, forget it). Also, my retention of facts seems to be hampered quite a bit. So, I'll be seeing a neuro-psychologist this month (hopefully).

Physical Changes

I can't remember whether or not I mentioned this the last time I wrote (go figure, eh?), but I've been able to start working out (weights and riding a stationary bike) for about the last 3 weeks. I work out for an hour or so at a time and my stamina has gone through the roof (at least as far as it compares to what it was right after I came home from the hospital in February).

My left shoulder is still causing me a LOT of discomfort. It's painful 24/7. But, thank the Lord, since I've been able to work out, I've actually gotten strong enough to lift up my smallest child (Danielle) and can now carry her without any problems. I've even developed enough shoulder strength to lift her onto my shoulders every now and then (although it's too painful to carry her like that for more than 10 minutes or so).

My taste buds and salivary glands are still severely disabled (especially my salivary glands). I'm able to taste meat fairly well and fruits and vegetables (cooked or raw) very well. Most sweets I'm still unable to taste so I just avoid them. The 'sad' thing is that my olfactory senses (my nose) are still working great so everything smells wonderful – it just doesn't taste the same as it used to. The deterioration of my taste buds probably has to do with the lack of salivary glands. I've not gotten a full night's sleep since I died because every hour my throat becomes so dry that I wake up and need to have a drink of water (I keep a bottle of water by my bed and drink almost the full 16 ounces. before I get up the next morning). Strangely enough (but thanks be to our Lord), prior to my salivary glands going out on me, I didn't like the taste of water all that much. Now, water has kind of a 'malted' taste to it and I actually crave it. So, now I drink over a gallon of water every day and I LOVE it. God is so gracious, isn't He?

Work

I'm still unable to work so I'd appreciate your continued prayers for our finances – this really does concern me quite a bit. Hopefully, my business will begin to pick up but, with the price of fuel getting out of hand, it doesn't look good.

Okay, now for...

My Ascension Into Heaven

[Note: This is the first time I placed 'in print' my experience in Heaven. I've noted it here as you've probably already read it in the preceding pages.]

Week 45

6-15-08 From: Lonnie Honeycutt

Subject: CB: Good News, Bad News, and Neuropsychologist

3-Months Coming Up!

I'm going back to the doctor's office on the 27th for my 3-month checkup to see if the cancer is back or if there are any new cancers for us to deal with. I'm honestly not worried much at all (just a little – but it's such a small amount that I don't think about it until I'm writing something like this or until someone I meet tells me a harrowing story about their cancer coming back).

In any case, please keep this office visit in your prayers for two reasons:

Reason 1: We (my wife and I and all of my friends and family) want the results to come back negative (i.e., that I don't have cancer) and...

Reason 2: My wife and I will not have insurance after this month.

Good News About My Weight

I've actually now gained back 2 pounds of what I'd lost (48 pounds)! Yay! Plus, I've found out that I can now taste cinnamon. This means that cinnamon toast, a childhood favorite of mine, is now back 'on the plate' as it were. I had 6 pieces of the toast last night!

Bad News About Headaches

I don't know if it's the stress of everything going on at once or something else, but I've been having monster headaches for the last week – I'm talking about 4 ibuprophen tablets a couple of times (or more) per day! It could just be because my shoulder is giving me fits. Regardless of why I'm having the headaches I'd like them to go away.

Neuropsychologist Update

I'll be going to see a neuropsychologist on Monday for testing to see if my brain can be trained to learn and retain new information.

Honestly, I'd made the determination not to go on Monday because of the expense involved in the testing (over $900), but my wife has convinced me to go ahead and go.

I am concerned about my memory simply because it's so bad. Dawn hit the nail on the head when she asked me this morning, *"Do you sometimes feel like a stranger in our home?"* My answer was *"Yes."* She asked me how often and my reply was simply *"Often."* It's really scary to me that I've forgotten so many things about our life. It's even more disconcerting that I'm having trouble retaining new information for more than a day or two and that time seems to be all but a phantom to me – Monday - Sunday I have a difficult time remembering when it was, exactly, that I do anything. But, I'm majorly blessed to have such a loving wife who can bring me up to speed about the memories I lack. Obviously, I'm hoping that the neuropsychologist can do something for me quickly because, otherwise, holding down a job is going to be difficult if not impossible.

Well, that's all for right now! We're off to church! I appreciate all of your prayers! Remember to let me know who I can pray for as I love to do this! In Christ, Lonnie

6-17-08 From: Lonnie Honeycutt

Subject: CB: Neuropsychology Testing, Prodisee Pantry, etc.

Yesterday I went for my visit with the neuropsychologist. She's a very, very nice lady – and a Christian (which is a definite plus)! I found this out because after I told her of my bout with cancer, she asked me if I'd ever heard of a fellow by the name of Bill Johnson, a pastor in Redding, California, who has a powerful ministry of healing for cancer. Surprise of all surprises, not only do I know of him, I actually know him. In fact, one of the parishioners of DLF Mobile paid our way to Bill Johnson's church so that I could get prayed for by him. Then, when he was down in this neck of the woods, I was prayed for by him. Needless to say, it was a relief to me to know that my neuropsychologist is a Sister in the Lord.

I was also able to tell her about Lee McDougald being miraculously healed from Parkinson's disease. If you haven't yet read his story you can do so by going to: http://www.thehealedguy.com. I've known Lee for about 5 years now (although I barely remember knowing him for the last 4 months or so) and I PROMISE you – he WAS healed (completely) from Parkinson's. Praise the Lord!

After meeting with the neuropsychologist, I underwent a series of mind-bogglingly difficult series of tests. At least they were difficult to me nowadays. I have a feeling that they wouldn't have been so difficult a year or so ago. But, as it is, I had a terribly hard time answering the mathematics questions and, believe it or not, repeating two short stories that were read to me. I say 'believe it or not' because, as some of you who know me know, I used to be more than capable of completing that task – in fact, I used to pride myself (in a good way) of being able to repeat, almost verbatim, what a person said to me. Yesterday, I did terrible on this exercise.

You know, I know that some of the questions are supposed to be harder than others and that there aren't any 'right' answers (I was simply supposed to try my best) but, still, I know that there were correct answers and I didn't give them in most cases. I couldn't even remember who had written *Faust* (it was Goethe) and I should have known that without question as I did a paper on the play. Honestly, that's about all of the questions I can remember being asked (if that doesn't tell you something about my mental state...).

In any case, I've got an appointment to go back for my results in a month and a half (July 30th). Please pray that whatever the results reveal that she'll be able to help me.

Well, thanks for listening and reading. In Christ, RevLon

Week 46

6-27-08 From: Lonnie Honeycutt

Subject: CB: Still Cancer Free!

I thought you'd want to know that I just came from my 3-month checkup and **I'm still Cancer Free** (Yay God – Praise His Holy, Holy Name)!!

The doctor was a bit concerned that I haven't gained any of my weight back (if you remember I'd lost nearly 50 pounds since this whole ordeal began) until I told him that I'd actually gained about 6 pounds of it back and then lost it because I've been able to workout really hard for the last month. I let him know that, with the exception of my memory, I felt and feel GREAT. Honestly, I think I'm just about as strong as I was before the cancer and the treatments – and I'm getting stronger every day.

A BIG Thanks to Everyone – Again!

Guys and gals, I want to THANK ALL OF YOU from the bottom of my heart for all that you've done for me and my family in recent months. As some of you know, I've been trying to write a book that details the events of the last year of my life (including my trip to Heaven). Part of the book (a MAJOR part) is going to be direct quotes – in their entirety – of the emails I sent to everyone and that were sent to me or to others. Well, in order to decide which ones I wanted to include in the book I've had to go back and read all of them. To be quite honest, doing so has been incredibly difficult. In fact, there have been times (several times) when I had to stop reading and writing about my experiences because the emails were so 'real' that they brought me to tears. Honestly, since I have no recollection of any of my treatments I was surprised that I reacted in such an emotional manner. I guess it just goes to show how connected I am to everyone. So, again, thank you so very much for all y'all have done for me and my family. I love all of you dearly! Lonnie (RevLon)

Week 50

7-27-08 From: Lonnie Honeycutt

Subject: CB: Doing Great But Need to Find Work

It looks like it's time for me to again update this journal since I've received so many inquiries as to how I'm doing.

Well, physically, I'm doing great! I feel as though I'm getting stronger each and every single day. There are times, however, when I do realize that my body is still somewhat traumatized by the recovery from cancer and dying. For instance, last week I was out late (after 10 p.m. a couple of nights in a row doing some type of ministry) and when I finally came home I was ready to drop. It took me about two more days to recover from the late night outings. Of course, that the two outings were also compounded by strong emotions, didn't help either.

Speaking of emotions, those have been a bit strained on my end as well the past week or so. This has been due, in part, because of the strain my wife and I are under as it concerns finances (more on that in a few lines). But, there's also been the added pressure of trying to remember things that I've forgotten. Dawn and I engaged in a Question and Answer session the other night to determine some of what I still don't remember and it was draining.

I still have a terrible time remembering certain things about my life prior to dying and the cancer and some of it goes back several more years than what I had previously thought it did. For example, while I don't remember preaching a single sermon at our church on the Eastern Shore, I do remember being the Associate Pastor at our church in Mobile. In fact, we recently visited them on their 5th birthday and I was able to 're-live' some of the moments I thought I may have forgotten through a short 30-minute video the Pastor (Mark Wyatt) had put together. The video was a history, of sorts, that contained many of the servant evangelism outreaches we'd done during that time. I was in most of the sections of the video and it was at that time I realized that I still felt as though I should still be part of the staff of DLF Mobile. It's sobering to know that I'm not but that I still feel like I am – does that sound weird or what?

Looking for Work

I'd appreciate your prayers for Dawn and me as we look for work. Both of us have been putting in applications for work over the past few weeks now (heavily for the past 2 weeks) and neither of us has heard a word from any of the prospective employers to which we've applied.

As many of you know, Dawn lost her second job in the past 8 months because the company she had been working for closed its doors. Thankfully, Dawn has a 1-day a week job with a friend of ours (Jorge) but, it's only 1 day for 4 hours a week. With the loss of her job, I also lost my insurance coverage which now means that ALL the expense for medical procedures (blood work and Pet Scans, etc.) are falling squarely on our shoulders.

Unfortunately, I don't know if anyone is going to want to hire me with the memory retention issues I have going on. Still, I've applied with bookstores, GNC, etc. and I'm sending out my resume for ministry positions all around the country. And, I'm doing odd jobs for a few different companies around the country. Suffice it to say that we're looking for anything that will bring in some income because we're on our last legs financially and we really need your prayers that God will step in and do something amazing again. I mean, He did bring me back from the dead so I'm certain that He can provide for us in this situation too.

DVDs Are Going Well

A few of you have asked how well the DVD sales are going. They're going well considering how few people actually know about them at the present time. We've sold around 25 of them at $12 each so that's not too bad. By the way, if you know of anyone who would like to see one, they can get them at: **www.DeeperLifeEast.com** for $12 and we can NOW take Credit Cards!

I'd appreciate it if you could spread the word about these DVDs because they are a great witnessing tool (to both the Saved and Unsaved) and because, as of right now, they are the only source of income generation I have.

Death, Heaven, and Back – *The Book*

I'm currently working on a book with a similar title as the DVD and I'll (hopefully) have it done in the next few weeks – then it'll be a matter of getting it edited and submitting it to publishers. Prayers that

I'll find the right publisher would be great, too! Well, that's it for right now. It's getting late and I need to hit the sack. Blessings to ALL! Love, Lonnie (RevLon)

Week 52

8-12-08 From: Lonnie Honeycutt

Subject: CB: **It's Been a Year Now! My Last Post on Caringbridge…**

Guys and gals, it's been a full year now since we began this adventure – and what an adventure it's been!

To everyone who has prayed for my family and me or who has helped out in any way (financially, meals, travel, giving us a shoulder to cry on, and more) I want to THANK YOU one more time. I don't have the words to express the gratitude I feel towards every single one of you.

To my wife (who also reads the Caringbridge Updates) I'd like to say *"I Love You."* You are the most beautiful woman in the world to me and you are certainly the best friend I have in this world. Thank you so much for loving me enough to care for me as you have during the last year. You've definitely lived up to your marriage vows to love me even in the worst part of life. Obviously I'll never be able to repay you for all you've done for our family but I promise to try.

More than anyone else I'd like to praise and honor my Lord and Savior, Jesus Christ who is the King of Kings, the Lord of Lords, and Jehovah God over all! It's impossible to fully articulate my thankfulness to You, my Lord. You've shown me the glories of Heaven and I can't wait to be with you again. You gave me the choice to come back to Earth and, once I'd chosen to do so, you gave me an assignment to spread the news that Heaven Is Real and that You want everyone to join you there. I'll do my best to make you proud of me in this task. Thank you, thank you, thank you for giving me this honor and responsibility. Thank you even more for being willing to die for me and everyone else who accepts your pardon for our sins so that we never have to face death – even though our mortal bodies may falter and wither away. Finally, thank you for giving all who truly accept You as our Lord and Savior the privilege of witnessing for you while we're here on Earth. I LOVE YOU!

My Last Post on Caringbridge...

Again, as I've already said, it's been a full year since I began to have serious concerns about what was going on in my neck. Since that time I've undergone surgery, survived cancer and death, gone to Heaven and came back, and have regrown my goatee (to some degree). I've also been able to celebrate my 11th anniversary with my wife, the 5th anniversary of Deeper Life Fellowship in Mobile, and the 9th birthday of my son Brance.

Interestingly enough, I just completed the book I've been working on for the past several months on the year anniversary of my first email to everyone. I didn't plan on doing this so, who knows, maybe there's some special significance to the date?? In any case, the book (tentatively titled: *Death, Heaven and Back (The True Story of One Man's Death and Resurrection)* is beginning to be edited as I type this. So, your prayers that the book and the DVD (of the same title) will be a blessing to all who see them would be greatly appreciated.

Through Caringbridge I've been able to communicate with hundreds of people with whom I've never had any face-to-face contact. So, since this site was designed to help people talk to others when the 'chips are down,' this will be my last post on it because my 'chips are up' again! Praise God!

If anyone wishes to write to me about anything, you can do so via the following email address: **lonniehoneycutt@yahoo.com** or **revlonnie@gmail.com or by visiting www.DeeperLifeEast.com**

That's all for now, folks!

I love all of you and hope to see every single one of you (and a LOT more) in Heaven! Love, Rev. Lonnie Honeycutt (RevLon)

Epilogue

Writing this book has definitely been cathartic for me. It's allowed me to express my thoughts and my thanks in a way that few other mediums can. As I write these last few sentences I'm a bit saddened by the fact that this project is over. With that being said, I hope you'll indulge me as I write a few more words concerning my overall feelings about my battle with cancer, my experience in Heaven, and my new life here on this side of eternity.

As far as being a cancer survivor goes, I don't think I'll ever be 'the same' in that I'll always have a fear that cancer will again crop up in my body. Even though I'm certain that the Lord has healed me completely (and radically) and though I'm convinced of His sovereignty over everything, in the back of my mind (mostly late at night), I'm scared that He'll again allow my body to come under attack by this disease.

I can honestly say that it's not me I'm scared for but my family. You see, at this time, I still don't remember having had cancer. But, I know that my wife and children remember and I don't ever want them to go through such trauma again. Of course, if given the choice, I'd choose to have the worst cancer imaginable before I'd allow them or anyone else to develop even the most minor form of the disease.

Should He allow cancer to invade my body again I can honestly say that I'll praise Him through it all – just like I did this time. There's a song by the group Mercy Me titled 'Bring the Rain' and the start of the song expresses exactly how I feel about the trials in my life and my relationship to the Father, The Son, and The Holy Spirit:

"I can count a million times, people asking me how I can praise You with all that I've gone through. The question just amazes me. Can circumstances possibly change who I forever am in You? Maybe since my life was changed long before these rainy days it's never really ever crossed my mind, to turn my back on you, oh Lord, my only shelter from the storm. But instead, I draw closer through these times."

My Experience In Heaven

What can I say about my time in Heaven that would truly do the experience justice except that it has forever changed me. Prior to my death on February 16, 2008, I wasn't scared to die. Now that I have died and I've seen 'the other side' my entire perspective on death has changed. Before that fateful and wonderful day, I used to think that I'd miss the people I'd left behind. Today I know that's not true. I now know what it means to be completely at peace with everything because I know that God is in complete control of everything. If there's one thing I long to 'know' again, it's that type of peace – it's something I look forward to knowing for all eternity. And, one day very soon, I will experience Heaven again and I won't be returning.

But, for now, until Jesus calls me home once and for all, I'll content myself with going about 'His business' of spreading the message that I've been given concerning Heaven. It is my most sincere desire that people take away from my experience, at the very least, hope that something better (much, much better) awaits those who accept Jesus as their Lord and Savior.

My New Life Here on Earth

I can't begin to express to you how dull everything on this side of eternity is – with the exception of relationships. My good friend, David F., made a statement after hearing my testimony of going to Heaven that I couldn't agree with more. He said, based on what I had told him about my time in Heaven, "*I believe the currency of Heaven is loving relationships.*" I believe that David has hit the proverbial nail on the head.

Throughout Scripture, from Genesis to Revelation, everything is about relationships – His relationship with us, our relationship with Him, and the relationships we have with each other.

I am more committed now than I have ever been in the past to help people develop a relationship with Christ – the King of Kings and Lord of Lords – so that they too will have a relationship with The Father, The Son and The Holy Spirit both now and in the hereafter. Further, I know that I desire a deep, abiding relationship with Him for myself. This is perhaps the strongest desire I have in my life at the moment. Lastly, I want to develop loving relations with people from all around the world – first with my own family members and then with others. The reason is simple: It is with these people, my Brothers- and Sisters-in-Christ that I will be spending eternity. How much better will it be whenever I step into eternity again to know that I'll already know people with whom I've begun a 'life' now? I can't think of any better way to go into glory than by being preceded by friends and by proceeding friends!

As for how I'm doing physically and mentally today, all I have is praise for God and His kindness. It's been nearly a year since my death and things have changed dramatically in this short period of time. For instance, God has miraculously protected me from the ravages that could have been brought about by the massive doses of radiation I received. Namely, I no longer suffer from photo-aging or capillary fragility. While I do have wrinkles, they are the type you'd expect to find on a 43-year-old man rather that those I was beginning to develop early on during the treatments I received. Also, water now tastes delicious to me – a fact that I'm very thankful for since before my death I detested the stuff. Speaking of water, I no longer have any problem with moisture for my eyes. If you'll remember, I talked repeatedly about the blisters that had formed on the inside of my mouth. Well, it seems that I've grown new skin on my lips and throat and my taste buds are akin to that of a child's. I also have no discernable scars from the radiation treatments that horribly burned my face and I've suffered no hearing loss. Further, my ear has regained all of the feeling it had prior to my undergoing surgery to remove the tumors that had lined the inside of my head, neck, and throat. This is a fact that the surgical oncologist simply marvels at since he removed a major nerve that should have caused me to be partially paralyzed.

Perhaps the most amazing testimony to the power and grace of my Lord and Savior is the fact that I have zero physical brain damage from the stroke I suffered. This, in and of itself, is nothing less than a miracle. In fact, since my death and resurrection I've begun to play my guitar and write music once again and, while I had experienced a major reduction in my ability to communicate with people, it was apparently temporary. I say this because I now speak on a regular basis to both large and small groups. Whereas, most people who have experienced what I have would be severely restricted in their ability to perform on a daily basis, I believe the Lord has supernaturally enabled me to function very well. For instance, I work with a couple of companies in the area of marketing which entails, among other things, doing higher level graphic work on a computer, talking to hundreds of individuals on a weekly basis, and corresponding with people from all over the country.

As for my energy levels, let's just say that they are out of this world. When I first returned home from the hospital in February 2008 I could barely walk. In fact, I had to ride around on a scooter for a short period of time. While my wife and I had arranged for a physical therapist to visit our home, by the time he arrived (two weeks after I returned home) I was doing so well that he never came back. Two months after dying, I was asked by another cancer survivor, Pam P., to join her on a Survivor's Walk sponsored by the American Cancer Society. At the time, I was told that they would have a wheelchair available for me in case I couldn't make it around the track. To their surprise and my delight, I was able to tell them that not only didn't I need the wheelchair but that I had actually been running. Since that time until today, I've been able to maintain a stable body weight and I'm actually physically stronger than I was prior to going in for cancer treatments.

As I've stated earlier in this book, my blood pressure is normal and I take no drugs whatsoever for pain, depression, or hypertension – all of which I'd been taking while undergoing chemo and radiation. Actually, that's not entirely true. I do occasionally take an ibuprofen for muscle aches when I've worked out too hard (what an awesome testimony to God that I can actually work out)!

All in all, I'm doing wonderfully and I have no other person to give the credit to but God Himself.

A Word About Near Death and Death Experiences

I would be remiss if I didn't provide a warning to anyone who reads this book or any book like it. The warning has to do with what to believe and what to reject. The first and foremost authority on death and near-death experiences has to come from the Bible for the simple fact that it is the inerrant (without error) Word of God. Any true death or near-death experience should serve only to clarify that which is stated in the Bible but it should never contradict Scripture. Should you find anything in what I've said herein to be in conflict with the revealed Word of God (i.e., Scripture – the 69 books of the Bible), please disregard my entire testimony. The same goes for any book, DVD, audio, or other presentation from anyone. The reason I make this request is because I believe that everything anyone states having to do with those things mentioned in the Bible should, without fail, line up with the Bible. Should one find that what I've said seems to be in conflict with God's revealed Word, I would like the chance to review and respond to the same.

As a Christian minister I'm always fearful of people being mislead by New Age theologies – theologies that deny the Trinity, the Deity of Christ, Salvation by Grace, the Bodily Resurrection of Christ, the Gospel (as defined in 1 Cor. 15:1-4), Sin, Hell, a real, personal satan (devil) and a number of other essential doctrines of the Christian faith. The purpose of this book is to simply spread the knowledge that Heaven and Hell are both very real and to let everyone know that there is a way to be certain that you escape the latter (Hell) and enter into the former (Heaven) and that way is through a personal relationship with Jesus Christ.

Please Do Me a Favor

If you take away nothing at all from my account of going to Heaven and from the emails you've just read, I'd like it to be that God really is in control. I believe this, I know this and I'll tell this to anyone who will listen from now until the day I die and go to be with Him forevermore.

If you believe this, then I have a favor to ask of you: The next time you meet someone, take the time to find out if they have a personal relationship with Jesus. If they don't, then tell them your story (the story of how you came to know Jesus), tell them my story, or tell them of someone else you know who is living a victorious life in Jesus Christ. Regardless of whose story it is that you relate, tell them of Jesus and His great love for them. Don't worry that you'll not know what to say. If you're scared of witnessing to people, pray to God that the Holy Spirit will give you the right words to say. I'll make you a promise right here and right now… No matter what words you use, (even if you're the best or the worst orator in history) it's not going to matter.

The reason is because you and I are simply extensions of God's grace (if you've personally accepted Him as your Savior) and, as such, all the pressure is off of us. No one who has ever lived, with the exception of God Himself, has ever brought anyone to God. Instead, He has always drawn people to Himself. What this means, to you and me, is that we can and should freely witness to everyone possible with the knowledge that regardless of how good or bad we do, salvation is His responsibility, not ours. But, when we do witness to people, we honor and glorify the One of whom we testify and we are rewarded for doing so. What a great 'job' we have as Christians. It's a win-win-win situation (they win, we win, and God wins)!

Write Me and Let Me Know How My Story Has Impacted You

I hope you'll take a few minutes to write me and tell me how my story has impacted you or those you love.

If you'd like me to come speak at your church or group, I'd be honored to do so as time permits me.

In case I'm unable to speak directly to your church or group, you might be interested in knowing that I've got a DVD of my testimony out titled:

What If It's True: Death, Heaven and Back (Risen to Live Again!) for $12
(plus S/H & Taxes, if applicable).

Please feel free to contact me by writing, calling, or emailing me at the following:

Rev. Lonnie Honeycutt (RevLon)
3350 Dawes Rd.
Mobile, AL. 36695
251-421-4166
www.DeeperLifeEast.com
LonnieHoneycutt@yahoo.com or RevLonnie@gmail.com

May the Kingdom of our Lord and God reign supreme in your life just as if you were already in Heaven.

With great love, Rev. Lonnie Honeycutt (RevLon).

Questions and Answers

Q: Was there any angst in Heaven concerning people who were there or who weren't? In other words, I've known people in my life who I honestly didn't think would ever be in Heaven or with whom I've had a lot of difficulty with. So, would I feel bad for them if they didn't make it to Heaven or sad if they did?

A: No. As I said in my testimony, when I met the people who greeted me as I came into New Jerusalem I felt a tangible sense of giddiness, of absolute happiness that I was going to be with Christ for eternity and that I was going to be with them eternally.

Bill Weiss, in his book, '23 Minutes In Hell,' says, *"Those twenty-three minutes were more than enough to convince me that I would never, ever want to return, not even for one more minute. And it has now become my life's purpose to tell others what I saw, heard, and felt so that whoever reads this story will be able to take the proper measures to steer clear of this place at all costs."* (Introduction, page 17-18)

I believe that on the DVD of my experience in Heaven (What If It's True: Death, Heaven, and Back) I believe I paraphrased this quote from Mr. Weiss as *"The terrors of Hell were such that I wouldn't want anyone to go there."* As far as Heaven goes, I say, *"The glories of Heaven are such that I want everyone to go there."*

There simply was not any sense of jealousy, ill will, or disappointment towards anyone in Heaven regardless of whether they were someone you liked or disliked while on Earth.

Q: Are you still 'You' in Heaven or do you lose part of yourself, such as your memories of things that you've done that were bad etc. when you go to Heaven?

A: Obviously, all I can do is answer this question based upon what I personally felt. I was definitely still 'me.' I still smiled and laughed the same, my voice was the same voice that I've had for a few decades now, and I was still short. As I came closer and closer to New Jerusalem I became more and more aware of the sins I had committed towards others and, ultimately, towards Christ Himself. I understood the gravity and the severity of these sins to a greater degree than I'd ever understood before. Still, even though I knew that I was going to be judged for how I'd conducted myself on Earth as far as it related to Jesus and His Kingdom, I wasn't 'threatened' by the coming judgment. Indeed, I was so focused on getting to meet my Lord and Savior face-to-face that everything else paled in comparison. Thus, having considered all of this, I'd say that we are still very much 'ourselves' only with heightened senses of exactly who God is (how great, wonderful and awesome He is), who we are in Him (I knew that I was one of the redeemed, His child and an heir to His Kingdom), and of who others are (I knew everyone I met just as if I'd known them for years on Earth and I was just as happy as they were that we were able to meet and be together worshipping Christ).

Q: Do we have bodies in Heaven or are we just disembodied spirits floating around?

A: Yes, we have bodies. In fact, those whom I met all looked 35ish in age, they were fit, trim, and seemed perfect in every way. The lady I met while there in Heaven, my Mother-in-Law, June, had flowing locks of dark brown wavy hair and even though she had died a horrible death (her body was emaciated from years of having suffered from emphysema) at close to 60 years of age, she too seemed to be in her early 30's.

Someone asked me if I had hair while I was in Heaven or if I wore contact lenses or glasses while I was there. Honestly, I didn't notice if I had hair (there were no mirrors that I saw) but I didn't require either contacts or glasses. My vision was better than I ever remember it being.

Q: Did you meet and speak to anyone else other than your mother-in-law during your time in Heaven?

A: Absolutely. In fact, I met dozens, if not hundreds of other people. One of the most notable persons I was reunited with, at least in my mind, was a relative who died when I was just a teenager. He was very, very old when he died and yet, like June, he seemed to be a young man. I have a clear recollection of many of the people I met while I was in Heaven and I've often wondered what, if any, connection that I may have to people they know and love here on Earth. For instance, one of the ladies I met told me her name was

Delia. She had come to Christ because of someone I'd witnessed to a long while ago. I often think about her and wonder whom I might know now who might be kin to her. I may never know on this side of Heaven but I definitely know that she'll be waiting for me when I go back.

Q: Where there people in Heaven who practiced other faiths while here on Earth?

A: No. The only people in Heaven whom I met (and I met quite a few people while I was there) were Christians and Old Testament Jews. No other faith (be it Islam, Mormon, Jehovah's Witness, Bahá'í, Buddhist, Taoist, or any number of other religions) was represented in my encounters with people who were in Heaven. However, there were a number of Christians who were from many different denominations and sects and, of course, every skin color known to man.

Q: Did you actually walk or did you float while you were in Heaven?

A: I walked as did the angels who were escorting me and all those that I met. I distinctly remember looking underneath my feet to see if there were any shadows (there weren't) and I remember the warmth of the road of gold I was on.

Q: Did you talk (as in verbally speak) or did you communicate with your mind (as in telepathy)?

A: I spoke with my own voice using my lips. Everyone I met communicated in the same manner with me.

Q: Were you able to communicate with the angels accompaning you and, if so, what did they say?

A: I never actually spoke to the angels who were escorting me although I know that they could speak because when I had crossed over into New Jerusalem they began talking to some of the people who were there to meet me. Other than being totally captivated by the beauties I saw in Heaven, there wasn't any reason I couldn't have talked to the angels; I simply didn't.

Q: Were there children, infants or animals in Heaven?

A: I didn't see any kids or animals in Heaven but, then again, I didn't get that far into New Jerusalem so my reference point on this question probably doesn't mean much. As I stated before, everyone I saw while I was in Heaven looked 35ish. There was a quality about those I met that allowed me to know if they had died at a much younger or much older age than what they looked like on the outside when I met them. Again, it was an intangible quality but I didn't recognize anyone as having died as an infant or even a child. Everyone I met I instinctively knew had died either as a much older teenager or as an older adult. So, as for the question of whether or not babies or children are in Heaven, I don't know. The same would apply to the question about animals. While I didn't see any animals in Heaven, there's no doubt that there are animals in Heaven or, at the very least, there *will* be animals once the Earth is transformed into a part of Heaven. I base this on the many Scriptures that reference animals as being a part of the Kingdom of God (in both the millennial reign as well as afterwards).

Q: Did you get any idea as to how close Jesus was to returning to Earth?

A: No. Not only wasn't I concerned about this I sincerely doubt that I would have been made privy to such information. This is especially the case since I know for a fact that one of the reasons I was allowed to return to Earth was to tell others about Christ, His Kingdom, and the part of Heaven I visited – not about end times.

If you've enjoyed this book and you have an Amazon.com account I'd like to ask for a favor. Please log into your account, look up the title of this book (Death, Heaven, and Back) and leave me a comment. Alternatively, you can contact me at the address(es) below to leave me feedback on how this book and the Lord has impacted you. Thanks, RevLon!

Rev. Lonnie Honeycutt (RevLon)
3350 Dawes Rd.
Mobile, AL. 36695
251-421-4166
www.DeeperLifeEast.com
LonnieHoneycutt@yahoo.com or RevLonnie@gmail.com
Death, Heaven and Back